The Patterns of Life

The Patterns of Life

by

Peter E. Connor

SterlingHouse
PUBLISHER
Pittsburgh, PA

ISBN 1-56315-110-3

Trade Paperback
© Copyright 1998 Peter Connor
All rights reserved
First Printing—1998

Library of Congress #: 98-85203

Request for information should be addressed to:

Sterling House Publisher
The Sterling Building
440 Friday Road
Department T-101
Pittsburgh, PA 15209

Cover design & Typesetting: Drawing Board Studios

All illustrations are used under permission of Thomas Kephart to the author.
©1997–1998 Thomas Kephart

Printed in the United States of America

PART I
THE SEEKER

MY REASONS FOR STARTING THE SEARCH

Of all the addictions that fight to possess a person's soul, the hardest, meanest, most cruel, and most unrelenting is the obsession to fill that inner emptiness in one's heart which is the desire to find God—to find the meaning of one's life.

Once a Seeker has started on this search he or she will be shaken, broken, and mended so many times he will feel like a rag doll with no stuffing left inside to be sacrificed. Luckily the Seeker will then be picked up, soothed, and put back on the path—only to find, sooner or later, the shaking and breaking happening all over again. Each time seems more violent than the last.

Still the obsession will not let go. The Seeker now needs to find God or die trying.

So it happened with me. When I was still in my early twenties, this unrelenting desire to find my God, and the meaning of life, grabbed hold of me. I didn't want to find a God I could worship, praise, sing or pray to. What I was looking for was my creator. I began to seek because the things I had always done in my life no longer gave me any real satisfaction.

No matter how many good friends surrounded and entertained me with their laughter and the pleasure of their company, I still felt lonely deep inside. It was as if I had eaten a big meal and was completely full—yet a hunger remained. Something was missing. So it was that my urge to find and know God became greater and stronger until finally it had to be satisfied.

It is a desire that is with me as a Seeker each moment of my waking and sleeping life. No matter how great my frustrations, it can't be willed away. It is just there...always! It is as impossible for any true Seeker to ignore this inner desire as it is to ignore, for a lifetime, your desire for food or your thirst for water. Moreover, for a true Seeker, trying to ignore this inner desire to know God more fully only brings greater frustration and torment.

This desire I have described is always within me, even when I go to the ocean and watch the waves coming in, endlessly repetitive, endlessly calming and beautiful. I love to feel the strong sea breeze ruffle my clothes and my hair. I breathe deeply and smell the mixture of fresh salt and fish scents that has always seemed so familiar, even the first time I experienced it.

I listen to the waves thunder, then splash, as they roll up onto the sandy beach, foaming and charging the sand, full of white bubbles that soon break apart, then fade away to nothing.

As I stare out at the ocean, its rolling rhythmic tide seems to get inside me, stirring awake some ancient memory of my own mysterious origins.

I get a similar feeling when I walk in a wet forest after a fresh rain. Softly moving air currents filled with the full odor of damp soil, of pine, and of leaves flood and delight my senses.

These scents, together with the sights and sounds of birds flying from branch to branch chirping their songs, of chipmunks and squirrels playing, wrap themselves around me, and my senses become truly awake. I smell the cool fragrance of a forest at peace with itself. A quietness comes over me and I begin to relax. The soothing, healing balm of nature and its wild animals has entered into my consciousness and has worked its wonders. A kind of primordial memory rises up from some hidden place inside me, and I feel both happy, and yet still lonely, at the same time.

What is it I unconsciously recognize in these scenes that makes me happy? And what is there about nature that prompts the lonely feeling, telling me something is missing from my life?

On warm summer nights I look up at the stars, and their beauty, incomprehensible distance, and awesome numbers create a panorama of majesty that overwhelms me with its splendor. When I look at the stars like this, I always seem so insignificant as one individual. Random thoughts tumble across my mind: I wonder... Why? Why was I created? Where is God? Am I looking at God now? Why do I thirst for this hidden knowledge about God? Why can't I just work, play golf or horseshoes, or even just passively enjoy watching sports, as other men do? Why am I so different? Why am I doomed to be a Seeker? Why do I so love nature?

Maybe in some mysterious subliminal way, nature is giving me a message which I sense but is so subtle I can't grasp it consciously. Yet there is some part of me that does get nature's message, because it changes my emotions for the better when I am in the natural world.

What if nature is saying that I am the meaning of my own life?

You and I are, at this moment, unique and unlike anything that has ever been created before in the whole Universe. You and I are humans. And, as you shall see, we have had an experience different from anything God originally intended when the Universe was created so many eons ago.

As with me, your opportunities during your human lifetime are a strange mixture of opposites, so that what is good for you mentally and physically is hard to do, and what is bad is easy. As a human, you may be in your middle age before the realization comes over you that life seems *more mental than physical.* Perhaps you begin to suspect that most of your pain is self-inflicted. Perhaps, although you rarely have major illnesses, you have periods of being definitely uncomfortable. But it isn't your body that hurts every day—it's your mind and your emotions that are your daily torment.

Successes and failures seem to strangely blend together, all occurring together in a kaleidoscope of emotions woven internally in a way that seems confusing and chaotic. You slide from one into the other in the same seamless way night slides into day and back into night again. You seem never to totally get it all together. So the very day you have your greatest business success is the day your marriage starts to irreversibly fail or that someone you love becomes gravely ill.

It is my purpose in this book to show that *you* are the creator of this individual universe of yours and that *you* must become its savior—to show that your destiny on earth is not to save *the* world, but to save *your* world.

"How?" you ask. "How in God's good name can I save myself when I don't even know for sure who I am?" Well, this is exactly what I hope to show you. I hope to show you who you really are, and it's going to be one of the sweetest surprises of your life.

Where do you begin? *Here, now, right where you are today, is the perfect starting place.* If you, a Seeker, are ever to find God, truth, and the meaning of your seemingly chaotic and meaningless journey through life, then first you have to *stop,* right where you are at this moment..

Stop just where you are, and begin to examine yourself and the personal world that surrounds you much like water surrounds a fish. The fish never looks at, or examines, the water it lives in. A fish seeks food by going left, then right, then circling back and starting over again.

So it is with us. We move through life faster and farther. We take the left path and then the right. We double back, often finding ourselves at the place we started, and feel we have accomplished nothing. But it is in this life that surrounds you, made up of family, friends, neighbors, bosses, and fellow workers, etc., that many secrets lie hidden: because much of the inner life is reflected in them.

I know this because I have spent a lifetime seeking. I have been the fish endlessly swimming. Right, left. A twenty-year-old Seeker full of dreams, youth, and idealism. A white haired sixty-three year old retiree, full of memories.

One reason my quest for the truth was so long and hard was because, like the fish, I thought truth was always ahead of me: if I could just push myself harder, go faster and farther, be first on the right path at the right time, then I'd find truth, God, and the meaning of my life.

What is necessary is to go back to our beginnings—to the reason we were created. This is where our happiness lies. Where we belong is home! And home is where we haven't been looking. Home is inside ourselves. The Kingdom of Heaven *is* within.

Ahhh...I know what you are thinking now. "I've heard all that before. I don't want some dumb religious book."

But wait a minute, don't get upset! *This is not a religious book, it is a book about you.*

You have rejected most of the nonsense that passes for today's religions. You have a sense of goodness about you, a personal pride, a sense of fair play that makes you see the hypocrisies that are being squeezed out of modern religion by logical thought and the latest scientific findings.

You watch the television ministers and see that more time is spent asking for your money than for your soul. You see these spiritual leaders abusing their positions, their competition, and even their spouses, while telling you that when *you* do these kinds of things, it is a sin.

You watch our spiritual leaders fail, our political leaders fight each other with a meanness that makes you shudder. Our neighborhoods are torn apart by the sounds of gunfire and you doubt there is such a thing as God.

Yes, there is! God is the essence, the peace, the inner feeling of self worth that you seek each day you live on Earth. Find this inner peace, this essence of self worth, and then you will find a God that will surprise you.

This will not be the God you knew as a child; or the God that in the past was offered bloody animal sacrifices, the God of statues, paintings, and icons; the God that wars were fought for. That God doesn't exist.

What you will find is the God that you, as an adult, can understand, can identify with and be comfortable with. Where can this *adult God* be found? Where is the God of the twentieth century, of the twenty-first century? What are the truths of the meaning of life, and where are they hidden?

Well, I have news for you. These truths in fact are not secret—the trouble is that we look for them everywhere except inside ourselves and in the world that surrounds us like the water surrounding the fish. I never really found the true meaning of life until I seemingly quit seeking. Then it came to me as a gift.

One warm autumn day in 1994 I sat on my south-facing back porch enjoying the sun, reading a physics book about a 1975 mathematical discovery called fractal patterns.

As I read, an awareness of life's meaning and the truth of God's creation flowed over me like the sunrise pouring light over an awakening land.

Suddenly, like pieces of a floating jigsaw puzzle, all the long years of searching through esoteric, metaphysical, theological, and scientific materials came together as one complete picture in my mind in a great excitement of knowledge. Finally I knew! Finally I realized how God made its great creation, I understood the fundamental truths about the meaning of life.

I am writing this book in the hope that it will help to make your journey less difficult, and shorter, than mine has been.

THE SEEKER

Because you want to read a book about the meaning of life I know that you, too, are a Seeker, a restless spirit. You want to understand the truth about life, but only find confusion and chaos and you wonder: "Why should I go on? Why should I keep seeking when I find no answers?"

For me, being a Seeker of God and of the fundamental truths was for most of my life like having some deep inner desire which never got satisfied but wouldn't go away. It stayed with me constantly as a hunger and a thirst, always keeping me aware that there was a certain emptiness, a crucial void, in my life.

I don't know for sure if you are yet a Seeker, but there's one good way to find out. Do you feel an emptiness, a void, in your life? Do you want to know all about God, or the meaning of life?

In my own case, what I wanted most of all was to take away the mystery of how God and the Universe came into being. I wanted to examine all the nuts and bolts that made up God and all of its creations, which included both the whole enormous Universe, and myself. My lifetime quest, my magnificent obsession, was to find where God hid and what God was made of.

I searched for forty long years, my own personal forty years of hunting for the promised land, my own mythical forty days in the desert.

So that you can understand how I found what I was looking for, it is necessary that you walk with me a little back into my past. Why? Because unless you understand how I lived my life, you won't be able to understand how I *found* my own life and therefore found God.

My own play of life created for me a hunger to know God and a thirst for the secret knowledge that had been hidden through the ages. As you read about my life, you will begin to realize that your own life, like mine, is nothing more than a huge stage play with a cast of hundreds and with yourself as the Superstar. You will also realize that there is nothing that will ever happen to you in your lifetime that can't be changed into an opportunity for soul growth.

To come to understand the meaning of life, you have to first realize that living a human life is one of the greatest gifts God has ever given. As a human, you go through life playing out each day's scene as if you were an actor in some worldwide stage play, a play that uses nature as real live sets and backgrounds, and real people as fellow actors.

The work you have chosen to do to earn a living, plus the country, state, city, and even the street and house you live in, are really nothing more than the scenic backgrounds for your play of life. These things provide the appropriate color and atmosphere that set the mood and tempo of your life's play.

Your family, relatives, friends, fellow workers, even your enemies, are the character actors you have chosen to give your life's play its emotion, its flavor and drama.

The people who are your most intimate associates will be the ones who will help manifest the humor, the fears, the anger, the sadness, and the happiness that are in you. These people become your mirror, your own personal looking glass, so that what you see, love, or hate in them is more fundamentally what you see, love, or hate in yourself.

At the same time that you are the star in your own life's play, you are also a character actor in the life play of each person you meet. In this latter role, you become the mirror that reflects back to them what they hate, or best like to see, in themselves.

These other people, and the places where you see them, also become dream symbols that your higher consciousness will use to guide you. Animals, for example, often become dream symbols of hidden emotions you fear to expose, symbols which appear in the dreams your higher self gives you so that spiritual growth can continue.

This game of life has funny rules. And in order to win the game, you have to first understand the rules the game is played by.

It is possible for all the failures you have in your physical life to become your greatest spiritual triumphs, and conversely, for your greatest physical successes to become your greatest spiritual failures. In a strange way you can actually win when you lose and lose when you win, because your spiritual and physical sides use two different ways of judging results. Your soul consciousness judges you by your intent, while your physical or human consciousness judges you by the results, by your actual successes in the physical world, the physical life.

The living of a full human life, with all its failures and successes, is a sacred thing to participate in. *A human lifetime is our gift from God.* And it is the living of a full life that enables us to find God. And this process is painful.

I believe I would have lived a normal, ordinary life except for one thing: I either developed very early, or was born with, the desire of a Seeker. And this was not a mild desire—it was a fully developed thirst for God and for knowledge of life's truths. It slowly changed me from a shy introvert into a mature extrovert, never bashful, sometimes too loud and too pushy, but change me it did!

I grew up just north of a town of about eighteen thousand people in western Pennsylvania called Butler. My family lived in a settlement of ninety families, called North Butler, nestled between two rolling hills with a large valley to the east. The hills were high enough so that the south side of the north hill would be in shadow while the south side of the north hill would be in sunlight. In the spring of the year it was like living in two different climates, since all the snow would be melted away on the south side, while a few thousand feet away on the north hill there was still snow to be played in.

North Butler had the reputation of being a tough neighborhood. The men who had moved their families there did hard physical work for a living in the local steel mill, in the coal mines, in the railroad car manufacturing plant, or at one of the three major railroad lines that crossed through the front of our valley.

Men who do hard physical work for a living tend to settle their differences in a physical way rather than talking them out, so fistfights between grown men were common. And of course the boys imitated their fathers, so fistfighting was the accepted way to settle differences. Girls and women tried to tame the savage beast in the males surrounding them, and were sometimes successful. My own parents fought long, bitterly, and loudly almost all the time, until my father left home when I was twelve.

Still, to me, North Butler was a playground paradise that made Huck Finn's childhood seem like sissy play. Most people didn't know anything about pollution back then, or toxic wastes, and the local railroad yard, fertilizer plant, cement block building plants, abandoned coal mines, coal tipples, and burning coal slag piles all seemed perfectly created for us to play in.

Connoquennessing Creek, an Indian name meaning crooked creek, flowed through our valley; in the hot humid summers we had favorite swimming holes in its deepest places and we swam all summer long, often in gangs of twenty or more boys. We also liked jumping off bridges onto loaded, slow moving railroad coal cars, and running alongside railroad cars and jumping in for a free ride. We loved the sound of the long mournful whistles of steam engines when we slept out on hot summer nights. We made torches by dipping cat-o-nine tails from the local swamp into kerosene so when we entered abandoned coal mines, we could look at the animal skeletons in the water. We would also see snake skins that had been shed on the coal shale and wonder if the live snakes were still nearby, maybe we could catch them.

We ran in a community gang of some thirty or more boys and it was the job of the older boys to look after their younger brothers; if a boy didn't have an older brother, one of the older boys in the gang looked after him. This was why no real bullies emerged to torment the younger kids. One of the tougher older kids would simply tell a bully to knock it off and he would do so quickly before he got hit himself. I had three older brothers and one younger, so I always had a guardian and a mentor. When some of the other older mentors got killed in the Second World War, we younger kids all felt as if our own older brothers had died.

It was in my Catholic school and in the church, with its ritual of the mass, of a priest in silk and gold garments and nuns in black silk or fine black mesh cloth, that I found spiritual comfort. Some things are either a natural fit, or they are not. For me the Catholic Church, with its ceremony, its pageantry, its saints, and its history that went back to Jesus and Saint Peter, was for many years a perfect fit. And I loved listening to the Gregorian chants.

The Catholic church in Butler, named Saint Paul's, was of a cathedral design and could seat about nine hundred people. It was one of the larger, richer churches in town. Both inside and out were constructed of marble blocks trimmed in fine dark hardwoods. All the windows were of expensive stained glass and looked especially beautiful when the sun shone through. The church had a large pipe organ, and it had a big choir loft in the back so that the sound of music and song flowed like a magical summer breeze over the congregation before completely filling the church. Life-sized wooden statues stood in wall niches and surrounded the main, left, and right altars. Behind the main altar was an especially huge series of stained glass windows. On the ceiling high, high above our heads were beautiful painted pictures with lots of gold trim, which added even greater richness to the church.

The beauty and opulence of Saint Paul's was in complete contrast to the poorness, the starkness, of my home and play environment. Going to this church was like having a consistent subliminal feedback that told me my physical life was drab and poor, but my spiritual life could be rich and beautiful.

In grade school I was taught by nuns of the Sisters of Mercy, who succeeded in being both kind and strict, no easy accomplishment. I remember always having hair that was too long because it was three or four weeks past when it should have been cut. My father had a long-term illness, and with four brothers, three older and one younger, and one younger sister (the baby of the family), there never seemed to be enough money to get haircuts on time.

I was always chubby, but active, and for some reason my pants kept splitting in the seat, so I'd walk home from school with my coat sleeves tied around my waist so the coat would cover the ripped out seat of my hand-me-down pants.

I was long into manhood before I understood that the reason my pants ripped was because they had been worn so long and washed so often before they were handed down to me that there was no strength left in either the fabric or the stitches.

One day a nun asked me to stay after class. When the classroom had cleared, she went to a closet and brought out a bag of used clothes and handed it to me. "These are for you and your brothers," she said gently. I got red in the face and said loudly, "My family don't need no charity!"

She smiled in the kind way nuns do and said quietly, "All right." I watched her put the bag back in the closet. Then she turned toward me, knelt down so our eye level was the same, and from one of her long flowing sleeves pulled out a white, lace embroidered handkerchief, wiped the tears from my eyes, and then stood up and shooed me out of the classroom. I still remember this as if it were yesterday.

I loved those nuns. In their mysterious black habits with the white starched face shields, they seemed to me like angels on earth.

In the public junior and senior high school I attended the Catholic religious education classes, receiving the Sacraments of First Communion and Confirmation at the appropriate ages.

In those days, high school classes were given IQ tests. Then the scores were handed out to the class a week later. My score was 120, which I assumed was normal, medium, average. I compared it with the two students on either side of me.

One had a score of 118 and the other had 120—the same as mine. Yet both of these boys were straight "A" honor students who would be going on to college. I was surprised that my IQ was the same as theirs and yet I was only getting average grades. Even when I did get an "A" or "B" in a class for a six week period, I would then goof off for the next six weeks and get a "C" or a "D", so my average stayed passing and I let it go at that through my senior year.

I seldom did homework assignments because of my parents' constant fighting at home. Also, I didn't like school because I was too shy, too introverted, to be able to participate in the class with ease. I would know the answers but be afraid to raise my hand. If I was called on, I would get red in the face, stammer, and be so uncomfortable I'd just sit down without answering. So school was very painful, as all shy people know.

Because of the way I was, I didn't want to go to college or get into any position of authority. I didn't want to be a boss or any kind of leader; I wanted to be just a follower, blending into the background, unnoticed and safe.

I graduated from high school in June of 1952 and by the end of July, I had been hired on at the local steel mill where my father and older brother worked.

The following spring, in March of 1953, I enlisted in the regular army to fight in the Korean War. My three older brothers were already overseas and it was the macho thing to do. My younger brother joined the army one year later, so all five of us were in the army at the same time, in 1954.

I was a paratrooper stationed at Fort Campbell, Kentucky, and never rose above the rank of Private First Class, nor did I want to. As the sixteen week basic training course was coming to an end, I was summoned to the company commander's office. I wondered why.

He told me that my army entrance scores were high enough for me to become an officer. He did his best to convince me to attend O.C.S. (Officer Candidate School).

I was still too shy to talk in a room full of people, so I definitely couldn't see myself in front of a company of men giving them orders. I had to sign a paper stating that I refused to attend Officer Candidate School.

After twenty-two months I returned home to Western Pennsylvania on a hardship discharge, so I could help my mother with my baby sister who had become blind from a brain tumor.

I went right back to work at the steel mill, and a year later married a girl I had been writing to while in the army. My seniority at the mill had run concurrent with my military service, so my job, though menial, was pretty well paid at that point.

Though I started as a laborer, one of the lowest paying jobs in a steel mill, I retired forty years later as a Rougher Roller in the hot strip mill department—one of the highest paid hourly positions in the steel industry. I ended up making more money than the turn foreman, the general foreman, and, in a good overtime year, the department superintendent. So I lost nothing but titles and the prestige of being a boss by staying an hourly worker.

But still, working all those years in a steel mill was humiliating to me because I always felt as if I were working beneath my potential, beneath my level of creative ability.

In the beginning, when I would be sweeping floors and would see a high school buddy coming down the aisle, I'd become embarrassed and, if I could do it quickly enough, I'd hide behind a steel column until he went by so he wouldn't see I was just a "clean up".

Meanwhile I was beginning to suspect there was something about myself that I didn't know about; I had this inner feeling that I was too good for this kind of work, that something inside of me felt superior. Yet I couldn't lay a finger on it; I couldn't identify this strange sense that inside of me something superior was hiding. It would come out as embarrassment when I saw an old friend on the street or in church, and would have to admit I was *just a millworker*.

I always had a love/hate feeling toward my job which I didn't understand. I felt a greater and greater emptiness inside of me. As the years as a steelworker started to accumulate, I wondered what it was that I was seeking, yet couldn't even identify.

I can see now that I was getting ready to become a Seeker; the thirst was coming; the hunger near. At the time, I thought that maybe it was a desire to become a boss or to become rich and successful, maybe even to go to college. But I always had a deep dread, a terrible fearful feeling, whenever I would think about going to college under the G.I. Bill, becoming a boss, or getting rich and successful.

Further, when I would actually try to do these things, I was always stopped dead in my tracks by an inner procrastination that absolutely would not let me go forward. I'd feel like a forty ton weight was anchored to my legs so that I couldn't take another step. I didn't know it then, but this was my inner guidance working when I didn't even know such a thing existed.

It was my dissatisfaction with my work, with myself, that caused me to begin my search for God. However what I discovered for many long years was not God, but the flaws in my own character. As I became painfully aware of my many defects, I worked long, hard, and not too successfully to change, to reach perfection.

While trying so hard to change myself, I couldn't stand it when others didn't also try to change. I could see with laser-like accuracy the flaws, the character defects, the shortcomings of others. I couldn't tolerate my own imperfections and I couldn't tolerate flaws in others either.

Meanwhile, so far in my life I was just drifting. I loved my wife and our four children and they were my only source of happiness. I had expected that in the intimacy of marriage and with children of my own, I would find an inner contentment.

But after a few years, as satisfying as my family was to me, I still had a deep sense of loneliness inside. I had a good wife and children, a safe, secure job with a good and steady paycheck—but it wasn't enough. I wanted my children to strive for perfection in their own lives. But my dreams weren't theirs, so they resisted.

When I would go out through the plant gates, weary to the bone after an exhausting 11 p.m. to 7 a.m. shift, I'd see the beautiful sunrise. Going home, playing the radio loud with the windows down so I wouldn't fall asleep driving, I'd ask God, "Why?"

"Why are you doing this to me? Why am I doing this to myself?" I'd cry out in agony, "I don't know you, God, you are cruel and heartless! Where is my hope for tomorrow? Why am I living? Why am I working turns in a steel mill?"

In the Christian religion of my youth I had been taught that God was my Father, my Creator; God was the creator of all things, visible and invisible. Yet I kept thinking, "If God is my Father, then why can't I see him?" and "Why doesn't God speak to me?"

I knew that God is apparently capable of speaking to humans, because in the Old Testament God spoke to Moses from a burning bush. In the New Testament God spoke to all the people who surrounded Jesus when he was baptized, and at other times during Jesus' ministry. So why couldn't, wouldn't God speak to me?

I would go to baseball games or play golf, and feel deep inside that I was wasting my time. I felt I should be doing more with the life God gave me. I also felt that if I could find God, then in the process I would also find a way to free myself from a numbing and repetitious mill job that seemed to be stealing all my creativity.

Year after year, I faithfully attended Mass with my wife and four children on Sundays and Holy Days. But I was getting more and more bored as I sat there and participated.

In the Catholic Church, the Mass is performed with the same ritual, using the exact same words, all over the world. This is done so that the religion is standardized. The format of the Mass is so exact that the mass for each Sunday or Holy Day is predictable five, ten, even twenty years in advance. Most of the ritual of the Mass is hundreds, or sometimes thousands, of years old.

After the Epistle and Gospel are read, the priest gives a Sunday sermon from his pulpit designed to elaborate and expand on the teachings in the Epistle and Gospel. Since the Bible text to be used had already been decided upon years or even centuries before, there was little, if any, latitude for the local priest in the writing and giving of his weekly sermon.

I have only an average memory, but after ten or fifteen years of attending Mass as an adult I started to realize, although I didn't want to admit it, that not only was I hearing the same yearly Epistles and Gospels, I was also hearing the same yearly sermons explaining them. I thought to myself that the priest must have written out a sermon for each week some time in the past, and instead of looking for new insights and revelations about the words written in the Bible, he just got out the last year's of the last decade's sermon for that Sunday or Holy Day and re-read it.

"Whoa," I thought after I realized what was going on. "How's this ever going to teach me more about God, or myself, or the meaning of life?" I realized that the religious teachers I was following were so bored by repetition of the ritual and the boundaries of the tight church dogma they had to work within that they seemed to have quit the search for God themselves.

The endless repetitions of Sunday sermons by a celibate priest who seemed to know less about life than I did, finally got to me. But the final straw that broke the camel's back was when I was trying to use self discipline to break a bad habit, which was beer drinking.

I wasn't having much success, so one Saturday afternoon as I prepared to go to Confession, I thought I'd just ask the priest about self discipline while I was inside the confessional.

That day I could see, by watching the priest enter the confessional, that I would be going to the head of our parish, a Monsignor. This particular Monsignor was not only the head priest of the three assigned to our church, he was also the head of the other Catholic churches in the area. He had a reputation, or so I had heard, of being an intellectually brilliant man, so I felt satisfied that I was going to the very best person available to ask my question.

After I had confessed all my sins I stopped and, as was the accepted procedure at that time, the priest then asked if there was anything else. This was a way of prying out that last deep sin you really were too embarrassed to confess, and it was also used by the priest as an opening to talk over anything that was bothering you.

When the Monsignor asked the question, I was ready. "Father," I said, "I'm having a problem trying to break some bad habits. How can I learn self discipline?" To me, my question seemed simple enough and directed to the appropriate person: "How can I learn self discipline"?

His answer was: "Well... Hmmm... it's something you have to work with... aah... no... work on. You see, you have to... " And then silence. I knew right then that this highly educated Monsignor *didn't know*. He didn't know how a person could develop self discipline when they didn't have it.

He knew what it was, but apparently his belief system was based on the idea that a person either had self discipline or they didn't; the winners had it, but the losers didn't. The idea of how someone who didn't have it could acquire it was absolutely foreign to him.

As the silence continued, I thought to myself in amazement, "He doesn't know... he's a priest, he's a *Monsignor* over sixty years old, he's in charge of other priests and of all the Catholic Churches in the area, and *he doesn't know*!" I was stunned.

Finally he mumbled something about praying that the Holy Spirit would guide me and said I should say ten "Hail Marys" and ten "Our Fathers" for penance. After that he became silent again and I knew the confession was over. I said my "Act of Contrition", got up from my kneeling position, and left.

In the whole period I spent inside organized religion, in my case the Catholic interpretation of Christianity, I kept getting three pat answers to all my questions about God and the meaning of myself, as a human, being born and living such a funny life, a life where everything that was bad for me was easy to do, and everything that was good was hard to do. These answers were:

1. *It's a mystery*! (Only God knows.)
2. *You have to accept these things with faith*! (The priests don't know and maybe God doesn't either.)
3. *The Biblical Quote*! (The old standby of all organized Christian religions, the skeleton on which the fabric of Christianity is hung.) Some ministers have made a whole career out of

nothing more than reading chapter and verse from the Bible to their congregation and then offering their interpretation. Having read the Bible two or three times from cover to cover myself, I knew it seemed to have something in it somewhere that duplicated or paraphrased every condition a human could ever encounter. Therefore, all a priest or minister (blessed with a good memory) had to do, when confronted with a parishioner's problem, was to wait until his internal memory banks kicked in and then give the Bible passage that just fitted the situation. The trouble is, one hundred people will give you one hundred interpretations, *all different*.

For years these three pat answers had satisfied me. But now I began to think, "Well, this is nice and the Biblical quote sort of fits my problems—but it's all based on a book thousands of years old. Isn't some more modern research available, aren't there some better answers than these three standard answers to *any* questions I ask about God or the meaning of life?"

It's a mystery, Have faith, or a *Biblical quote* just weren't cutting it anymore.

I quit going to church; I quit listening to those three stock answers and to the endlessly repetitive sermons that I had heard each Sunday at Mass for so many years.

I was ready now to start my own private search for God—all because I couldn't get a simple answer to a simple question: "How can I learn self discipline?"

I began to look for a way to truly find God and really understand the nuts and bolts of God's creation. I was determined to accept nothing less as I made my break with the Catholic Church and started out on my own.

THE PRIVATE SEARCH BEGINS

The first decision I made after I quit attending Mass was that my search for the meaning of life would be a secret one. I was already spending a larger part of my life praying to God and trying to find answers about how God operated than did most of the so called religious people I knew, and I didn't want to be thought weird or crazy.

I began my search in the religious and occult sections of book stores. (These are now called the "New Age" sections.) Whenever I'd take my family on vacation, to a Fourth of July parade and fireworks show, etc., I'd always have an esoteric or religious paperback in my rear pants pocket in case the action slowed and I got bored.

Within a few years I had a thousand or more books in my basement that had been read at least once, some of them two or three times until I was certain I understood the author's meaning. After a while, storage became a problem. The books were getting musty in my semi-damp basement, so I took a bunch of them to a used book store. The owner wrinkled up her nose at the musty smell, and with the back of her hand waved me and my beloved books away.

Unfortunately, this was before the days of yard sales. I went through my books over and over again, picking out real favorites and setting them aside. Then I hired a trash truck to haul away the rejected books and a few other things I wanted to get rid off. In addition, I threw out forty or fifty large paper grocery bags of paperback books. It kind of broke my heart to do it, but now I was finally down to four or five hundred of my favorite occult, metaphysical, scientific, religious, and ancient mystical teaching books.

I re-read and studied the old and new parts of the Bible. I read the Jewish book of mysticism called the Cabala which tells of God's creation through emanation (coming from a single source), and explains their cipher method of interpreting scripture. It was a heavy read, folks. I read about numerology, palmistry, head and face reading, and astrology.

I realized that somehow God and creation were tied into man's consciousness, so I got books from the library by Sigmund Freud. I couldn't take Freud, with his simplistic "Sex causes everything" kind of thinking, although I did like his work on dreams. But Freud was too abstract in his reasoning for me, so I set him aside and tried Carl Jung.

I had more success with Jung's ideas, and an easier time reading and understanding his writing. I liked his ideas on symbolism and mythology, and I liked the fact that he could recognize that the basic truths in the spiritual and mythological religions of American Indians and other primitive peoples had a universal application.

I tried to read books on philosophy, starting with the old masters, Plato and Socrates, but got too impatient. I wanted knowledge of God, not an abstract thesis on some psychological trait in a human. If they had the time and interest to sit around thinking up problems to solve, then why didn't they try to solve the problem of why they were sitting there solving problems? (Maybe I didn't have the right books.) It seemed to me that what they were doing was examining the parts instead of the whole. I wanted to find the writers and thinkers who were trying to find God, the totality, and the reason for their own existence.

I began reading books that could be classified as metaphysical, a widely misunderstood word often associated with cults, fortune tellers, etc. The real meaning of this word, according to *The New Merriam-Webster Dictionary* is as follows:

METAPHYSICS (met-a-fiz-iks) N. (ML Metaphysica, title of Aristotle's treatise on the subject. Fr. GK (ta) meta (ta) Physika, Lit., the (works) after the physical (works): Fr. its position in his collected (works): The part of Philosophy concerned with the study of the ultimate causes and underlying nature of things.
Metaphysical (fiz-i-kal) Adj.-Metaphysician

I also began studying books about the occult.

Today the word occult has a sinister, evil connotation because it is usually associated with cults or devil worshippers. The real meaning of the word, according to *The New Merriam-Webster Dictionary*, is as follows:

OCCULT (A-'kalt) Adj. 1: Not revealed; secret. 2: Abstruse, mysterious. 3: Of or relating to supernatural agencies, their effects, or knowledge of them.

In plain English, the metaphysical books were more concerned with the study of the ultimate causes and underlying nature of things, while the occult books dealt with secret, mysterious, and hidden things that had no apparent "natural" explanation.

Today's scientists, in the various disciplines of medicine, psychiatry, psychology, and physics, are really our modern occultists and metaphysicians according to the above dictionary meanings.

I read the Seth books, Baird Spalding's *Life and Teachings of the Masters of the Far East*, Rudolph Steiner's *Cosmic Memory*, I read *The Secret Teaching of the Ages* by Manly P. Hall, *The Unobstructed Universe* by Steward Edward White, the out-of-the-body books by Robert Monroe, the Carlos Casteneda series, a book by the Native American Black Elk, books about mythology and American Indian mysticism, books about the Navaho and Hopi Indians, and hundreds of the current pop psychology books. I read the writings of Swedenborg describing out of body experiences where he entered heaven and talked to angels and others who had died.

Then one lucky day I came across *There is a River*, a book by Thomas Sugrue about the great American psychic Edgar Cayce, and about the current work of his followers at the Association for Research and Enlightenment (A.R.E.) located in Virginia Beach, Virginia. In the late 1960's I joined this group as an associate member.

One beauty of the Edgar Cayce and A.R.E. material was that it was non-denominational. Baptists, Hindus, Catholics, Buddhists, Jews, Protestants, and members of many other faiths were all studying the Cayce material and receiving valuable spiritual insights from their studies.

It was through the Edgar Cayce readings and my association with the A.R.E. that I discovered the importance of writing down my dreams and how to interpret them. Fortunately, I seemed to have a natural affinity for dream recall and interpretation. Even as a small child, my nightly experiences were vivid and scary and I still remember them.

When I was five to ten years old, before I would fall asleep, when my eyes would just close, I'd see dot flashes of light like looking at a star filled sky, then I'd see faces looking at me. As a teenager, before I slept, I could close my eyes and sometimes only one or two beautiful faces in full front view were looking back at me. This was never frightening, but seemed a soft and pleasant sight as I fell asleep.

Another thing I experienced up to the time I was about fourteen was spontaneously hearing classical music in my mind instead of thoughts when I was exhausted and tired from playing or working at home chores, and needed rest. Sometimes I'd just stop, lean against something, and with my eyes closed listen to the beautiful music. I never studied classical music or even just listened to it, so to this day I can't identify what it was I was hearing.

I also remember that when I was five or six years old I could lie very still in my bed and the bed then seemed to get bigger and bigger as I was getting smaller and smaller. When it seemed I was just a dot between my own eyes, I would start to accelerate up into a tunnel. I'd become scared halfway through the tunnel and would return back to my bed.

I wish now that I could have allowed myself to go deeper into that tunnel, but I was too young and inexperienced to realize I was having the beginnings of an out of body experience. This, by the way, is a classical example of what one can do in deep meditation when all of one's consciousness is focused on one's pineal gland—then an out of body experience becomes possible.

By the time I reached my twenties, these things had stopped occurring. Then I began having vivid nightly dreams.

Over the years I would have many, many dreams of failing life's tests—because I was undisciplined, or for some other reason. After I woke up from one of the failure dreams I would think to myself, "I can't believe this. Surely I'm doing something right some of the time just by pure dumb luck if nothing else." Once in a while I'd have a dream which showed me graduating from grade school, high school, or college. The dreams I disliked most were the ones where I had to go back to one of these schools because I had to relearn a lesson I had already known.

Most of my dreams with these kinds of recurring themes were telling me I wasn't willing to pay the price for what needed to be done in my life. These were the ones I had the most trouble interpreting because I could never be sure what price I was supposed to pay or what it was I was trying so hard to get.

One of the mistakes I was making was not recording my daily thoughts or the various things that happened to me during the day before the dream. If I had done this, then as I reviewed my dreams on a weekly or monthly basis I could have seen a correlation between my daily activities, my thoughts, and my nightly dreams.

As a rule of thumb, a dream is a review by my own oversoul of each day's activities or current unresolved problem—like a comment by a teacher on how well I am using my free will choice to become a more complete and evolved person. If I could continually become a more evolved person, then I should eventually find God in that great ecstasy of light and emotion that the saints of old seemed to find. Apparently, though, I wasn't walking the same path they had, because I wasn't finding light and an ecstasy of emotion; what I was finding was more and more old fashioned flaws in my personality.

Try as I might, though, I just couldn't bring myself to write down my innermost thoughts, desires, and emotions about myself and the people I was meeting on a daily basis. In order for it to be truthful, it would have to be uncensored and raw, just the way I felt and thought. But I knew my wife would read what I wrote; she couldn't help herself; she was curious or just plain nosey. I couldn't always understand my own dreams, and she didn't understand them at all.

I only realized she was reading my dream book when I came home from work one day and she met me at the front door absolutely livid with anger. "So, I'm not good enough for you," she screamed. "You had to dream about having sex with her!" (a woman we both knew who was a regular dream symbol for me).

I asked, "What in the world are you talking about?" She ran into our bedroom, came back out with my spiral notebook and threw it at me.

I tried to explain about the idea that each of us is composed of a male and a female side and as we strive to bring them into balance, we sometimes have dreams that show us having intercourse with this portion of ourselves.

"Why were you dreaming about her?" she shouted, "she's not inside of you!" Then I got mad too and started screaming back and we didn't talk for three days.

After a few of these experiences I knew I was never going to keep a personal diary, and I even quit recording my sex dreams, putting them down in a sort of shorthand code so I could remember them. I even thought about getting a strongbox, but I knew this would so infuriate my red haired wife as to make a daily ongoing battle. To be honest about it, if my wife was reading a lot of odd books and waking up in the middle of the night to write in a notebook, I'd be tempted to sneak a peek inside it myself just to see what was going on.

As I continued to read more A.R.E. material I was surprised by the number of A.R.E. staff members with different religious backgrounds who had Ph.D.s or other graduate degrees in a number of different disciplines including theology, medicine, and psychology, who were helping people study and apply the Cayce readings to their own lives.

I read a great deal about the Cayce material from such authors as Gina Cerminara, Harmon Bro, Elsie Sechrist, Hugh Lynn Cayce, and others.

However, in all this reading I still wasn't finding what I was truly looking for. It was as if all these authors were describing how beautiful the car was, while I was looking for a mechanic's shop manual that described where all the nuts and bolts were located and how they worked. I wanted to know how the car ran, how it was designed and put together. I wanted to know the actual mechanics of how God created the Universe. I wanted to know why I was created with the shape I had and with the diverse intellectual and emotional drives that were so often in conflict with one another.

It didn't make sense to me why I, or any other human, wasn't created clean and neat by God. Why such diversity? Why such pain and horror in the human experience? Furthermore, why couldn't I see, hear or touch God? Why did it choose to hide itself from its own creation—from us? I figured that if I could find the pattern, the inner workings of God's creation, then like backtracking footprints in sand, I could backtrack God to where it stayed hidden. It was that simple. Therefore, I needed to know how the nuts and bolts of creation went together.

Over the following decades I would remain a member of A.R.E. for three or four years, quit while I explored some other avenue of interest that suddenly opened up, then go back to A.R.E. for another stint.

It was the A.R.E. that became my anchor. Whenever I drifted too far into the strange land of occult and metaphysical study and got lost or confused, I'd rejoin the A.R.E. and get centered again. And I'd always be welcomed back without comment or reproach.

The Bible says, "Seek and Ye Shall Find". After years of seeking with the A.R.E. and reading so much metaphysical material, I realized I was developing an inner feeling about the information I was reading. If it was true and right for me, then I'd feel comfortable and satisfied deep inside, like everything was all right. If the information was wrong, then I'd get agitated and uncomfortable inside. When this happened, I'd put the book aside and read no further.

I had tried to interest my wife, and then each of my four children as they entered into puberty and as they became young adults, into searching with me for the meaning of life. They all thought I was off in loo-loo land somewhere, and weren't interested. God, to my family, has always remained the God of the Catholic Catechism, of Sunday School Bible teachings, of Michelangelo's Sistine Chapel paintings.

I became quiet and didn't discuss my internal longings, my thirst, with my family anymore, because I could see it was making them uncomfortable. Even though I knew no one can become a Seeker until he or she is ready for the experience, this hurt.

I also couldn't find anyone in the steel mill who had a similar interest, so I stayed quiet about my search there, too. I was learning with some pain that the quest of a Seeker can be not only frustrating, but very lonely. The frustration would come and go as I got new insights into God's mysterious world, but the loneliness was always there and just became worse and worse. I had the feeling I was the only one in the world searching for God—*no one else cared*. This was wrong, of course, and I knew it was, yet it was a feeling that would stay with me for many long and lonely years.

Meanwhile the more I prayed, meditated, studied my dreams and searched for God's light, the more I just kept encountering my own darkness.

I wanted God to tell me what a great guy I was because I spent so much time praying and searching for him. I thought I ought, at the least, to have nightly visions of angels tending to my needs, soothing my daily hurts. Yet all I was being shown was yet another thing wrong in my character. Sometimes after recording a nightly dream that revealed yet another flaw, I'd throw down my pen in disgust and say, "This is all bull! I'm not finding God; I'm only discovering how screwed up I am."

When I would have an outburst like this, my dreams would stop for days, weeks, and sometimes even months at a time. Then, like a dog licking its wounds to induce healing, I'd grudgingly admit to myself that maybe the dream was right and I should try to correct my ways. I would have dreams of looking at myself in a mirror, which is a dream symbol of self examining self, and I'd get so upset by what I saw and its obvious symbolic meaning that the realization would make me depressed and moody for weeks. No one likes to look at their weaknesses, their bad side, and I was no exception. Yet I now have twenty spiral notebooks filled with the dreams I have recorded for over twenty years. Some of the experiences, visions, and revelations that I had as dreams were awesome, and would shake me to the very core of my being. Others made no sense at all.

Gradually, after years of study, I started developing an inner sense of some oncoming disaster, of some imminent doom of Biblical catastrophic proportions, and it was going to happen to me. For years I carried this sense of dread inside of me, cloaked over with a black cape of depression.

Winston Churchill once commented that each day, after he awakened, his first job was to fight off the black dog that followed and tried to attack him—his depression. I, too, started to fight off my black dog each day, but luckily it never stopped me for long from continuing my search.

CHAPTER

THE WORLD OF GUIDANCE DREAMS

It is essential to realize that you are never alone in your journey through life. There is someone, something, that always seems to be guarding and guiding you. In your waking hours, this guarding or guiding is felt as urges to do or not to do something or as a deep emotional flush of satisfaction, happiness, or well being. If negative, it will be felt as dissatisfaction, unhappiness, and a sense of hurt, or dread. This guidance has been called consciousness, but that is too pat, too limiting—it is much more than that.

Remember how you feel when you give someone a gift they really enjoy? Remember how you feel when you knowingly do or say some nasty thing to another? These feedbacks are from this special guidance—your guardian angel if you are inclined to identify it that way.

It is when you are sleeping, though, that your greatest guidance in your journey of life takes place. The idea that we have an inner guidance that speaks to us through dreams is thousands of years old, and is well documented in the Bible as well as in extensive modern psychological research. I have never ceased to be amazed at the depth and wide range of guidance that I've received in the last twenty-seven years from my nightly dreams.

Through the many years of confusion and sometimes despair, what kept me going was my involvement with the A.R.E. There, at least, I was having success learning how to meditate, and how to remember my nightly dreams and interpret them.

To interpret dreams in this system, it is necessary to consider the dream as if it were a one, two, or three act play. You then identify the general theme of the play in a sentence or two. If you, or others, are in the dream, separate each one as a meaning, a symbol, of your own complex personality. Each individual in a dream represents a living part of your own human ego. Remember that ninety percent of all dreams are given for our personal guidance to tell you what you did right or wrong in the day that just passed, or in the current period of your life.

Just as a good stage play has background settings or scenes, identify each of these in your dream as a symbol. Next, identify all the props that are on stage (in your dream) that help create mood, effect, or a time period. This last could be daily, yearly, or, for example, centuries ago.

This idea of understanding each dream as a play with acts, and with scenes within each act, is very important for dream interpretation. Think of each day's activities as one complete act, with many different scenes played out within the daily acts. We can even break our life's play into four separate stages: child, young adult, middle aged adult, and old adult. Then realize that the period from the day we are born until the day we die is to be considered the whole play.

It is said by many people who have had near death experiences that at that time the whole play of their life is fed back to them almost in an instant, so that an understanding of their life to that point can be experienced.

The other thing that must be done in analyzing your dreams is to try to remember how you felt emotionally and mentally in the dream.

Then try to figure out what the play was about: what was the play or scene trying to depict, what was the theme of the play?

What is going on in my unconscious mind, and where do these dreams come from, I wondered. And why are they always in symbols that have to be broken down and interpreted?

One of the first significant dreams I had that convinced me of the wisdom of recording and interpreting dreams occurred soon after I joined the A.R.E. and began to seriously work on understanding my dreams.

THE DREAM

I had just entered a nice big living room which was furnished with expensive parlor furniture, and I was standing in that room looking at a big, expensive grandfather clock. The clock hands were at 11:59, or one minute to midnight. I somehow knew it was going to be midnight rather than 12 noon.

End of Dream

This short dream had only one act and one scene. To start out, I wrote out the dream as I remembered it. Then I started to break it apart like this:

THEME: I am in a nice house, in a nice room, looking at a
   grandfather clock and noticing the time.

Dream Symbols	Earthly or Physical Interpretation
House	Place where a human lives.
Living Room	Place in house where human spends most of his/her time when not working or asleep.
Nice Furnishings, Expensive, in Room	This would make this house and living space a desirable and comfortable place to live.
Grandfather clock, Expensive	Clocks are used by humans to tell the passing of time by the second, minute, hour. Clock is of good quality—and therefore reliable and enduring
Clock set at 1 minute to midnight	In a human's life, midnight is the beginning of a new day. It is one minute, or a short period of time, before a new day (or new life period) begins.
Emotion of Self in dream	I seem to be calm and relaxed like I was just an observer.
Emotional feedback that scenic setting of room seemed to give to the dreamer pro and con	I feel the room felt comfortable, a nice place to stay in. It was not loud, hostile, or intimidating as some rooms are.

There are only four categories of symbols in a dream: people, places, animals, and things. Their conscious or mental and emotional equivalents in *broad* categories are:

People	Symbol of mind or intellect.
Animals	Symbol of emotion.
Places	Symbol of state of consciousness where one's whole body and soul stays or is at home.

Things   Symbol of a mental state of consciousness that
                                shows mental conditions that surround self.

In order to get the meaning for this dream, or any dream, it is helpful to use the terms "*Just As*" and "*So Also*" to transfer the symbols into their spiritual meaning. After you do this, then change each physical symbol that was used in the dream into its mental and emotional counterpart and you can usually solve the dream. Furthermore, notice how you feel when you wake up. In this dream of the clock, for instance, I felt it was a positive dream because I felt when I woke up that something had happened that was wonderful. I felt happy.

Here is how I solved the clock and room dream, using "*Just As*" and "*So Also*".

Dream Symbol	Category	Spiritual or Conscious Mind Interpretation
House	Place	"*Just As*" this house is a place my human body calls home, *so also* is this a place my soul or spiritual consciousness calls home.
Living Room	Place	"*Just As*" my body sometimes stays in my living room, *so also* does my soul or spiritual consciousness sometimes stay in certain rooms of my soul.
Expensive room, nicely furnished	Things	"*Just As*" these things make this room more attractive and desirable to live in, *so also* does my soul or spiritual consciousness like to stay in attractive and desirable surroundings.
Expensive old grandfather clock	Things	"*Just As*" a grandfather clock that is old and reliable keeps track of the progress of the day, *so also* does something old and valuable keep track of my soul or spiritual consciousness's progress.
Clock's time	Thing	"*Just As*", in a human's life, a clock set at 11:59 p.m. means it is one minute before a new day or a new beginning, *so also* do souls or spiritual consciousnesses have a new beginning or a new day with its opportunity for new awarenesses.

When I was finished breaking the dream down into its symbols, and then transferred the physical symbols into their spiritual conscious meaning by using the words *Just As* and *So Also*, the meaning of the dream became clear to me.

It told me that I, my own spiritual state of consciousness, was just about to enter into a new day, a new state of awareness. The dream showed that my consciousness was in a comfortable environment, with nothing threatening or attempting to overwhelm it at this time in my life.

This was a good positive dream about a new awareness that was about to occur. It wasn't about something I was currently doing right or wrong, and there were no problems that needed to be solved.

The house and room symbols still appear in my dreams and I can tell by the room I'm in what part of my consciousness needs to be worked on. For example, sometimes I'm in the kitchen and then I know that *Just As* this is a place where food for the body is prepared, *So Also* does it symbolize that this is where food for thought or for my consciousness is being prepared. I can tell by the food being prepared or served whether the thoughts or things I am studying are junk or are a good nourishing meal.

Sometimes I'm in the bathroom, and I know a cleansing of attitudes is needed. Sometimes I'm sitting on a bathroom commode and I know I have to get rid of the waste that my mind or emotions have accumulated in a current situation.

When I'm dreaming I'm in a bedroom, I know that the issue is one I should sleep on, or let rest for a while. The other parts of the dream tell me what the situation is that I need to let rest.

"Ahh, those damn symbols!" I would struggle with them and implore God or whoever was guiding me to please just talk to me in plain English. But the answer I always got back was, "Learn Symbols!"

When humans get to the last stage of their lives, as I have, then it becomes easier to look back over the parts of their lives so far, and to examine the acts and scenes that have formed these many parts.

For example, the thirty some years I had children in my home and was personally responsible for them is a separate part of my life play that had many acts and thousands of scenes—most pleasant, some nasty and loud.

After my last child left home, I reflected for a long period of time over my efforts to guide and raise my children. There were so many ways I could have done things differently in the formative years that shaped their adulthood that I got on a major guilt trip. For some time I could think of nothing else.

I worried that I had been too selfish and self-preoccupied in my search for meaning, that I hadn't devoted enough time to them. But then one night I had this dream:

A major war battle was over and I was standing in my army uniform in front of other soldiers and was being decorated. A soldier in uniform, in this case, symbolized one who does his duty by serving his country rather than himself.

I knew, because I was being decorated after the battle was over, that I had done my duty as a father in an honorable way, and I no longer felt guilty about the adults my children had become.

It's not that my children turned out bad, they weren't criminals or drug addicts; it's just that I had wanted each one to be a college graduate and work as a professional—as I had *not* done myself. Only my oldest daughter graduated from college, while the other three were ordinary normal workers like I was. Why parents want to have their children live their own dreams instead of letting them live *their* dreams is one of life's mysteries. But most children will always have things their way anyhow, so no real damage was done. The guidance from my dream when I was a soldier being decorated allowed me to put away another obstacle in my path and get on with my search.

I would dream of being high up on mountains, which symbolized attaining a high level of consciousness. I'd be riding a motorcycle or bicycle, easily and well, and know that I had obtained a good balance during the day that had just passed. I rarely ever had a falling dream. If I did, I would catch hold of something, then stop and begin to pull myself back up.

I would dream often of the everyday things I did and about the people I worked with or was friends with. When I would dream about riding on boats, railroads, planes, or buses, I knew this was about my activities with the public—with other groups of people such family members, fellow workers, friends, etc.—or with my role playing consciousness, with all its diverse parts.

Some nights I would have sex dreams with scenes so graphic, earthy, erotic, and vivid that I didn't want to write them out in full for fear my wife or someone else might read them and think I was writing pornography.

These dreams I would just remember, then think about them all day long. I would wonder, as I tried to interpret them, why I was even having them. Why, I thought, would a superior intelligence like my unconscious or superconsciousness be interested in something so earthy as sex unless it symbolized something sacred and spiritual? I'd ask myself, what is this really all about, this sex act between a male and a female? I felt there was only one way to really understand this, and that was by studying sex manuals, watching the public television shows on sex, and getting books on the human anatomy.

In the beginning I didn't know enough psychology to get this all figured out correctly, but in later years, after getting deeper into Freud, Jung, and others, I realized that the primary purpose nature had in having a male and female join together in intercourse was to produce a baby, a new creation that would perpetuate the human race on Earth. Sex was also a pleasurable thing to do.

Once I was sure in my own mind of all the emotions, excitements, physical attractions, satisfactions, and scientific reasons that could be found in physical sex, then I was ready to find their correspondent or equivalent meaning in the spiritual or consciousness side of myself.

Remember that a dream is showing that *Just As* we do a physical act, such as a sex act between a male and a female, *So Also* are we doing it spiritually to ourselves. In some way, in other words, two parts of our own consciousness are joining together in order to create.

I realized that the sexual act in a dream symbolized an act of creation, the start of a new beginning of some sort, in my own life or consciousness. Somehow, I had two forms of consciousness that were joining together, just as two people do in sexual intercourse.

It is rare to have dreams that are warnings for other people. Their own guidance will warn them, if they are in touch with it. Most of the time, even when a future event is predicted for a friend or loved one, it is nonetheless meant to be a personal message for *the dreamer*.

Your dream is telling you that *Just As* this future thing could happen to a friend or loved one in the near future, *So Also* is it going to happen to *you* unless you change your ways. If you dream of an airplane or car crash, then realize that even though this might also happen somewhere soon on earth, your dream is telling you that *your* plane or *your* car (symbols of vehicles that carry *your* consciousness around) is in danger of crashing.

As the years rolled by, I began to get a lot of dream symbols that kept reappearing, and I was able to make up my own personal dream dictionary. Sometimes, if enough old dream symbols were present, I could write out a dream and almost interpret it verbatim immediately.

Many of the personal dream symbols that I have identified, which are a permanent part of my dream dictionary, have to do with the work I did in the western Pennsylvania specialty steel mill where I worked for forty years. For this reason I want to describe here in a little detail what the work processes of my various jobs involved.

I started out as a clean-up worker in the hot mill. After working ten different dirty, undesirable jobs that were on the seniority promotion progressive route to the top, I finally got a crack at the department's top job—Rougher Roller in a hot strip mill.

My job as a Rougher Roller gave me both satisfaction and a pay rate which would be the envy of most college graduates. I told people who admired my job and its pay that it was easy to get: all you needed to do was serve a twenty-five year apprenticeship, and the job was yours.

The hot strip mill is a department where advertising companies shooting film for commercials like to come because of the great visual images they can capture. Beer companies have shot film, used as background for their beer commercials, of a red hot slab entering into a huge rolling mill with lots of sparks, steam, and water flying back as the slab enters and is rolled.

This is what I did as the rougher roller. I took an eight-inch thick slab of steel eighteen feet long and started a "reduction in size" rolling sequence.

These red hot slabs that I rolled were cast into the shape they had when they came to me at the Continuous Casting Department that was not a part of, nor near, the hot mill at all, but was located a mile or more away.

In that department, molten liquid steel from a giant electric furnace is poured out of an upright furnace into a giant ladle. This ladle is made of cast iron and is brick-lined to keep the molten steel from melting it also.

These huge ladles hold from a hundred and fifty to a hundred and eighty tons of red hot liquid metal. The cranes that move the ladles are even larger, with a lifting capacity of over two hundred tons. These enormous cranes, on overhead railroad rails, carry the ladle of liquid steel from the melt shop into the casting department and, from a spout on the bottom of the ladle, drain the liquid steel into a continuous casting machine, or "caster".

In the late 1980's a man I'd been friends with in high school, but hadn't seen much of since, committed suicide by jumping down into one of these ladles filled with molten steel. He didn't go down into the molten metal as you might think, because a black chill scab forms over the top of the molten steel almost immediately as the top steel slightly chills and becomes firm.

He just lay spread eagled on top of the steel chill scab covering, and melted away as a sizzling sound and a cloud of black smoke poured off the top of the ladle. The smell, the sight, and the sound made everyone in the melt shop sick and they all went home. All received counseling before they returned to work.

At that time my older brother was a railroad engineer whose job it was to move railroad cars in and out of various departments in the mill using a railroad locomotive. He was given the task of hauling away the ladle my friend had jumped on, to be buried. It was now a solid, round pot of cold steel with the outline of a spread eagled body still showing on the top. My brother took the ladle to a slag dump where a minister and a few other people were waiting. Without much ceremony, the ladle was buried. What could one really say or do?

Even though death while working in a steel mill is now rare because of more extensive safety programs, it still shakes people up when these things happen. I think of Bill occasionally, and wonder what was tormenting his mind so greatly that he committed suicide in that terrible way.

During my forty years in the steel mill, we averaged one fatality every eight years or so. Much more often, we had major accidents where a worker was hurt badly enough so that he could never come back to work. These accidents happened at a rate of twelve to eighteen a year for every year I worked at the plant.

From the ladle, the molten metal is poured into a continuous casting machine and the steel comes out the other end of a mold as a red hot, solid, continuous strand of steel, the mold usually set for a thickness of eight inches and a constant width.

After that, an automatic gas and oxygen torch cuts through this solid ribbon of steel so that pieces, or slabs, eighteen feet long and eight inches thick, are made for further processing by the next department.

The next department, of course, was the hot mill department where I worked as a rougher roller. I would advance and then reverse the red hot slab, weighing from five to eleven tons, back and forth and in and out of the roughing mill five to seven times depending on the hardness of the steel. By doing this I could reduce the thickness by one inch or more each advancing and reversing time, so that when I was finished, the slab would only be three-fourths of an inch thick and would now be one hundred and eighty feet long.

Further up the hot mill aisle, another sequence of mills would accept this three-fourth inch strip and further reduce its thickness to eighty thousandths of an inch, and elongate it to one thousand eight hundred feet.

During the heyday of America's space program, we even rolled hundreds of titanium steel slabs. Titanium is an extremely light weight metal and for a while was used in rocket construction. It was a beautiful sight to roll on the night shift, because the surrounding aisle was darker. This made it easier to see the millions of sparks that jumped off of the steel as it was being hot rolled. They looked like fireflies in a dark field on a starlit night.

The huge size and savage power of a hot mill department's roughing mill was awesome to see and, for newcomers in the department, frightening to hear. The 7,000 horsepower motor that ran the roughing mill was about twenty feet high. The rougher mill housings that held the large round rolls that shaped the steel in place were over forty feet high. The mill and rolls weighed hundreds of tons and were gear driven so that even more power could be delivered to roll down the slabs of steel.

I wasn't pussyfooting around finessing anything while doing my job. Things weren't done in the soft hushed tones of a librarian handing a book to a scholar. I was shaping and rolling steel the *old fashioned way*, by using *pure brute force*. When high pressure cold water is put onto the surface of a steel slab heated to 2,500 degrees, it causes a violent reaction as the cold water hits the hot steel; scale that has formed on the red hot slab surface is literally exploded and blown off in a fury of sparks, steam, and a thunder bolt that can be heard half a mile away from the steel plant. This is done so the scale isn't rolled into the steel slab.

I worked in a glass paneled room about twenty feet above the mill. It was a room anchored onto upright steel columns that was soundproofed and air conditioned so the noise and heat were bearable to both the human operators of the mill and to the electronic equipment and computers used to control the rougher mill.

Sometimes as I rolled slabs, the rougher mill shook and groaned from the heavy load, the deep strain. Sometimes the ampere pull on the 7,000 horsepower motor was so great in the substation that the overhead aisle lights would start to dim from the overload, giving an eerie dark look to the rougher and the slab being rolled, and to me.

When this happened, it would take great skill and courage from me to keep on rolling the slab. Butterflies would start up in my stomach and my heart would thump against my chest like I was running a marathon. When I succeeded, and sometimes I didn't, it felt good—and I mentally and emotionally got tougher because of it.

I have sometimes wondered if my job in a steel mill wasn't predestined because of how this very tough physical environment helped shape and reform my own mental personality, my own mental attitude. I needed toughening up and I succeeded in unconsciously placing myself in a job that would do just that—a work environment that could shape me mentally, emotionally, and physically in the same way I was shaping steel. The steel I was rolling was becoming the steel backbone of myself.

Because I was shy, soft, and introverted, I needed to reshape my own emotions, my mental outlook and belief system about life. I now think that somehow, some way, I was subliminally absorbing the raw physical toughness of a steel mill into myself. This strength, this toughness, this dirt and noise of a hot mill department, permeated me, became a part of me.

The steel mill was about twelve miles away from where I lived and when I would close the front door of my house behind me to get into my car and drive to work, I'd sense what a warm, comfortable, secure environment I was leaving. Getting to work in the winter time during the midnight shift, sometimes with a blizzard blowing snow drifts across roads faster than snow plows could keep them open, with the temperature at zero and still falling, took some doing.

Getting to work on time, never missing a day because of bad weather in thirty-five years, developed a toughness in me. Changing turns each week, working double turns for extra money, staying always in an all-male environment, and finding out that I could hold my own with other men, developed and compounded this new toughness in me.

In this all-male environment I learned to scream, holler, threaten, and challenge anyone who would dare to invade my turf. I went from a shy introvert who blushed when he raised his hand in a grade school classroom to a full blown extrovert who loved confrontation. I actually went through a period when I *sought* confrontation like a shark seeking its next prey! I loved to intimidate and flaunt my newly acquired extrovert power. As time passed, I learned from the violent playback I got from my dreams how to balance myself and stay more centered, being neither an extreme introvert nor an extreme extrovert. But I want to tell you, I loved those days when I won my battles of confrontation after having been a shy introvert for all of my early life.

As a rougher roller, I would sometimes have to roll some stainless grade that our research department had come up with which had never been rolled before. These experimental grades were extremely difficult to do, and it would become a test of a roller's own personal ability as to whether the slab could be rolled successfully down to the required thickness. These kinds of slabs would become a challenge for me. I would always want to roll these slabs successfully because of the personal satisfaction I got from doing it.

These slabs were hard and tough! They would resist my efforts to roll them just as strongly as I resisted change in my own life. When the slabs entered the rougher mill, dust clouds would fly into the air and the mill would actually shake from the enormous strain put on the work rolls by the resistance of the hard slab to being shaped and reduced in size.

Often the mill couldn't take the strain and the thirty-six inch diameter rolls would break in half; then the maintenance men would have to work for eight hours or more to repair the damage I had done to the mill. This is when I was glad I was in a union.

As I became a more experienced roller, I learned not to even try to roll certain kinds of steel slabs because of the damage they could cause, and my mill wrecks became rare.

All these things being done to form or change the shape of red hot metal became major dream symbols as I strived to form, shape, and change my own character.

As I became more experienced and a more mature Seeker, I would have dreams where a decision or action I had taken had just wrecked my own rougher mill, my own personal part of myself that I used to temper and shape the steel in me. Sometimes I had dreams that showed me absolutely destroying "my rougher" or the part of me that shaped change.

My very first dream that used extensive steel mill symbols was also the first dream that was a pure guidance and not a correction dream.

THE DREAM

I'm back in the neighborhood where I lived as a teenage boy. I'm standing by the home of a bachelor who later died in his middle age. (Also in this neighborhood, about 200 yards away, another man was found early one Sunday morning by other neighborhood kids, dead in his car from the effects of alcoholism).

I sit down next to the house of the old neighborhood bachelor and build a fire. Then, as it gets roaring, I start to put rods of iron about one half inch thick and three feet long into this fire. I keep taking them out again and looking at the tips, which have been heated red hot, and then I stick them back into the fire to heat some more.

Then, as easily happens in dreams, I am suddenly standing by the last mill of a five mill hot strip finishing mill (this is the beginning of the dream's second act). I'm standing at the last of these five rolling stands with the oldest, most competent finish mill roller in the hot mill department. He is trying to show me how to adjust the mill so I always get the desired finish gauge or strip thickness ordered. Then the strip exits this mill and goes down the table rolls to be coiled up by a set of down coiler machines.

End of Dream.

After writing down the dream, I did as had been suggested by the many books and the dream interpretation course I studied at the A.R.E. When I was done, my paper looked something like this:

THEME: I was being shown, in a two act play, as a boy and a man, in two different places doing something with steel. One time I am heating it with fire—the other time it is in a finish mill shaping stand being completed as ordered.

Individual Symbol	Category	Physical Interpretation
Old Neighborhood	Place	Place where I once lived.
Bachelor's Home	Place	Where someone lives.
Man Who Died in Car	Person	Alcoholic who died from alcohol near where I once lived.
My self Starting Fire	Person	My self as a young boy.
Putting Steel Rods in a Fire	Thing	My self doing this.
Hot Strip Mill Location in a Steel Mill	Place	A steel mill was now my life's work. Location was where the finished gauge was given to hot strip steel.
Finish Mill Roller and Myself	People	A teacher symbol. But I didn't understand what I was being shown.

Location of Finish	Place	This is the actual place where the strip being rolled
Mill Roller by		and shaped was actually finished.
Last Stand		
Problem		I didn't understand what process was going on in my life.

I was just getting into dream interpretation at that time and I had a strong desire to do this one right. I looked at and studied this dream and these symbols for three days straight.

But, I couldn't come up with any kind of interpretation. I knew that since this was such a strange dream, it had to be important. However, the more I thought about it, the more puzzled I became. Finally after three full days of trying, I admitted to myself and to my higher self that I was stumped.

I didn't know what the dream meant.

That night I went to sleep still thinking about this strange, out of place dream. As I slept, I had the same dream again, and as I got to the part where as a boy I was building a fire and putting steel rods in and out of the fire for examination, a voice spoke to me in my mind:

"Peter, don't you understand that the fire you have built is to be used to temper the steel rods you are moving in and out of the fire? These rods represent the parts of your personality that have to be tempered by the test of fire?"

Then I woke up. It was 4 a.m.—a time of night I would wake up from dreaming for the next thirty years.

I got out of bed, feeling very excited. Who was talking to me? Was it my guardian angel, or my higher self, or, better yet, God? I didn't know, but I was sure of one thing: I had it made now. I had my own personal dream interpreter, speaking to me in plain English. This is great, I thought.

I opened up my spiral notebook, my dream book, looked at the symbols and interpretations I had written down, and saw that they now made sense.

The old neighborhood where I grew up represented an immature place where my consciousness was now residing. The fire I started symbolized the spiritual process I had started within my own personality whereby I would begin to test and temper parts of the iron that was in me, that was still too soft.

Then I remembered that in high school I had taken an industrial arts course (what is now called Votech, short for vocational technology). In metal shop, I made a steel chisel by heating one end of a one inch rod, then hammering it on an anvil until I got a nice flat end. After the end was wedge shaped, I put the end in a hot fire until it heated to an orange-red color. Then I quickly cooled it by quenching it in water.

This is called the tempering process for steel. And, it is what I was doing with the steel rods in the dream—checking the ends to see if the heat had given it an orange-red color yet, before I tempered it.

The steel mill symbolized my *life's work*. The finish mill was the place in my life's work where I did the actual "shaping to a finish" to parts of my personality that had already been heated and tempered. The finish mill roller was the symbol for the teacher who would show me how to correctly do this process.

The dream symbols showed me that *Just As* I had to do this or that by heating up and shaping steel, *So Also* did I have to do these same things to a part of my own psyche that needed to be put into a test of fire, reheated, then reformed and reshaped before it could be used by me as a finished product.

I was now happy that I had an interpretation for my dream. And of course I was even happier with my new internal interpreter who explained dreams to me in plain English.

Because of my new understanding, I rewrote the dream symbols and they now looked like this:

THEME: I'm being shown that the younger and more mature parts of my consciousness were starting to be "tested by fire" and to temper the soft parts of my personality.

Individual Symbol	Category	Spiritual Interpretation
Old Neighborhood	Place	*"Just As"* my body sometimes lived in a childhood place, *so also* does my soul have childhood places where it dwells.
Bachelor's Home	Place	*"Just As"* my body lives in one home in a neighborhood, *so also* does my spiritual self live in me—its home.
Man Who Died in a Car Who Was an Alcoholic	Person	*"Just As"* a human moves around by using a car, *so also* does my soul move through various states of consciousness. A car represents the particular state my soul is now being moved in. I didn't understand the alcoholic part.
Self Starting Fire	Person	*"Just As"* a human starts a physical fire to transform matter into different forms, *so also* is my soul consciousness *"fired up"* so it can transform or transmute parts of its own consciousness.
Steel Rods Being Placed in a Fire by Self	Thing	*"Just As"* a human can build a fire to temper the softness of steel, *so also* can the soul ignite itself in a *baptism of fire* so portions of its soul personality can be tempered.
Steel Mill	Place	*"Just As"* a steel mill is now my physical life's work, *so also* does my spirit or consciousness have a life work to do.
Finishing Stand in a Hot Strip Mill	Place	*"Just As"* the hot strip mill is the particular place where my life's work is concentrated, and the finish mill is a place where the last shape and gauge is given to a steel strip before it can be considered *finished*, *so also* does my soul need to have parts of itself given a final shape and finish before it can be considered complete.
Finish Mill Roller and My Self	People	*"Just As"* the finish mill roller is the person responsible for the final gauge and strip shape and is teaching me how to do this, *so also* is there a higher part of my consciousness, my soul, that is responsible for teaching me how to shape and finish parts of my personality.
Problems		*"Just As"* I had to be taught how to finish steel strip, *so also* would a teacher have to show me how I could *finish* parts of my personality, and I was having trouble understanding this process, which is why I needed a teacher.

After getting over the excitement of having a voice speak to me in a dream and tell me what the symbols meant, I thought complacently that dream interpretation was going to be a cinch from now on.

But this wasn't to be. In the next twenty years, I would be spoken to only four other times in my dreams, and these would only be when I was getting so far off the path, using my free will freedom of choice, that I was in danger of becoming permanently lost. One big trouble with dream interpretation is that there is a part of the human ego that is very self protective. This is because some parts of a human ego or consciousness consist of a lot of false beliefs and wrong conclusions that almost seem to create a life of their own, and the human mind doesn't want to let go of them *regardless of the cost*. This part of the human consciousness works hard to protect itself from exposure to truth. It becomes a trickster.

If you have ever had a family member or friend who has reached a wrong conclusion, or holds onto a false belief about something that you know for a fact is wrong, then you know what I'm talking about.

You try with speech and physical examples to prove to the person the error of their conclusion or belief, or even of their way of doing things; they quickly become extremely defensive and will then resist all rules of logic and plain common sense as to why they should even consider seeing things differently.

Often when you have this sort of encounter with a person, then that person will become a permanent dream symbol for you. When *you* become stubborn or bullheaded and won't change a wrong conclusion or a false belief, then that person will appear in *your* dreams as a symbol of your own stubbornness and bullheaded ways.

In future dreams, maybe years later, this person will continue to personify in human form the *trait of stubbornness*. It is the resistance your own mind or ego is putting up against a logical or common sense change in your belief system, a desirable change that your oversoul or unconscious mind is pointing out in scene play dreams using human characters to personify mental and emotional traits.

Your oversoul is telling you that it is necessary to change those beliefs or ways of doing things if you are to get any more growth in your life.

Your dream is showing you that *Just As* Jane or Joe was wrong and stubborn about changing, *so also* are you wrong and stubborn in some current context. Then a scene with your self and other humans or animals is shown to you to clarify exactly what situation and what part of yourself needs to be worked on, and what part is stubbornly resisting.

It was many years before I realized why I was building my fire near the bachelor's house in the dream, and also close to where an alcoholic died in his car. The bachelor had also been an extremely heavy drinker—a "working" alcoholic as they are sometimes called. This bachelor and the dead alcoholic were the only alcoholics I knew of at that time. In thinking about this dream over the years, I finally realized that I, too, had alcoholic tendencies which needed to be tested by fire and tempered (this was why my dream showed an immature part of me staying in the neighborhood of two alcoholics).

How I loved the taste of a cold beer, especially after a hot summer day sweating in the mill. I would go to a bar after work, wrap my hands around a tall frosted glass of beer, then pull my hand off the glass and watch beads of moisture form on the glass where my hand had been. The beads would run down the frosted glass, washing away the frost so I could see the gold color of the beer behind it.

Looking at the glass of beer, enjoying the sight, smelling the rich malt that gave it its flavor, I'd grab the glass with one hand, raise it to my lips and drink deep and long. Then I'd set the almost empty glass down, tasting the bitter sweet white foam on my upper lip as I swiped it clean with my tongue, almost without realizing I was doing it.

"Yeah," I'd think. "This is what it is all about!" The trouble was, it was *too* good—I'd keep upending glasses of beer until I got drunk.

The next day I'd be disgusted with myself and when I'd go to church with my family on Sunday (I was still attending the Catholic Church at this time), I would vow to God never to do it again. But the next week, and for years to come, I *would* do it again. It was during this period that I asked the priest in confession how I could acquire will power, and you remember how that story went.

After finally understanding the dream so many years after I first had it, I went to work on my beer drinking problem. Finally I quit "cold turkey". I quit for five years or so and then decided, while on a vacation trip to Texas with my family to see an older brother, that it would be okay to start drinking again. I was positive that after five long years away from beer I could be a social drinker just like other people.

That night I dreamed I had come to a fork in a road and had chosen to take the left fork. I knew what that meant as soon as I woke up! It meant I had taken the wrong turn on my path, on my journey, by deciding to drink again. In dreams, when you see a fork in the road, then the correct way to go is down the right fork or right path. This is a sort of play on words, a cute-humor dream mechanism that can befuddle attempts at interpretation.

However, I ignored the dream, and within a month was completely hooked on beer once again. Each week I'd drink more than the week before, until finally I started to get drunk again. I continued on this path for six months or so until I got so thoroughly disgusted with myself that I went "cold turkey" again, and just quit.

I reached a point where I got mad and said to myself, "I'll be damned if I am going to let booze or tobacco run my life!" What created the anger was my own overwhelming desire to be free—which was one of the driving forces that had made me a Seeker.

I just couldn't stand the thought that I wasn't in complete control of my own body. The thought that there was a desire inside of me that was stronger than my own will power made me mad. I was also angry because my drinking was interfering with my search for God. And it was the strength I got from my own anger that allowed me to break free.

As often happens when you stop a bad habit that has a strong hold on you, there is a later recycling effect that becomes a test. I woke up one morning about a year or so after I'd stopped drinking for the second time, and felt like I'd just stopped an hour before. The desire for a beer became more intense as the day went on. I fought off this desire that day, and all during the week that followed.

Finally, on Saturday (my favorite day to get drunk), the desire became seemingly almost irresistible. But I thought about how pleasant it had been for the last year to wake up in the mornings with a clear head and be able to greet God, as I do each morning, with a simple out loud "Hello, God" and not feel ashamed.

So I said to myself, "No, sir, I'm never going to walk down that road again. No beer for me, not now, not ever!" And the desire seemed to strangely go away entirely.

That night I dreamed I was walking on a dirt road and a swamp was nearby. Suddenly, out of the swamp, rose up a huge snake, a boa constrictor. It came at me and wrapped itself around me in coils. We rolled over and over and went down into the swamp, getting covered with mud as we struggled.

Wow, was that snake strong! I could feel its physical strength and power as its coils squeezed me tighter and tighter and we continued to roll and thrash around in the water and muck.

Finally I got the snake by the head, and started to twist and twist until the head was torn off the snake's body.

Then the snake started to shrink and shrink until it was the size of a fishing worm, and it just disappeared. I woke up and looked at the clock. 4:00 a.m.. I was very happy about the dream, which I could immediately interpret because of the biblical and archetypal symbols being used. I also knew enough about my self and my personal dream symbols by then, to be sure what the dream meant.

The snake was the temptation of alcohol which had come out of the swampy recesses of my own consciousness to wrap itself around me like the coils of a huge snake. It was still big and strong and perfectly capable of attacking and killing me even though I hadn't drunk alcohol for a year.

When I had made a permanent, *irreversible* decision *in my own consciousness* never to drink again, never to let alcohol take control of my life, I had, in effect, twisted off the head of the snake of temptation and killed it. I had killed the conscious desire for alcohol that had still been lurking deep inside my own unconscious mind.

I knew, as I lay still in my bed, that I would never be tempted by alcohol again—and I never have been.

At this time in my life, I still had no desire to be any kind of a leader. I was elected twice as a union representative, but I didn't like other people bringing their troubles to me to solve—in those days I always thought a *real man* solved his own problems. To my relief, at the next election they chose somebody else.

I had many steel mill location dreams that really upset me. Once I dreamed I was operating the up-cut shear, a shear powerful enough to cut through a steel plate three quarters of an inch thick and fifty inches wide with one cut. In the dream I wasn't cutting the front edge of steel strips, instead I was cutting up human beings. One after another I'd put them into the shear and cut their heads and arms off, or else cut them in half. I awoke, scared and shook up because in the dream *I had been enjoying doing this.* "I would *never* do anything like that," I thought to myself as I lay in bed. "I'm a safe, conscientious shear operator. I'd never cut people in half! What an awful dream!"

Later that day, after I calmed down, I began to try to analyze the dream and go for its hidden meaning. And as I thought about it during the day, the meaning suddenly became painfully clear. The dream was a play on words put forth in scenes. It meant I was supposed to *quit cutting people up*!, which is what I was verbally doing by talking behind their backs and criticizing their shortcomings—and enjoying doing it.

This backbiting, gossiping, and criticizing the faults of others was a strong impulse lodged deep inside me because I didn't like to see my own faults. This one major fault of gossiping and criticizing would take years for me to conquer; years before the desire to talk about people behind their backs, to *cut them up*, would finally leave me and this flaw, too, would be tempered.

Now I've finally learned to be non-judgmental toward my wife, my children, my fellow workers, and my friends. And at last *I have even become non-judgmental toward myself.* I've gotten to where I can laugh at myself and some of the silly ideas and old ways that I still have.

THE SEEKER STUMBLES

Three years after the tempering by fire dream, I was again spoken to in a dream. During this period I had continued to study the books available through the A.R.E. about dreaming and about the psychic Edgar Cayce. I was also getting books on metaphysical and religious theories and the occult from my home town book stores.

One day I ran across a book called *The Tiger's Fang*, which explained an ancient art of soul travel called Eckankar. The author, Paul Twitchell, described how he could leave his body while sleeping at night, and do this in a conscious way rather than in a dream state. He would then meet an Ascended Master or guru, in his case a Tibetan monk, who would show him how to explore the Seven Planes of Awareness which is the invisible universe of God. Twitchell described how, after passing through the lower six planes successfully with the assistance of the Ascended Master, the soul reaches the Seventh and final plane where all is a balance of unity and oneness. Here at last is God itself, the sum total of all creation. Best of all, Twitchell claimed he could teach this art of soul travel to others.

I was particularly susceptible to the concept of Ascended Masters helping earthbound people because of my initial training in the Roman Catholic Church. This had included information that holy people who died had to have a record provable to the Church of performing miracles that helped people on earth after they (the saint candidates) had died before they could be declared saints.

I was fascinated both by the theory of soul travel and by the concept that a person could leave his body while sleeping at night—in a conscious way, not a dream state, and explore God more or less like one could explore different parts of the physical world.

The idea really grabbed me. You might say I took to the concept of soul travel like a bird takes to air. I was convinced it was my destiny to learn this short cut to God. And, I had lately been having recurring dreams where I had been accepted as an initiate in some secret society.

At this time I was thirty-four years old, had been married for thirteen years, and had two sons and two daughters. The book had been published in 1967 and I was reading, in 1968, the second printing in that year. I immediately sat down and wrote to the address inside the book which was in Las Vegas, Nevada. I thought this a little strange. A religion claiming the ability to teach people how to explore God's universe headquartered in the capital of gambling and prostitution in the U.S.A.? (This was before Las Vegas partially cleaned up its image to that of an entertainment capital).

I soon received the books I had ordered and read them greedily.

Eckankar had an inexpensive training program for beginners and I signed up. If I remember right, the beginning set took twelve lessons of fifteen to twenty pages each, and twelve months, to complete. One then qualified as a *chela* (beginner). A second set of twelve lessons made the student an *initiate*. The third and final set put The Seeker on the way to becoming a *master* in the soul travel business.

I only made it through one and a half or two years of lessons, however, before I crash landed.

The Eck Master I was supposed to meet in the spirit world, after I had learned how to leave my body at night as I slept, was Paul Twitchell. Just before I went to sleep each night, I faithfully practiced Twitchell's methods for leaving my body. You were ready to consciously leave your body when you started to hear a buzzing noise like bees around their nest; then you waited for a popping sound, caused by the soul leaving the body through the top of the head. I had had the experience of hearing a loud popping sound sometimes when I was in deep meditation, but it had always brought my attention back to myself and I would become alert and come out of the meditative state of consciousness immediately.

For a long period of time I continued to study and try to leave my body, but had no apparent success—no buzzing, no popping. This was still in my heavy beer drinking and tobacco chewing days, and the lessons had warned never to attempt the exercises with alcohol or drugs in the body. But I was only drinking heavy on the weekends, so I told myself it would be okay to do the exercises during the week. This is a good example of the trickster ego at work

One night I dreamed I was floating high above the Earth, which looked like the photographs taken by astronauts from the moon: a beautiful round globe of green forests, blue water, and white clouds.

I was floating above this Earth and I looked down at my body. I realized that I *had* no body; I was just a shiny white globe of light with my head and face on top of the light globe. I thought to myself, "So, this is what my soul body looks like." Then I woke up.

This had to be a real out of the body experience, I thought excitedly, so I got even more committed to Eckankar and the training exercises. But, I was still drinking and I wasn't too disciplined with the rest of my body habits, either. I did have dreams where I met Twitchell, but I don't remember going anywhere with him.

Then one night, about a year into the lessons, I had a really bad nightmare. This was thirty some years ago, yet I can still remember it as if I'd dreamed it last night. I was traveling through the sky and all at once I was attacked by some kind of evil spirits. I felt like an evil presence was chasing me—all the more horrible because they couldn't be seen. They seemed to be radiating an electrical energy from their bodies.

They chased me across the sky and were right behind me as I flew home as fast as I could and entered into my bedroom through a closed glass window. For some reason I could pass through the glass but they could not, so they just kept buzzing around outside the window like bees, obviously furious they couldn't get in. They kept looking through the glass window panes at me.

I woke up at that point, terrified, my heart thumping like my chest was being pounded apart from the inside. I was more scared than I had ever been in my life. I could feel electrical energy vibrating off my body, then going around and around it like static electricity. Both my body and the bed seemed to be vibrating.

I was still only half awake and kind of groggy when I heard a voice speak to me inside my head. It said only one sentence: "We are sorry we had to frighten you so badly, but it is necessary." And that was all. It was a clear, bell-like sounding voice.

Immediately after the voice spoke, the vibrating energy that was shaking my body and circling me gradually slowed, then stopped. Years later when I'd watch Star Trek or a science fiction movie which showed blue static electricity flow all around and through a person, I'd think of that dream. That's what it had felt like, except there was no blue color—just the vibrations.

I calmed down, got out of bed, dressed, and went downstairs. It was 4 a.m. I got a glass of water and, in the darkness, so my family wouldn't be disturbed, thought about the strange frightening thing that had just happened. My wife had been lying beside me and apparently what had happened had no effect on her.

I sat in the darkness and then turned on a lamp because I was still frightened. I wondered why I'd had this dream experience of being chased by evil spirits through the sky. And why had my body vibrated so? I thought, "What *has* just happened to me?"

To this day, I'm not sure what that experience was all about. I can only guess. I think I had succeeded that night in leaving my body and I went somewhere I should not have gone. Maybe this was because I was still so undisciplined, or because of the alcohol in my system. I do know one thing for sure—I didn't meet Paul Twitchell or any other Eck Master. I was out there all alone.

For weeks I could think of nothing but the experience of being chased by the terrifying evil spirits, of vibrating in bed and then being spoken to. It was the voice that held my attention and fascination: "We are sorry to frighten you, but it was necessary."

I would be spoken to a few more times in future dreams, but this was the only time the voice identified itself as a plural or group, and also the first and only time I was ever apologized to for being frightened by something in a dream.

What could the dream possibly mean? With my inborn habit of always asking "Why?" to everything I saw, felt, or experienced, I took the next step and began to analyze the dream experience and the voice. Who was "we"? Who or what is it that speaks to me when I'm in a crisis or emergency situation I can't handle? Who were the persons or things watching over me? Ascended masters? Members of Eckankar, the secret society? Guardian angels?

Was it God speaking to me? No, it spoke of itself as "we", so it couldn't be God. Besides, why would God bother speaking to *me*? I was only a high school graduate, a shift worker working in a steel mill. At that time, I ran a jack hammer to clean steel slag from the hot mill reheat furnaces when the slag got so thick it had to be broken up and shoveled away to clean the hearth.

God talks to ministers, priests, bishops, saints, and holy people—not to mill workers. Still, *someone* was talking to me; *someone* was guiding me through troubled waters. But *I* wasn't saint material, so why me? I had no answer. And I soon got so wrapped up in everyday living that I just went on to other things and put the dream and the voice out of my mind.

The experience did make me wonder, though, if I should go on with Eckankar. I had a weekend free, and decided to re-read the three or four books Twitchell had written about the ancient society of soul travelers, along with the training manuals.

As I read through the material I began noticing inaccuracies and statements that were inconsistent from book to book or with statements made in the training manuals. I hadn't noticed these the first time, but when I read all the materials together they stuck out like a red flag.

As a Seeker of the truth, as a struggling perfectionist, one thing I couldn't stand was inaccuracies. And here was Paul Twitchell, a man of God, a self-professed avatar, a man capable of soul travel and of teaching others how to do the same, making statements that just didn't add up.

I had a couple of pages of these examples and, with a cover letter expressing my deep concern, I mailed them to Eckankar headquarters in Las Vegas.

I waited several months for a reply. Silence. Meanwhile I continued the nightly Eckankar practice, but still with no results. Then I received a flyer that Paul Twitchell was coming to Cincinnati, Ohio, to give a weekend seminar on Eckankar for his followers.

Since Cincinnati was only a few hours drive away I thought "I'll just go and talk to this Mr. Twitchell in person and get my information straight from the horse's mouth."

I arrived Friday evening and after checking into the hotel for the weekend, went to the assembly room where the seminar was to be held. As I entered, everyone seemed to be in a hushed, subdued mood. "This is sure a sad bunch of soul travelers," I thought as I looked around. I went over to the arrival desk to register for the seminar and get the ever present name tag. After a moment the woman registrar looked up at me and said, "There will be no seminar, Mr. Twitchell died in his room last night."

Well, I mean to tell you. I was stunned! I just could not believe it. How could this be? Wasn't he an avatar? A spiritual adept? Surely anyone that far advanced on the spiritual path ought to at least have some idea of when they are going to die; they don't do it away from home in some hotel room.

The registrar told me I could stay for the weekend—that there were other leaders from the Las Vegas headquarters who would be guest lecturers.

Disappointed, disillusioned, I don't remember answering. I just turned around, walked out of the lobby and up to my room to be alone. After a while I called my wife and said I'd be home sometime the next day because the speaker I had come to hear lecture had just died. She said, "Okay," and I hung up.

That night I dreamed I walked into the hotel room where Mr. Twitchell had just died, and saw his wrist watch lying on a night stand. I picked it up, put it on my wrist, then turned and left the room. End of dream.

"Oh, great," I thought as I woke up. "Does this mean it's now my time to take up his watch? No way," I said to myself, puzzled as to the dream's meaning and symbols, "I'm going home." And I did.

A week or so after I got back, a notice came from Eckankar headquarters announcing Twitchell's death. The invisible members of the Secret Order were meeting to pick a new Avatar.

The flyer showed Mr. Twitchell's young wife, dressed in mourning. She appeared in the pictures to be considerably younger than her husband, but that was no concern of mine; I was only interested in spiritual guidance, not in the leader's family. I was still doing the practice faithfully every night—but if I ever did succeed in leaving my body, I wondered what Ascended Master would be meeting me now. Finally another announcement came: a new Avatar had been appointed by the spiritual masters. A photograph showed what appeared to be a nice enough young fellow. I think he had been either a mechanical or electrical engineer for some large car manufacturer, and I wondered what his working friends thought of his latest promotion. About a year later an announcement came that the new avatar had just married Mr. Twitchell's young widow. After I read the marriage announcement, I thought, "Oh, yeah, nothing like keeping the business in the family."

But even then, I somehow didn't want to admit to myself that I was wrong about Eckankar; I didn't want to say it was the wrong path for me or even to try to decide if it was a true path. I kept right on doing the spiritual exercises that were supposed to lead me to out-of-the-body travel while I slept.

One night three months after the marriage announcement, still not getting anywhere with soul travel, I had another major dream.

THE DREAM

I was out walking somewhere, crossing over a huge valley. Its hills were really high and the valley floor deep. After I crossed over I looked back, and realized that both the valley floor and the sides of the hills were lined with thousands and thousands of empty steel drums. Somehow I knew they were empty.

Then I looked ahead and saw a big, beautiful, shiny archway, studded all over with jewels. Standing right under the archway was an extremely ancient man with long white hair and a long white beard. He had on a full length metallic shiny blue one-piece garment. It was beautiful cloth and he looked like pictures I had seen of Merlin, the ancient sorcerer, but he didn't identify himself.

He came further out in front of the archway and we sat down somehow, on something, so we could talk. He pointed back at the hills and valley I had just crossed which were lined with fifty-five gallon steel drums.

He told me it was very dangerous for me to keep trying to cross over the valley in the manner I was now doing and that I was to stop doing it right now!

Then he looked at me and said, "It won't do you any good to cross over because I won't let you through this gate anyhow!"

End of Dream

I had been reading occult and metaphysical books long enough to know what this dream meant without bothering to write it out in symbol form. I had just met the ancient Old Man, the Ancient Wisdom, who in our modern mythology used in songs and jokes is St. Peter at his pearly gates.

This old man is in effect the guardian, the protector of the gates between the visible physical world and the invisible spiritual world. We are not supposed to go through these gates until we die. This guardian was telling me that the way I was trying to cross over to the spiritual world was very dangerous, and also that it was senseless to keep trying because he wasn't going to let me inside the spiritual world.

I also knew what the symbol meant of the barrels covering both the hills and the floor of the valley I was trying to cross.

As a young boy I often played in a local fertilizer plant's storage yard after the workers went home. In those days there was no fence around the plant, nor was there a guard at night.

This plant received many kinds of liquid chemicals, shipped in steel drums, which were ingredients in the powdered fertilizer they made for the local farmers. After the barrels were empty the barrels were laid out in rows twenty barrels long and four high. A wooden 2 x 4 block at each end of the row kept the barrels from rolling.

We neighborhood kids would crawl to the top of these piles of barrels and play "it". We ran and leapt from pile to pile and across rows to keep from being tagged and becoming the new "it".

The trouble was, so many kids would be running and jumping on top that the barrels would begin to rock and bump together. When this got violent enough, the end barrels would jump over the wooden 2 x 4 stops, and then the whole long pile would start to roll out.

I've been on top of barrel piles when this happened. In quick succession the second row of barrels would follow the first; then the third and fourth rows would follow those until the whole pile was rolling out onto the ground.

If you had good balance and could spin or walk barrels, like lumberjacks do when they spin logs in the water, then you could stay upright by moving your feet in rhythm with the spin of the barrel. Some of the older, best coordinated kids could do this from the fourth row all the way through the other rows and down onto the ground, and then actually stay on the barrel as it rolled across the storage yard. Then they would jump off the still moving barrel, always raising their arms up in a self proclaimed cheer of accomplishment.

For my part, after a barrel would make one or two revolutions, I'd fall down on my butt and bump, bump down to the ground.

The real danger was if you *lost your balance* and fell forward, getting ahead of and in front of the rolling pile. This meant a lot of heavy, not always empty, steel barrels were going to hit you. Going across a barrel pile that started to move could mean serious injury, even death if a whole pile rolled over you.

Remembering this dangerous childhood game, I easily understood the valley and two hills covered with barrels as a symbol of danger. If they started to roll while I was crossing over them, I could be crushed and killed. I further remembered that what would cause the trouble in the first place was being *out of balance.*

All that day I was depressed, almost broken hearted. My dreams of being a great soul traveler in the spirit world were evaporating because I had been clearly told that it was wrong, dangerous, and in any case of no use, for me to continue to do it. That I was danger-ously out of balance in pursuing this path.

I remembered the earlier dream where I was out in space being chased by evil spirits and the voice spoke to me. I belatedly admitted to myself that that dream, also, had warned me of the dangers of attempting out of the body travel, of trying to cross over to the spirit world in my sleep.

I quit all the Eckankar monthly and daily lessons, but with a deep sense of sadness. I somehow felt that it was I who had failed; it was I who had not been worthy enough to be-come an initiate in the Ancient Society of Soul Travelers.

About ten years later I read somewhere that Paul Twitchell had had a group of paid ghost writers (if one dare use that term with spirit travelers). If he did, it would sure account for the many discrepancies I'd noticed. Maybe I was just nitpicking. Maybe Eckankar was right for some people, but it definitely wasn't right for me. I had been so sure that I'd finally arrived at a wonderful shortcut to God and ultimate truth, that when I failed my entire path seemed to end. I had thought I could use soul travel to bypass my earthly woes and any need to discipline myself. Now, like a stream of water flowing out into the desert to just disappear in the sand, my path just faded into nothing.

Unless you've ever been a disappointed Seeker, you can't understand the feeling of total loss when you completely and utterly fail. I was disillusioned, my expectations were shattered. I didn't know where to go next.

I wasn't even sure if I wanted to find God anymore. It was the same emotional feeling you have when you go into a relationship with someone believing that the person is Mr. or Miss Right. When the relationship unravels just as it was starting to get meaningful, you are left with nothing but the pain of rejection and the hopeless, helpless feeling of failure.

The months passed and became a year. I couldn't bear the thought of beginning over. I had made such a deep emotional and intellectual commitment to Eckankar that I just couldn't seem to accept that it was over. I'd go down to my basement study and pick up some old Eckankar book or literature. But my dream warnings had been too clear, and the dangers and implications of continuing soul travel too vivid. I would put the book aside after a few pages and go for a long walk in the woods back of my house.

It was a black time of life for me, that year after I quit Eckankar. I wondered if I had enough humility and tenderness of spirit to ever find God and that worried me some. Often that year, I thought the thirst to find God had finally left, was gone forever.

But suddenly, well after a year had passed, it came back. One morning I woke up and discovered that once more I wanted to find God.

"Where do I go now?" I asked myself.

The answer was suddenly quite obvious: back to the A.R.E.; I rejoined, and reading and restudying the A.R.E. material soon got me centered and feeling calmer. I began to meditate again, and I returned to the practice of recording and interpreting my nightly dreams.

THE SEEKER STUMBLES A THIRD TIME

That summer for our family vacation I rented an eight person tent trailer and we headed south toward the Virginia Beach area. We found a trailer park near the ocean which was also just a few miles from the A.R.E. headquarters. After I got the tent trailer camp set up, we were ready to swim in the ocean and enjoy camping out in the great outdoors. Instead it rained for three days and three nights, a steady and unrelenting downpour.

I quickly found out that having a wife and four young children inside a tent trailer for three long, long, rainy days and nights was nothing like the wonderful camping life shown in the brochures. I also discovered that tent trailers have a major problem—canvas tops. They shed rain all right—but only the light shower kind of rain. As the heavy deluge continued, day and night, the canvas top got damp. If you touched the canvas or rubbed against it, the canvas acted like a water wick and outside moisture would start to drip and drop inside the trailer. These drips didn't stop until the rain stopped.

Forced to stay inside the tent because of the heavy rain, we made more living space available by pushing the blankets and clothes against the canvas sides. Naturally touching the sides with blankets and clothes, especially on the upper bunk beds, made moisture seep through and we soon had a trailer full of wet clothing and bedding. As the bedding and clothing got wetter and the water-wick drops more numerous, the mood of my family of happy campers dropped like the drips.

Finally after the three interminable days, the sun came out. I think we had clotheslines strung over half an acre of the campground.

Never again would I daydream at work about sitting around a campfire encircled by my family, singing songs and swaying in rhythm, or about waiting all night for the plaintive howl of a wolf outlined against a full moon (some fifteen or twenty miles from a major city (my wife's idea of wilderness). From that time on vacations were spent in hard roofed hotels and motels, places with room service and cable TV, where stairs instead of elevators was as rough as it ever got.

Toward the end of that week in Virginia Beach, when the kids were at last having their fun on the beach, I told my wife I'd like to drive down to the A.R.E. headquarters for a few hours and look it over. She knew I'd been a long time member because I always kept her current on the events of my search in the secret hope that she would join me, though she never did.

At noon I drove over to the headquarters, at that time just the big wooden building which had originally been Edgar Cayce's hospital. As soon as I got inside I asked directions and went to the library. A gentle looking lady sitting behind a desk asked in a soft, southern accented voice if she could help me. "Ah," I thought as I listened to her speak, "doesn't she sound soft and sweet?" Southern and Irish accents! I could listen to the rhythm of their speech by the hour, like some people listen to music.

I asked if it might be possible to meet with Hugh Lynn Cayce, at that time the president of the A.R.E.. She answered in her lovely voice that Hugh Lynn was in the middle of his personal meditation time; she would see if he would be available. Within a few minutes, a pleasant looking man in his late fifties or early sixties came through a side door and greeted me. He had a plump, red cheeked, round face, kind of like a little cherubic boy. He introduced himself as Hugh Lynn Cayce and said he was glad to meet me.

I was impressed that he would break off his meditation to meet a stranger. When I'm meditating, I get in so deep that I don't even like to hear noise, let alone be disturbed by anyone. Yet from his personal meditation time he came to see me. I told him how much I enjoyed the A.R.E. material and how it had helped me over the years. I told him I was a Seeker trying to find God. He smiled and said, "We all are."

Somehow, meeting Hugh Lynn Cayce, the actual son of Edgar Cayce, made Edgar Cayce more real to me.

A.R.E. people in general, as a group and as individuals, always seem to me the most polite, cordial, "I'll do anything I can to help you" kind of people that I have met in my many years of searching for God. They always seem willing to go to any length to answer a question or to help in finding a solution to any personal problems I was trying to get answers for. But over the years I finally found that the answers for personal problems can ultimately be found only inside the one creating them; sooner or later I would have to look inside myself to find my answers.

After the vacation was over and the tent trailer returned, I began reading the new books I had bought while at Virginia Beach and soon ran across a reference to something called the Great White Brotherhood. This wasn't a racial supremacy group; I was never bothered by this problem and racial hatred was never one of the steel rods I had to temper.

The Great White Brotherhood was supposed to be made up of saints who had ascended and were now in heaven surrounded by a white light, hence the name. Their job, as ascended beings who had mastered themselves and the Earth, was to help souls still on Earth who were struggling to better themselves. Once again, my early training in Catholicism, the belief that holy people helped those on Earth after they died, made this concept easily believable. "Here is the help I've been looking for," I thought happily. (This was a big part of my problem in my earlier years as a Seeker—I was always looking for someone to help me, or do it for me, rather than doing it for myself.)

I was particularly susceptible to the concept of ascended masters helping earthbound people because of my early childhood Roman Catholic training. It had included information that holy people who died, before they were declared saints, had to have a record, provable to the Catholic Church, of performing miracles that helped people on earth after they, the saint candidates, had died.

Another thing that made me susceptible was that I had long been having dreams that showed me being accepted by some secret society as a candidate for membership. The problem was that, months or years later, I would have another dream that told me I had been thrown out because I had failed all the tests or something like that.

Anyway, because of dreams I was having, my Catholic training, and my current choice of reading material, the concept of a Great White Brotherhood seemed to be just what I was looking for at this time and place in my life.

This organization, which they called The Church, was headquartered in Los Angeles. At least, I thought, "a City of Angels seems to be a more fitting place for a God centered organization than Las Vegas." The leaders of The Church were a husband and wife who claimed they had the ability to channel all of the Ascended Masters including Jesus himself—which did seem a little too much of a good thing to be true.

As I read, or listened to the channeled messages on the tapes the organization sent me, I found I was getting new insights into Biblical writings and the reasons humans were on earth. The various channeled messages appeared to agree with most of what I had picked up out of the A.R.E. material. Only, sometimes, The Church's interpretation seemed to roll back towards itself so that everything that had been written in the Bible was a justification for The Church to exist—they were the leaders of the New Age and, as such, only *their* material should be listened to.

I was skeptical about people or organizations that claimed they had sole control of the one and only path to God, so I was really slow to make any kind of deep commitment to The Great White Brotherhood and their Church. I had gotten mentally and emotionally beaten up twice already dealing with organized religions, the Catholic Church and Eckankar, yet here I was thinking seriously of going at it again.

I realized that people like myself can make an emotional commitment to religion that can become stronger than the love they have for their spouse or even their children; every day people leave their husband/wife/children to follow some religious leader or join some cult.

I also knew now that once people do this breakaway act it becomes very, very difficult to leave the cult or religion; before they can quit, they first have to admit to themselves that they were wrong, a gullible fool maybe, and this is tough to do.

So I waded into the waters of The Church's teachings with a great deal of caution. But gradually I got in deeper and began to send for more and more of their literature and tapes. Finally, after a year or so, I decided to become an initiate in the Great White Brotherhood using The Church as the teaching vehicle.

Their course for the Chela (initiate) would culminate, if I was successful, in my being one who had passed all of The Church's tests and also my own personal life tests. Then I would be on the way to becoming a Master myself. And I also would be accepted as a secret member of the Great White Brotherhood via The Church.

All the big names were being channelled by the husband and wife team: Jesus, Michael the Archangel, St. Germaine, the Virgin Mary, and more. So if this was for real, a really impressive cast of saints would be helping me.

And this was what I thought I wanted—a chance to be in the big leagues, to be shoulder to shoulder with all the heavies of sainthood. At last, instead of my lonely search I'd be with others who had the same desire, the same thirst.

I was informed by the Los Angeles office that a Saturday evening study group met in Pittsburgh, only a forty minute drive away; I phoned the group leader and was invited to attend. I was still keeping my wife current about what I was doing, without expecting her to join me, but I asked if she wanted to go along. She just bit her lower lip and shook her head, then turned away.

When the first set of The Church's initiation lessons came in the mail, I eagerly read through it. At the end there was a printed declaration of beliefs that I was supposed to read, then follow and strictly adhere to—the same thing Eckankar had had me do. These declarations had to be accepted and believed without reservation, first in Eckankar and now in The Church, just like the Apostles Creed of Catholicism. It is a basic outline of all the Catholic Church's teachings and doctrine which specifies that you, as a Catholic, must believe and accept without reservation.

This Creed was the first thing the nuns taught after the "Our Father" that had to be memorized. Then, at each mass I attended on Sundays or Holy Days of Obligation, I would repeat it out loud as part of the congregation.

Each time I got into another form of organized religion, the first thing they would roll out was their "Creed" or list of beliefs that *had to be* accepted and adhered to by a new member.

I understood many years later, after receiving a lot more of life's hard lessons and reading many more psychology books, that each man and woman, when they reach adulthood, needs to write out their own personal "Creed" or outline of the beliefs they live by, including their fears. This list of personal beliefs becomes the myth you live out each hour and day of your life, the narrative of your life based on your belief system. You can never change your life for better or worse until you first change your belief system: the "Creed" you live by is the fence that holds you in.

As I looked at the "Creed" of The Church, I wondered why it was necessary. I was joining their organization so they could train me how to find God on a one-to-one basis. I didn't want or need any intermediator between myself and God—I'd had quite enough of this in Roman Catholicism. I didn't want to find the Catholic Church or Eckankar or The Church of the White Brotherhood, I wanted to find God! So why did I have to accept *any* organized church's beliefs? As I looked over their lists of beliefs, I began to feel skeptical again.

However, I had no other path to explore right then, and I had already found that many of The Church's written teachings verified conclusions I had already arrived at in my own search. So I decided to dive head first into The Church and I began attending the weekly Saturday evening meetings with an open mind and an anxious heart.

The meetings were held in the basement of the leader's home, remodeled into a family game room with paneling, a dropped ceiling, and a blue carpet on the floor.

The leader, who I will call Gail, had been a member of The Church for a good many years, trained at the Los Angeles headquarters. She was a happy, spirited, bubbly person and seemed genuinely glad to meet me. She introduced me to the people already present and, as new members arrived, made sure I knew them also.

As I still had a good deal of skepticism when it came to organized religions, I looked around this basement temple, appraising and evaluating everything I saw and heard. I wondered if this finally might be the place where I would find God and truth.

A card table was set against the back wall and a pot of coffee brewing. There was also a fruit punch and some cookies. As more members came, some placed cookies they had brought onto the card table on paper plates.

Against another wall was a homemade altar covered with a white linen cloth. Hanging behind it was some kind of centerpiece picture, with a picture of Jesus to the right and one of St. Germaine to the left. St. Germaine was supposed to be the member of the Great White Brotherhood who used his light to be the primary sponsor, or the Ascended Master, responsible for the creation of The Church on Earth sometime during the 1950's.

The center picture, up close, showed what looked like the outline of a short, wide, white candle. Within this outline were three forms stacked one on top of the other. A figure outline of a human man on the bottom, an outline of Jesus that somehow blended into the top of the man, and God itself on the top. God seemed to stand on formless legs atop Jesus.

I learned that this center picture symbolized that man, Jesus, and finally God were all parts of one whole, joined together in the symbolic candle that showed they really were all made up of the same light. The picture also symbolized that the only way to God for man was through Jesus.

As I viewed the hanging pictures I automatically compared them, and the altar, with the Catholic Church of my youth and young manhood. The Catholic Church went in for more life sized statues and expensive portraits and altars. Of course they had more money, and had had a longer period of time to collect their icons.

When about eight people besides myself and the leader were present, I was handed a thick booklet of songs and also what I took to be poems.

First we sang some songs together as a group. Then the leader looked at me, the new member, and explained that we would next repeat Decrees—what I had thought were poems. These Decrees were a half or full page of wisdom channeled by the Church's founders—either the husband or the wife—from one of the various saints or Ascended Masters. They were intended to cleanse the mind of carnal thoughts or thoughts of the personal ego.

As a courtesy to me, Gail explained that they would start the decreeing slowly for a while and increase the speed until the words were being repeated in a singsong chant. They did this for ten minutes or so. At that point they went into high gear, repeating whole words and passages faster than I could even read them. I stopped trying to keep up and just listened. Their words got faster and higher pitched until they seemed to hum together as one sound. It was almost like the humming sound a swarm of bees makes flying through the air or around their nest, the sound I was supposed to hear in Eckankar, I remembered, before taking off for space travel.

When the chanting stopped, I was given a decree book of my own to take home and study. Gail told me to read the decrees aloud and practice going faster and faster until I could keep up with the group.

I did this for months and months at home by myself and also with the group each Saturday evening. I sent for all the books and literature The Church had that interested me. If I'd ordered all the literature and audio cassette tapes they had, I would have been broke because the quantity available was enormous.

Finally after six months or so, during which I had both good and bad dreams as to how my journey on the path to God was progressing, I was able to keep up with the group as they chanted at the slow and moderate speeds—but when they really got to smoking, when they sounded like bees in flight, I still had to quit and just listen. They all assured me it was only a matter of time and that soon I would be able to reach those speeds also.

The people in the Saturday evening group were all nice, sincere, polite, family people with children. I was happy that I had finally met some of my own kind, people whose lives involved a search for God. Often, during a halfway break or after the meeting was over, we would sit around having cookies and coffee or fruit punch, and compare notes. I would tell of my experiences with Eckankar and they would laugh at the funny parts, then tell stories on themselves of how they too had stumbled or gotten off the path. I was really beginning to like these people.

One Saturday evening as we all arrived and got ready to begin, the phone rang. Gail picked it up and after saying "Hello", just listened.

The phone never rang at our meetings and so we all watched curiously. As Gail listened her face became pale and she asked, "Who is this?" A frightened look came over her face. She listened a bit longer, then put the receiver down.

We all looked at her, puzzled because she was so pale and frightened. One of the women asked, "What is the matter?"

"It was the devil," Gail whispered.

"What do you mean?" another woman asked.

"It was the devil," Gail repeated, louder this time. "He wouldn't identify himself when I asked, but I know who it was. He said for us to quit praying and chanting so loud because it was disturbing him!"

The group mumbled aloud and turned to each other, looking surprised but nodding their heads in acceptance.

"We must decree immediately," Gail proclaimed, then turned to me and added, "We have to surround ourselves with light for protection." I nodded and joined in the decree chants, but what I was thinking was, "She's paranoid as hell if she really thinks the devil phoned her."

As we continued to decree, I thought about what had happened and figured it was probably a close neighbor who was tired of the loud singing and praying, and had called to complain. I thought and thought about her statement "It was the devil!" I knew AT&T and ITT had done a good job stringing communication wires all over the planet, but I had never read where they'd run a phone line to hell. I got this mental picture of the devil sitting with his feet up on a desk calling a basement phone in Western Pennsylvania.

But, I realized, the rest of the group had immediately accepted Gail's interpretation without reservation. This wasn't the first time I'd witnessed an odd group reaction. Often when I'd asked a question that called for a private, personal opinion, no one had given one; they would always defer to the group leader or repeat from memory what The Church's view on the subject was. I realized that none of them were thinking for themselves anymore. The phone call added considerably to my uneasiness about the group—but I kept studying and going to group meetings anyway.

One evening a few weeks later we chanted an unusual type of decree, supposedly channeled through The Church's male leader. About halfway through, the Ascended Master said "God Bless Andrew," or some name or other; then like a dam bursting apart, other names flowed out in a torrent, one after the other: "God bless Saint Helen, Saint Sam... John... Michael... Arthur... Sarah...." On and on the names poured forth.

After thirty or forty names I thought, "We have them all now but the butcher, the baker, and an Indian chief." Then the decree finished, and as we took a break another member asked me what I thought of that last decree. I smiled, and said, "He must have been a politician in his last Earth incarnation because he sure didn't want to offend anyone." Then I added, "Maybe he's still campaigning, trying for a higher office in heaven."

You could have heard a pin drop in that room. Talk about saying the wrong thing, in the wrong place, at the wrong time! Whew! I was glad to get out of there that night. Now I had not only a paranoid group of people, but one with no sense of humor.

I was still upset about the so-called phone call from the devil incident and seriously considered leaving The Church. But on the other hand, when I read the written literature and listened to the channeled messages on the tapes, I felt the information the husband and wife team were channeling and teaching had a strong element of truth.

The Church Masters explained secret insights about the Earth and humans, and how mankind should live a God-aware life. After all my years as a Catholic, where my religious education consisted of memorizing the Our Father, The Creed, the Hail Marys, plus stories from the Bible and the correct way to participate at Sunday Mass, these teachings were a revelation. Taken with my dream interpretations, I was really on a roll. This was what I had left the Catholic Church to find, and I was finding it. Even if some of what I was learning would not prove to be true or practical in actual practice, it was still better than the boring repetitious worship of God I had found in Catholicism.

But—there was something about the application of these truths within The Church's membership that I didn't feel comfortable with.

A few weeks later I received a notice from the Los Angeles headquarters that the husband of the husband/wife team who were the co-founders and channelers, had suddenly died. He didn't look to be that old a man and seemed in good physical shape from what I could see in the photographs. I wasn't sure I was ready to follow a woman spiritual leader. "Oh, no,," I thought, "I hope this isn't going to be Eckankar all over again."

The widow would now be the sole channeler for The Church and the exclusive spokesperson for all the Ascended Masters. After Christ and his apostles and the male dominated Catholic Church, I had followed male spiritual leaders all my life, even in Eckankar, and I wasn't sure I was ready to follow a woman spiritual leader. Still, having an open mind was what started me on my search, so I stayed on as a member.

A few months went by and then another announcement came proclaiming the husband who had died to have passed all the tests needed to be an Ascended Master. The man's picture as an Ascended Master, with a new name, was now to be placed above the altar beside Jesus and Saint Germaine. I looked at the photo, the name change, and the announcement for a long time. Finally, I put them down and thought, "At least the moves up are fast in this organization, but I don't know... somehow..." "Hmmm," I thought, "the Catholic Church takes a hundred years or so before they declare someone a saint and The Church does it in less than a hundred days."

It wasn't long after this that I started to notice something new happening to me. Suddenly, at work or at home, without consciously wanting to chant I would spontaneously start having a chant come through my mind instead of the usual random thoughts. I mentioned this to one of the group members I'd become friendly with. He told me not to worry about it—it was just my false human ego being cleansed.

I had understood that the chanting was a form of praying. Now I was learning that it was being used to keep under control the supposedly useless stream of random thoughts that people have all day long. I didn't know about that!

Something that seemed even stranger happened next. As I kept listening to the many audio tapes and continued chanting, I began to have the strongest desire to sell my house, quit my job, and go to California to join The Church's commune. In almost every mailing were pictures of the commune and the great life they were having together, as well as an invitation to join. I had never before had any desire to be part of a commune; my natural tendencies are those of a loner who studies. When I started with The Church, I only wanted to milk from them all the truths they had discovered to help me with my own search.

And now I had this strong desire to join their commune. I asked my wife what she thought about it and she said flatly, "No way!" (I might have trouble understanding my dreams, or God, but I never had any trouble at all understanding my wife when it came to matters of The Search.)

By now I had over fifteen years service at the steel mill, a wife, four children—and I wanted to join a commune.

One Saturday evening the group leader announced good news: the widow and co-founder of The Church was coming to Pittsburgh as the main speaker at a big meeting. We were all expected to be there to see our leader in person. Gail told us she was going to channel one of the Ascended Masters right on stage, just for us.

I wondered if the co-founder could explain why I was suddenly developing this strong desire to drop everything and join her commune, and why I had spontaneous chanting running through my head rather than my usual thoughts.

While I was at home getting ready to go to the meeting, I sat down and wrote out a short letter of introduction requesting a brief individual meeting. I put her name on an envelope and put the short letter inside, unsealed. I had no idea how I would get the letter to her because I sure wasn't one of the elite in The Church—not even among the Saturday group. But I put the envelope in my coat pocket and left for the meeting, about an hour's drive away. (I forgot to say that my wife's response to my invitation to join me that night was short and punctuated with the kind of glare she had mastered lately when it came to matters of "the Search". I always thought if I could patent that glare I could make cheap ice cubes and get rich quick.)

Pittsburgh has the worst laid out streets of any city in the world. I've always thought it was laid out the same way pioneers or Indian scouts, at least in the movies, decide which way they want to go when they come to a crossroad or are in the middle of a plain: they spit in their hand and then hit it with a finger—whatever way the moisture flows, that is the direction they go.

When a new street was needed in Pittsburgh, someone in the street planning department puts a little water on a map and hits it with a finger; then they painstakingly trace the moisture outline for the route for the new road. I'm always getting lost in Pittsburgh, or there's no place to park.

That night was no exception, and as I hurried to the auditorium I was a little late. Inside, the place was full and no more seats seemed to be available. I walked further in and as I got closer to the stage I spotted three empty seats on my left. I quickly took the third seat in and as I sat down the house lights dimmed and a spotlight lit up the stage: the grand widow, the channeler of Ascended Masters, appeared. I was thrilled! I was close enough to see her well. She was in her early forties and quite attractive. She had rings on each finger of both hands and there appeared to be large stones or jewels set on each one. They were conspicuous and she told us the jewels brought in the right vibrations to channel the Ascended Masters.

She spoke for forty-five minutes or so on the need to be prepared for the coming changes that would affect both the physical Earth and society in general, as we got closer to the millennium. We should all have extra food and water in our homes.

She then told us she would channel St. Germaine or any other Ascended Master who chose to come through. After about twenty-five minutes of channeling, she paused. Frankly, I was disappointed. I had expected some really earth-shaking information. Instead, what had come through were general, run of the mill occult teachings that I already knew about.

Then she announced that The Church's choir would sing some hymns. The audience could join in, and she would be back later to channel a message from the Ascended Master. She left the stage, the choir began, and I settled back to listen.

Suddenly the widow and a young man in a nice suit came from the back left side of the stage, down the aisle, and stopped at my row. The co-founder looked at me, smiled, nodded her head in greeting, and sat down next to me while the young man took the aisle seat.

I kept glancing at her out of the corner of my eye, and looking at the big expensive rings on her fingers. Her hands were folded on her lap or, at other times, on her knees. She wore a sweet smelling lavender scented perfume. Usually lavender is a heavy, overpowering scent, but somehow hers seemed light and nice. There was no doubt in my mind. I was sure I was sitting next to a holy person!

I kept thinking of the note in my coat pocket. Should I get it out and hand it over? Or would that be too tacky, maybe even frighten her? I sat, hardly hearing the choir, wondering what to do.

When the choir finished the co-founder got up and walked back up the aisle to the stage, but the young man stayed in his seat. When the program was over and the audience rose to leave, I quickly turned him, pulled the letter from my pocket and handed it over, explaining how I had written the note with the hope of somehow meeting the widow.

I can't emphasize strongly enough how great was my commitment to the teachings of The Church at this time. I believed The Church's leaders were being guided by the Ascended Masters of the Great White Brotherhood. When I read their books and listened to the audio tapes that held the secret teachings of the ages, I felt they went to the core of the truth I was searching for, agreeing with my own basic belief system like a hand fitting into a glove, especially anything that described God's and my own consciousness. I wanted to believe with my whole heart that everything about The Church was on the up and up. But the phone call from the devil and the total lack of independent thinking by church members kept waving a red flag I just couldn't ignore.

The young man asked me to wait and came back with the message the leader would meet with me. I followed him into a side room, where she was waiting. I don't remember shaking her hand or anything formal in the way of a greeting. We were just standing, facing each other. The young man leaned against a wall, watching and listening.

I told the widow I had recently started to get this strong desire to quit everything and go to Los Angeles to join her commune, yet at the same time I had an equally strong feeling that told me this was the wrong thing to do. Then I looked her in the eye and asked point blank why I was receiving these conflicting feelings. She thought for a while, then asked what I did for a living and how many children I had, and their ages.

I felt a sense of caring from her, of wanting to help. She seemed sincere and self assured, soft spoken and attractive. I told her of my four children, their ages, and I explained my job working in a strip mill rolling red hot steel all day long. The widow seemed genuinely surprised and sort of awed by what I did for a living. "You mean you work different hours of the day each week and you also work all night long for a week at a time?"

I said, "That's right—it's called shift work."

She didn't say anything for a few moments and then told me we are all given different responsibilities in life. That sometimes we don't always like the tasks assigned to us, but we have to accept the responsibilities we are given. She thought my primary responsibility was to continue working in the mill and raising my family, that I should forget about going to California. Then she sort of glanced at her bodyguard and he moved to my side.

I have a tendency to be gullible and slow to pick up hints people give me: sometimes I'm like the mule that has to be hit with a 2 x 4 to get its attention, but I picked up her glance and its meaning immediately. It said, "This meeting is over!"

As I drove home I thought about having a one-on-one meeting with the great co-founding channeler of The Church. I thought about how softspoken she was and how caring she seemed. I was also still in awe of the incredible set of circumstances that had allowed this meeting to happen—from my writing the letter before I left home to the hard time I had parking, which made me late, which then made me take a front seat which I normally would not have done. I thought about how synchronicity had been working in my life that evening, as it had at other troubled times in my life. Synchronicity is a term used by Carl Jung and others to describe how events or people suddenly come together from many different paths to suddenly merge at a particular crossroad in a person's life journey. In this brief merging together, help occurs to solve a deep personal problem. The people and events, though not *causally* related, are nevertheless in a relationship of deep significance that has to do with their occurring at the same time. After this brief meeting, each moves through the crossroad and they will probably never meet again.

This concept is in some ways similar to the idea that when you need or are looking for something to fill a void in your life or to help you through the next stop along the path, you will meet just the person who can give it to you at the exact time you can assimilate it: "When the pupil is ready, the teacher will appear".

It was many years before it occurred to me that the widow had been checking me out, and what I did for a living, concluding that the last thing their commune needed was a steel worker with a wife and four children and not too much money. I sometimes wondered, over the years, if they had known I am also a good carpenter, plumber, and electrician who re-models houses on the side whether I still would have been rejected.

I continued reading, chanting, listening to tapes and going to meetings. The messages started getting very weird, emphasizing that the millennium was coming upon us. We were advised and expected to get a year's supply of food stored in our houses, non-perishables such as canned goods and dried food and fruit, plus drinking water. We were also to get our savings changed over to gold and silver because paper money would be worthless in the days of upheaval soon to come. And we should get guns and be willing to use them to protect our families, our food, and our gold and silver.

For some reason I bought into this idea that the end was near. I had extra food and water, ammunition, and even gold and silver, stored in my house, and the fear and dread of an enormous social chaos would stay with me for years.

Then another "jolt awake" letter came in the mail. It announced that the widow had de-cided to re-marry.

A channeled message from The Church said they had met and chosen a man from among those in the commune. Enclosed was the wedding picture, and when I looked at the picture I did a double take: the new husband was the young man who played the role of bodyguard at our meeting.

"Wait a minute," I thought, "this kid's in his twenties and she's well into her forties. Aah... not again, not Eckankar all over again!" I sat down in a chair and just stared at that wedding picture.

In the Catholic church I got repetitive ceremonies and a vague, tired message of Bible quotes, "it's a mystery", and "trust me, I know what I'm doing."

Now with The Church I was getting fresh new answers and ideas, but the messengers were acting in an unpleasantly familiar pattern. I had nowhere else to go so I decided once again to stay open minded and give The Church the benefit of the doubt. I liked going to the weekly Saturday evening sessions because I just liked to talk to others who were seeking a spiritual path. I didn't feel so lonely and unsure of myself when I was with them and knew there were other people in the world besides myself who had this unquenchable thirst, this desire to find God. Meanwhile however, my desire to quit everything and go to California kept getting stronger in spite of what the widow had advised.

I was by now becoming very proficient at speed chanting. I could keep up with the group and we would get going so fast that the sound was like a giant bumblebee in flight. And at various times during the day, both at home and at work, the chants spontaneously flowed into my mind. As I would think about why I was having so much spontaneous chant-ing in my mind, the chants would start up again and interrupt my chain of logical thought.

It was at this point that I had one of the most significant dreams of my life.

THE DREAM

I dreamed I was in some kind of church or chapel. The whole room was filled with a soft white light. I was up front where an altar should be. I raised my eyes and saw in front of me, back against where the altar background wall should be, the large presence of the top figure (God) used by The Church in the central picture on the altar. Only this figure, this pres-ence, covered the entire wall. The figure was by itself, without either Jesus or the symbolic figure of man under Jesus.

I was looking at a huge symbol of God surrounded by a white bath of light and radiating out halos of different colors from its head.

God then looked at me and spoke: "Peter, don't you realize that chanting is a form of mass hypnosis that is affecting and paralyzing all of the United States?"

At that point I was shown, in picture form or as a vision, how a chant would flow like an arctic cold air current that froze or paralyzed everything it passed over, anywhere in the whole United States.

End of Dream.

I woke up, feeling frightened. I wrote the dream down in my spiral notebook, and got out of bed.

I had just been told *by a voice speaking to me personally* that chanting is a form of mass hypnosis which freezes and paralyzes everything it touches. I could understand that part, but the part about *my* chanting paralyzing all of the *United States?* That made no sense to me at all.

Then I realized that not only had I just received a significant *message*, I had also received it from a significant *messenger*. Was this the voice of God written about in the Bible, the same voice that Moses heard from a burning bush?

I tried to pull every smallest memory of the dream back into my now awake consciousness.

The symbols were few and almost self explanatory. The church or chapel location is symbolic of that most sacred place in my own consciousness, my own church or chapel where my own consciousness goes in some mysterious way to worship God in pure spirit form.

God, in the dream, came in the form of The Church's God so I would have no doubt as to the context of the statement. And this God told me personally that chanting, in the context in which I had been doing it, in The Church, is a form of mass hypnosis.

I still had free will choice. This God didn't tell me that I could keep chanting or that I couldn't. But the dream meaning was obvious. Chanting is a form of *group* hypnosis. I didn't quite understand why it was a group hypnosis thing, nor did I understand how all of the United States could be frozen and hypnotized because I was chanting. But it was clear enough. I was being *brain washed* by my chanting in The Church. I was being warned about this, and because of this warning I was going to stop chanting right then and forever. And I did. It was an instant "cold turkey" withdrawal from The Church.

As I worked on the dream, I realized that it was also showing me I still had a place deep inside my consciousness, a church or chapel, where I could go to see God personally and have God talk to and advise me.

I went back and forth between a state of ecstasy, the knowledge that God really knew who I was and was giving me a personal warning, and the Doubting Thomas part of me. "Naw... Come off it, Pete, get real! You are *nobody*, an hourly paid, run of the mill steel worker who has problems with self discipline, swearing, overeating, and all the rest. Why on earth would God ever personally speak to you? You're the low man on the totem pole."

Yet, the dream! I couldn't ignore it or deny it. Try as I might, I couldn't rationalize away what I had just experienced. Then I felt humble, and in awe of what had happened.

I knew I'd never get a dream warning that was more clear than this one.

The next evening I called up Gail, in Pittsburgh (to whose house I had been going for over two years) and told her I would not be coming to any more Saturday evening meetings. Gail wanted to know why and after thinking about it, I told her about the dream.

She suggested I come to one more meeting and tell her all about it. I went, because I thought the dream warning was so vivid and the dream imagery so compelling that perhaps the others should be warned about the dangers of chanting, too.

So I went to the meeting, and was surprised to see that another group leader from another area was present. I told the group of the dream warning me against chanting. The other group leader immediately told me I was misinterpreting the dream. "What was really happening," he said, "was that your human ego created this dream manifestation as a defense mechanism to keep the human mind, or ego, from being conquered." He then explained that the human ego had to be conquered before one could really begin to advance on the spiritual path.

I looked him in the eye while I remembered my thoughts about how paranoid they all seemed and how quickly they deferred to their leaders when asked personal questions, how they all seemed to have lost the ability to think for themselves. I told this man that I believed my human ego was one of God's gifts, along with free will; that my human ego was what gave me my sense of self and I wasn't about to give up what gave character to my personality.

He told me to think about it and they would get some other Church people, who were especially trained to deal with this problem of cleansing the human ego, to talk with me and explain what my dream meant. I said, "I don't think so."

I left and never went back.

One morning a week or so later I was lying in bed thinking. I had been blue and depressed for the past week, I assumed from the effects of quitting The Church. I kept going through in my mind how much of a failure I was.

I had failed at *soul travel* and I still wasn't sure whether it was my fault for being so undisciplined, or whether it was the fault of the *messenger*, or whether it was just a false path. Now the same thing had happened again with The Church, and again I wasn't sure if it was me or the *messenger* or if this, too, was just another false path.

I thought about the boxes of literature I'd accumulated from Eckankar and from The Church. The day before, in disgust but with sadness, I had thrown away and burned most of what I had received from the two organizations for over seven years—the mail order lessons that had filled my soul with hope as I tried to work each of these paths, so sure I had now at last found the way to God. At this time a thought came to me—a thought so strong that I said it out loud: "God, it sure is tough trying to be a mail order saint." After I said it, I started to smile, then I laughed out loud. "Yeah, that was me, all right," I thought, "trying hard to be a mail order saint!"

Where do thoughts come from? Are they from God? Or do we all have some kind of a thought processing machine in our heads that spews out thoughts like a newspaper teletype machine spews out sentences?

I've analyzed lots of my thoughts over the years, but this one spontaneous thought would stay with me for the rest of my life: "God, it sure is tough trying to be a mail order saint."

I'd think of it at work and laugh at myself all over again. Even so many years later, I still smile when I think of it; I've even thought it would make a great line in a country western song.

Maybe this was a thought that was sent from my guardian angel, or from my own highest spiritual part. Wherever it came from, it sure was a winner. I felt a lot better as I got out of bed and got on with my life.

For a long time after I stopped attending the meetings, I would get personal phone calls from the leader or one of the group members inviting me back. I never resented their calls because I sincerely liked them as individuals, and I knew that in their minds I was *lost* and needed help.

As time passed and I was no longer chanting or doing any more of the spiritual practices of The Church, I stopped having spontaneous chants come and disrupt my thinking patterns. And after six months or so, I realized I no longer had the intense desire to go to Los Angeles and join their commune—a desire that had been accompanied by a feeling just as strong *not* to go. These two strongly conflicting desires had created anxiety.

When the desire to join the commune left and I felt at peace with myself again, I thought about why this was happening. It is now a lifetime habit to analyze my internal thoughts and emotions by asking myself "Why? Why do I or don't I have this emotion or that emotion today?"

I had read books on how advertising uses subliminal messages and symbols to get hidden messages into people's minds. I wondered if hidden subliminal messages were put into the audio tapes and chants The Church had sent me which I had listened to and repeated so faithfully.

About ten years after I had the dream about chanting, and had matured more, I was studying some psychology material about how a human is made up of many states of consciousness (such as human consciousness, unconsciousness, and superconsciousness), and about how we humans role play characters in consciousness. I role play a father, a brother, a husband, a friend, an enemy, a sinner, a saint, a steel worker, and have an awareness of each one of these states of consciousness held both by my conscious and unconscious minds so that I can shift in and out of these roles with ease.

I walk down the main street of my small home town and meet someone I've been friends with since our school days and instantly I smile, open up inside, and prepare to greet him or her. If it is someone I have never been able to generate a good feeling about, I instantly become stern, closed up, and silent. I am role playing an enemy. The friend and enemy can be only four feet apart as I walk from one to the other, but I instantly change character.

It was during this period of time that I began having dreams about meeting various presidents of the United States who I admired. I would meet them in the dream and they would greet me and tell me what a great job I was doing. Naturally, when I woke up I'd have no idea what the dream meant. So I decided to break a dream apart into individual symbols and try to finally figure out what president symbols meant.

I asked myself, "What is the spiritual or mind conscious equivalent of being a president of America?" Then I thought suddenly, "It's not America I should be saying, but United States."

Then I tried it again. I thought, "*Just As If* I am the president of the United States of... America, then *so also* am I the president of my own United States of... *consciousness!*" After a couple of days of thinking about it the answer arrived as a flash of inspiration. Just as my personality is a composite of many characters who I role play, as states of consciousness, so also is there one ruler or one president who controls or rules over all these various consciousnesses.

I thought back to the God dream so many years before: "Peter, don't you realize that chanting is a form of mass hypnosis that is affecting and paralyzing all of the United States?"

Now, after all these years, I finally understood. God was telling me that chanting was a form of mass hypnosis that was affecting and paralyzing all of *my* united states of consciousness. The scene of the cold arctic air flowing over the United States of America symbolized the effect of the chants as they flowed over my various united states of consciousness: they were freezing them immobile!

No wonder my chanting friends of the Great White Brotherhood no longer seemed to have any will or opinion of their own. All their individuality had been frozen together. They were all brain washed. Or maybe it would be a better analogy to say their brains were all freeze dried. They just didn't have any individuality left. I felt very thankful my dream had gotten me out of that religion of The Church.

Then I thought about God in that dream. Was it really God, or was it a symbol personifying the leader of my religious consciousness in the same way a president personifies aspects of my physical conscious life?

Was this God who talked to me really only a symbol for the highest spiritual leader that was in my own consciousness? Was this God symbol really my own highest part of me, my own oversoul or super soul who coordinated and ruled over all the various conscious and unconscious parts of me?

THE SEEKER STRUGGLES WITH PERSONAL FAILURES

I had been on three main paths so far in my search for God: the path of Christianity in the Catholic Church, the path of soul travel in Eckankar, and then the latest New Age fad religion—The Church of The Great White Brotherhood. This last, blending the imagery of the Catholic Church with the New Age concept of channeling, had turned out to be the most hokey, bizarre blend of brain washing and mind control that I had yet exposed myself to. It was also the most dangerous. If it hadn't been for my warning dream, I'd probably have left my wife and family, and be marching on a California mountain top carrying a sign "The End is Near".

However, I just couldn't seem to drop the idea that it was *me* that was the problem. If I had been more disciplined, more spiritual, then maybe things would have worked out differently. I kept thinking, "Many are called, but few are chosen." Nobody wanted me!

After a while, however, I regained a modicum of calm and reason. I had quit the last two organizations *because of my dream warnings*. And I had left the Catholic Church because it had provided no answers for me in the years and years I had been a faithful member.

Finally I realized that the only real guidance I had ever received was from my own dreams. *It was my own dreams and my own inner guidance I should be following, not churches or individuals.*

What should I do? I thought, fretted, wondered, and finally decided I would just give up my search for God. All I had accomplished in all the long years was to make a fool out of myself.

I was at this point extremely glad I had kept my search secret. No one knew but my wife and maybe my kids, depending on how much my wife confided in them, but that was all.

It was now the early 1980's, and I was forty-seven years old. My years as a great Seeker of truth and of God had only succeeded in revealing to myself how badly put together I was. I had more weaknesses than strengths, and the wisdom I had gained from my studies had only showed me how bad I was. And after all, I hadn't gotten on the path to find out how bad I was—I got on the path to find God!

I was also discovering that each time I uncovered a personality defect and scoured it clean, perfection didn't appear. Instead of purity of purpose with the white light of good intentions shining through, the scouring seemed only to reveal another blacker, deeper personality defect that would require even more care and scouring to clear up than the defect which had hidden it.

Was there no limit to the depths I had to go in order to find the pure goodness my soul surely had to possess? But maybe I didn't have any purity, any truth in me. All I had found was temper tantrums, cynicism, and ridicule toward others, impatience, and a lack of staying power in myself.

I felt I was failing as a father, as a husband, and as a Seeker. At the mill I was difficult to work with or even be around. I was miserable inside and just as miserable outside.

Inside my failures I dug a hole to hide in, and then covered myself with depression as the condiment I best liked to taste. I wallowed in self pity and dejection like a pig rolling in a favorite mud hole. I didn't love myself; therefore no one else loved me. I knew it! I stayed depressed in this way for several years.

Still, through habit, I did keep recording my nightly dreams. I was so good at interpreting my personal dream symbols, I could usually interpret one verbatim as soon as I'd written it down.

There was no let up in their damn messages.

"You are wrong, wrong, wrong! What you said or did yesterday was wrong. This reaction was emotionally wrong. That action was intellectually wrong. Your thinking is wrong! What you did last week, last month was wrong then and wrong now."

My dreams kept telling me not to act, talk, swear, or think the way I was doing. Day after day the feeling of failure and the sense of depression hung on me. Even my choice of clothes was dark because somehow black matched my mood.

Then for a year or so, I sunk even lower. I quit bothering even to record my dreams, much less interpret them, though I could still remember each one every mornings. In addition, the deep and unceasing anxiety my search had produced, coupled with concern over the righteousness of the path I was on, plus worry over how my actions were affecting my wife and children, caused me to react by overeating. I stayed thirty to forty pounds overweight from then on.

The misery and stress, along no doubt with the right (or wrong) genes, had also produced premature grey hair starting in my late twenties, so that by my late forties I was completely grey.

I didn't realize it at the time, but this long period was my *black night of the soul*. I couldn't find God, I didn't understand God, and I also didn't understand myself, my wife, or my children. I hated my job, I hated the endless shift changes, but believed I couldn't find a better job.

It wasn't simply that I didn't know which way to turn—I couldn't even see a path anymore so I could get to a fork in the road.

During this time I'd have dreams of being in storms with lightning, thunder, and rain. I'd be standing at one end of a bridge, afraid to cross it, or I'd be swept away in a flooded, muddy rush of water in huge rivers and I'd know I was passing through an emotional storm in my own life. I'd go into swamps and be attacked by swarms of black poisonous snakes that I'd kill and then escape from. I knew that the bridge was a way across this emotional stormy river but I was scared to take it; I couldn't start across.

Other dreams would show something costing a given amount of money and I wouldn't pay because the price was too high. I knew that these dreams meant I was unwilling to pay the high price that had to be paid in order to get soul growth.

I would scream at my higher self, "Why do you keep giving me dreams that show I have failed a test when I don't even know I'm taking a test?" I didn't want to know I had failed a test! I wanted the test shown to me in advance so I could identify it and then cram for it so I would pass. But no, I never got dreams like that. I would just have a dream one night showing me in a classroom taking a test; then a teacher would tell me I had failed.

Once I dreamed I was taking a test with forty questions. I was expected to get the highest marks of anyone in the class. Then I was shown I had missed all forty questions and had finished last; the teacher and my classmates couldn't believe I had failed like that. I woke up with no idea where the class was or what the questions were; all I knew was that I had just failed again, and badly.

These dreams made me feel even worse, and there was no let up. I'd dream I had fallen into a muddy lake and was struggling to get out, to get on dry secure ground. I knew it was the muddy lake of my own emotions surrounding me. Other times I would have dreams of finding clear water springs in mud banks or in my cellar and knew it meant I had found spiritual guidance.

I would scream out loud as I walked in the woods, "Talk to me, higher self. Tell me in clear English like you have in the past what it is I'm doing wrong. I don't want any more damn symbolic dreams... give it to me straight!" Pause. Silence. "All right, don't talk to me. I don't need you. You sucker punched me into thinking you would always be there when I needed help. *Where are you now?*"

When I'd try to force my dreams into certain directions or to reveal their wisdom to me, the dreams would suddenly stop and for weeks at a time I could remember nothing.

I began to have what I called my "trapped" dreams. I was a soldier in the second world war and was trapped inside of Nazi Germany. I knew Nazi Germany was a symbol for arrogance of power used with discipline of purpose to conquer and subdue other people. I knew that *Just As* this human trait surfaced in Germany as a nation, *so also* had it surfaced in me as an individual and was trapping me. I was trying, with discipline of purpose and the arrogant use of my own will, to force the rest of my own personality into submission. And my dreams kept telling me, "No way, Jose!"

I dreamed of being trapped in a building that was on fire. I knew that this meant I was trapped in the fires, the passion and heat of my own anger and didn't see a way to break clear.

I had dreams of being in a boxing ring, slugging it out with another person who looked just like me and I knew this meant I was only fighting myself.

I had dreams of being in great Civil War battles which meant that parts of my own personality were at war with each other to see who would have final authority.

I said to myself, "Enough of this! I'm done! I quit! It's too hard! I've been at this too, too long! There is no light in the tunnel and I see no end. Where is this God I've prayed to all my life?" I'd always thought, "I'll be saved tomorrow." Was I?.... No!.... Why wasn't I? Wasn't I a Seeker? Wasn't I a true believer? "Ask and you shall receive," the Bible said; I'd been asking and asking, yet what had I received? Only enough wisdom and insight to see my own terrible imperfections.

Self esteem, self worth, a good feeling of accomplishment—I had none of these after at least twenty years on the path. Instead I had a feeling of loss, of quiet desperation, a sense that I was endlessly wandering in and out of the shadows of life. I couldn't find the light, with its warmth and strength. I seemed always cursed to travel in the light's shadows, and this shadow land of life's light was cold and lonely.

God, how lonely I felt. "Oh, God... Oh, God, how could you desert me!" I would think this so strongly and emotionally that I almost cried it aloud as I lay in bed trying to sleep, miserable and totally alone even though my wife was sleeping right beside me.

In those nights of mental agony I would roll in bed as I slept; twisting the bed covers, even pulling off the corner of the fitted sheet. When my wife would make the bed or rather completely remake it, after these nights, she would always make it a point to ask, "What in the world was bothering you last night?"—as if by answering the question I would be able to justify the extra work I was causing her. I always answered, "Nothing." What was the use of trying to explain my torment to someone who wasn't a Seeker herself?

During those nights I would wake up every three hours. Sometimes I'd be so wide awake that I'd just get up and read a book until five or so in the morning. I'd sit at the kitchen table with a cup of coffee and think and wonder at my life. If I was working the daylight shift, I would just get ready and went to work.

Finally one night as I laid in bed trying to sleep, I began to think more clearly about the past few years. I wondered again why I was suffering so. Why were anger and negative thoughts and emotions racing across my mind and filling my body? Why was I having so many negative experiences in my life? And not only in my life—negative things were also happening to my wife and children. It seemed like all I was ever doing was putting out someone else's fires or solving their problems. And before I could get a moment's rest after solving that problem, I would get a major problem of my own.

This had been going on for years now—deaths in my family, accidents, angry words and fights that had to be soothed over, emotional fences that always needed mending. When would it ever end?

At that moment I found myself praying: "God, I can't go on having one bad experience after another come into my life. What possible good can a negative experience do me or anyone? Why did you create a world that is so full of negative, just plain bad experiences?" Then I fell asleep and started to dream.

THE DREAM

I'm somewhere near the old "white building" where I attended seventh and eighth grades in Saint Paul's parochial school. I wasn't in the classroom, but outside near this white building (symbolizing a place of learning which I was near).

Then I'm in a situation where every positive and negative experience I had ever had in my life was lined up as a picture stream above me in the exact order they happened.

As I watched, this stream descended toward me and began to go around my body. These life experiences were postage-stamp size scenes that flowed around and through me.

Before they got one third of the way around my body, all of the negative scenes started to change into positive experiences. About halfway down my body, or near my stomach, these scene experiences started to change into individual musical notes that were shaped like bells.

As these individual notes also descended, still going in a circle around and through my body, they began to group together and blend to form chords and even whole musical movements. I could hear the bell notes, chords, and movements begin to vibrate together in harmony. Then, the individual notes that had clustered into combinations left my body. The whole movement sounded like a classical symphonic score made up of hundreds of tiny bells tinkling in perfect harmony.

Somehow, as we can sometimes do in dreams, I could understand as I watched, what the interpretation was: even though bad experiences are combined with good experiences in my life, no experience will stay negative if I can learn a good lesson from it.

End of Dream

Just As my stomach was a place where I digested food—both good and bad—*so also* if I digested this bad experience that was entering into me I could also transform it into a good lesson that would nourish my spiritual body.

It was never the negative experience that would cause me trouble, but my reaction to it that was important. If I allowed the experience to be digested and to remain a part of myself (which is what digested food does), then I would learn a good lesson from a bad experience.

Just as the postage-stamp size scenes were transformed, so also was the bad experience transformed into something beautiful to see, to hear, to have happen in my life.

I understood that I should accept these bad experiences into my life and let them flow in and around me as a good lesson that had to be learned. Then, by allowing this flow to continue, I was surrounding my life with good lessons learned. And these good lessons would make up the musical notes that formed my personal symphony, my own song of life that I was creating and playing each day I lived.

It was a beautiful dream! The imagery, the colors, the sights of the individual notes that looked like crystal bells, the beautiful music that was the end result, can't be described in words.

This dream would help transform my life, as so many other dreams had already done. I thought about nothing but the dream for weeks afterwards.

Most of my deepest insights into life had come from dreams—but only after I had read or obtained enough material from other sources so that I was capable of understanding what the dream was explaining to me in its symbolic way of talking.

When I had gotten eighty percent of the answers by my own efforts or by the way I lived my life, then I would either get a dream that gave me the other twenty percent or I would get a wrap-up dream. These are the dreams which wrap together many things into one so there can be an understanding of the whole that can't be seen when looking at the separate pieces.

The idea that the way I was actually living my life was how I acted or reacted to the diverse life experiences of not only myself but my family, relatives, friends, and co-workers, was new to me.

The idea that the most negative thing that I could ever do, or that could ever be done to me, could be transformed into a good life-lesson that would create harmony for my soul, was truly transforming, transcendental. I could see that my entire previous outlook on life had been wrong!

This included both the Catholic Church with their rigid, no exceptions allowed, strict interpretation of Christianity, and the occult teachings I had been exposed to in Eckankar and The Church. I had never liked the way the channelers would always slide in an advertisement for themselves, or an appeal for money right in the middle of a message that was supposed to come from an ascended master.

I thought about what my dream really meant, what it was really saying: Yes, there are bad personal experiences, but... *the effect of those bad experiences cannot be bad in themselves as long as my reaction to them is good.*

If I am in a car wreck and break a leg and an arm, or I fall, or get badly burned, or am wrongly accused of a crime, or am physically and emotionally hurt, but I can still say, "God, or higher self, I didn't like that last negative experience you gave me, or I gave myself, but it's okay because I learned a good lesson from it and I forgive everyone involved, *even myself*, and I won't repeat it again."

What does this mean? I know what it means for me—*No Guilt!* I no longer had to weigh myself down with a false belief system that said because bad things happened to me, I myself must be bad!

Knowing how to react to a bad experience is the greatest teaching Jesus gave mankind, and it became the backbone of Christianity: the doctrine of forgiveness. Forgive seventy times if necessary. Forgiveness releases the history, the negative experience, outward and it never reappears again. So I learned that if I could forgive and forget a negative experience so it was no longer a part of my history, then it would be changed into beautiful silver bell notes that made my life song and my symphony more full and complete.

If men as individuals, races and other groups of individuals, and nations that combine both individuals and groups, could learn to forget and therefore lose their negative history, we would finally have peace within and peace on earth.

With modern life-saving techniques bringing people back from death every day, many people are comparing their near death experiences and they all seem to have a similar theme. The person who has just died is shown all his life experiences in picture form, and there is neither a judgment given by the spirit that is the guide nor by the person who is watching his own life flash by. Why? Because it wasn't the experience, good or bad, that was important, but what was done with the experience.

If we create negative experiences in our own or in other people's lives, then to find peace and happiness we are obliged to go back, make restitution, and ask for forgiveness both for ourselves and for our victims.

As I got beat up, fought back, and returned to the path again and again, I developed a favorite saying: "You have to play the game with the cards you are dealt." I said this to myself as a way of staying on the path as a Seeker while more and more of my flawed personality became exposed. When I'd see another black side pop up in an area I thought I had purged clean, I no longer became angry at myself. I was learning to be non-judgmental towards myself and to recognize that it's okay not to be perfect, to just be human. I had finally gotten to the point where I was no longer looking for perfection either in myself or in others; I was playing the game of life with the cards I had been dealt and letting it go at that.

A few months later I had this dream:

THE DREAM

I was in a field and suddenly I saw a large vicious dog running toward me ready to attack and bite. As the dog jumped up at me, I grabbed it by the throat and somehow twisted its head off. As I was twisting, I saw that it didn't have a dog's head at all, but the head of a small white baby. I threw down the baby's head and the dog's body in disgust at having even handled and killed it.

End of Dream

A dog is a dream symbol of man's best friend that also can have a tendency to be mean and vicious. The dream meant that *Just As* a dog can be friendly, then mean and vicious, *so also* did I have a part of my consciousness that could be innocent and friendly and then quickly change into being mean and vicious.

This symbolized the conscious sense and need for perfection that I had always wanted. When I saw perfection mirrored in others, then I was friendly. However, because I hated my own imperfections, when I saw imperfections mirrored in others, I'd attack them by talking behind their backs or by the use of sarcasm and ridicule if I talked to them face to face.

This out of balance perfection/imperfection part of myself that was both innocent and friendly and mean and vicious was symbolized in my dream as a dog with a human baby's head of innocence and the body of an animal. It was both innocent and mean, and to stop it from repeatedly attacking me (or my conscious personality), I had to kill it.

I had to choke and twist off the *head of innocence* that was the head or the guiding force of this cruel trait in myself, the trait of being sarcastic and using ridicule to attack others while rationalizing to myself I was really just doing something innocent: helping them see their own faults.

My own higher self had repeatedly shown me in dreams that I took delight in *cutting people up*, which is what ridicule and sarcasm does.

Now, after so many years of trying, I knew that my dream was showing me I had successfully killed this animal trait in myself. Still, when I woke up shuddering as I remembered looking at the baby's head on a dog's body that I had just twisted off, it was a bit too vivid of an image for my taste.

I thought to myself, "Come on, higher self, let's tone down the dream graphics a bit." Then I grinned at what I had just thought. I did have to admit that there was no danger of misinterpreting that dream symbol. From that night on, I have never had the desire to cut people up by using sarcasm or ridicule or talking behind their backs.

CHAPTER

NEXT STEPS ON THE PATH

I felt much better now that I'd had the dream explaining the usefulness of my bad life experiences, and I vowed to come out of my depression. It seemed to me that this dream had come to me directly from God, because the wisdom contained in it was so profound and the imagery so beautiful. But in spite of the dream there was a residual emotional feeling I carried inside that would not go away, a feeling I had developed about ten years after my search began.

As I had studied, prayed, and meditated, I had gained wisdom about myself and the world I lived in. And as I did this, a fear began to develop in me. Deep in my heart, I felt that the end of the world was coming upon me and all others in the human race.

I felt increasingly that it would happen exactly as St. John had predicted in the Book of Revelations. The "final days" would be a thing of horror, with endless wars and rumors of destruction (sounds like the whole 20th century). The belief that the end was near was also something that The Church had preached about heavily and was part of the reason I had joined it. Also, at this time there were many books being written about predicted earth changes that had California dropping into the ocean as well as many other calamities.

It got to the point that any psychic worth his or her salt had a book or pamphlet telling their version of how the end would occur. Even members of the A.R.E. had written books that described Cayce's version of the terrible things that would happen as a thousand year cycle came to an end.

After the dream, I decided I had better come to terms with my fear that "the end is near."

As has happened many times in my life, synchronicity played a role at this point in my search. And so it happened that just when I determined to purge myself of my long standing fear of the world's destruction, I got a flyer in the mail from the A.R.E. inviting me to a three day seminar on "Earth Changes" to be held at Virginia Beach.

The main speaker at the seminar was a professional geologist, John Peterson. I listened intently from a front row seat as he spoke. After the lecture was over I went back to my hotel, where most of those attending the lecture were also staying. A lounge had been set aside for the A.R.E. people; I sat down at the first table inside the door where another seminar attendee soon joined me. We introduced ourselves and when a waiter appeared, ordered soft drinks. As we waited and made small talk, I looked up and was surprised to see the main speaker, the geologist, come in. I waved a greeting, and to my surprise he came over and sat down just as the waiter reappeared with our drinks.

For the next hour, like flood gates opening, John Peterson talked and answered the questions I asked. He was familiar with the Cayce readings on "Earth Changes", as was the other person at the table.

Peterson knew the "Cayce Readings" inside out and quoted from them liberally as he explained the errors and misunderstandings that some people were drawing from the

"Cayce Prophecies" by misreading them. He said that these people were taking statements out of context.

His belief, and the main thrust of the whole seminar, was that there need be no instant catastrophic earth changes. If the "Cayce Readings" were kept in their proper context, then it was as easy to conclude that the earth changes would be slow as it was to say that they would happen in "the wink of an eye".

As a geologist, it was his opinion and also that of most of his colleagues that constant earth changes are natural on our planet. He didn't deny Cayce's predictions of coming earth changes that might include California and New York City falling into the sea; he just emphasized that there need be no fear, for the changes would be slow enough to allow people to adjust to them as they happened, to be warned in plenty of time to leave a dangerous area and go to safety.

After we decided to call it a night, I went up to my room. As I lay in bed rethinking the evening's events, it dawned on me that a synchronicity experience had happened to me again—as is always the case, spontaneously and without thought or preplanning by me. This time I had been given the information I needed by a professional geologist at just the right time and place in my life, in a way I could understand and assimilate. And only a professional geologist who was also an A.R.E. lecturer and knew Cayce's writings could be the authority figure I could have trusted, accepted, and believed.

As I lay in bed I thought more about this strange fear I had developed that a "future doom, end-of-the-world catastrophe" was imminent. Was this fear a defense mechanism produced because of the positive results I was having in certain parts of my search? Was my human ego realizing that soon it could be destroyed—if I was successful in my search to find God and the truth about the meaning of life?

If I did succeed, then I would never think or see things in the same way again. Indeed, my human ego, the old world of my conscious mind, *would* be destroyed. It would be the ultimate doom and catastrophe that could possibly happen to it—to my human ego.

Then I expanded from myself, as an individual, to all people now on Earth. I had long ago realized, after reading Jung and searching for meaning in my own dreams, that all the people on Earth, at any given time, plus those who had already died, represent the whole of human consciousness.

If I could experience a feedback feeling of fear and imminent doom as enlightenment came into my consciousness, then would the collective consciousness of mankind send sensations of doom and of imminent catastrophe back to all the humans on Earth?

Was this why, if the collective consciousness of mankind was beginning to change, that in the 1960's and early 1970's, cults, hippies, communes, flower children, love-ins in San Francisco and at other locations began to sprout up out of nowhere? This was a time about love, individual freedom, and generosity. The drug used was for the most part marijuana, which usually makes people happy and mellow and which is completely different from alcohol, as well as crack cocaine and other drugs of the 80's and 90's which make people angry and violent.

The 60's and 70's were an exciting time to be young, to be in love, to be in college, or just hanging out, trying group living, growing your own organic vegetables and so forth. However, as we moved into the 80's and 90's, getting closer to the millennium, the drugs got harder and stronger, and the music began to lack harmony, with death, destruction, sex, and violence predominating in the lyrics.

It was is if humans' collective consciousness was also out of harmony, in chaos. As the turbulence and chaos of this consciousness became wilder, the physical equivalent was a break in historical weather patterns, with earthquakes, tornados, hurricanes, and violent weather the norm rather than the exception. Or, looked at another way, the harsh lack of balance in human consciousness manifested in our gross mistreatment and disturbance of the Earth and its balance, causing, among other things, the change in weather patterns. This breakdown in consciousness is reflected also in the general mindless and out-of-control violence of our society and politics.

As I lay in the hotel bed and reflected on all of this and my talk with the geologist, I no longer worried about the violence. I felt as if a burden had been lifted from me. I finally rejected the fear completely. And, I thought, no one ever gets out of this world alive anyway. So...I might as well live until I died.

That night I had this dream:

THE DREAM

I went up to the cold arctic to hunt for my car. I found it buried deep inside a snow bank. It had been buried for a long, long time and was covered with a thick blanket of ice. I chopped away until the car was completely free of snow and ice. I dug a path out of the snow bank. Then I got into the car, started it up, and drove away.

End of Dream.

I didn't need to write out the symbols of this one in order to interpret it; I understood my own dream symbols by now and I knew what had happened to me the day before. My dream was showing me that *Just As* my car was a vehicle that carried my human body around, *so also* was there a vehicle that carried my consciousness around.

Just As my car had been buried deep in snow and frozen in place for a long period of time, *so also* was there a portion of the vehicle that carried my consciousness around frozen in place for a long period of time and needing to be dug out and freed of the ice and snow.

Just As I did this, got in my car, started it up, and drove out of the snow bank and the arctic cold, *so also* did I manage to find the part of my consciousness that was frozen in place, and I was able to dig this trapped frozen conscious carrier free and start moving forward with the journey down my path of life. I knew this because I didn't back up, but drove forward as I freed my car or my consciousness.

I was naturally very happy with this dream. The feeling of impending doom had been a hangup of mine for many long years. And I have never had another fear or worry about coming earth changes or the end of the world since that night, since the conversation with the geologist and the dream.

As is my lifetime habit, several weeks later I did an overall analysis of what had been happening to me. I had realized, after starting to do this kind of review of both my dreams and daily events years before, that things that I never noticed in my daily living were trends that could easily be spotted when doing a review. Now I was able to see the full scope of the recent events as a total play or package, rather than as the individual scenes in which they had daily been played out.

I analyzed the events which caused me to attend the seminar and realized that if I hadn't had the individual hour long conversation with the main seminar speaker, I would never have been satisfied that my beliefs and fears about imminent doom were all wrong. It wouldn't have been the same just sitting in the audience listening to him; I had to have the personal meeting.

Then I had two more insights into what was occurring in my life. The Bible quote "Seek and Ye Shall Find" came into my mind and I knew it meant that only Seekers would be guided to the place where answers could be found.

The second thought was "Because of free will". God had given me the gift of free will, therefore I had to consciously use my gift of free will choice to constantly seek out and physically go after the answers or I would never find them. *I had to have the desire and determination to find answers before I could find them.* Sometimes I would be led on a path through the Catholic Church, or through Eckankar, or through a cult like The Church. I found truths in each of these organizations that I use and apply to this day.

I realized something else about God's gift of free will: in over twenty-eight years of recording and interpreting my nightly dreams—*I had never been shown by my dreams what to do next*! No matter how hard I prayed, threatened, cried out, or pouted, there was no guidance given until I first made a conscious free will choice. After I made the choice, I was shown in symbolic dreams whether the choice I'd made was the correct or the wrong one for my soul's growth.

THE SEEKER DETOURS FROM THE PATH TO SEEK RICHES

I came home from the seminar on a Sunday evening now realizing the world wasn't going to end any time soon and maybe never. Since the world and myself were going to be around for a while, I decided I might as well get rich so I could really enjoy my long life.

I came to this conclusion rather easily because for the last few years a strong desire had been surfacing in my mind—the idea that I needed to be rich! Not just comfortable and secure, but rich, rich, like maybe becoming a millionaire.

Few people, when they think of becoming millionaires, realize the intense effort that is usually needed to become rich. Becoming a millionaire *can* happen almost instantly, for instance by winning the lottery or when a sports star signs a big contract. It happens to rock groups with a string of hit songs, to movie actors with two hot films back to back (or sometimes only one), to software inventors, wall street investors, food chain developers, mall builders... the list is as endless as the opportunities.

So to me, the idea of becoming a millionaire was a small-change dream. It wasn't wishful thinking but a very doable thing. I was going to get rich. First I had to find out about the success secrets and formulas that the rich and successful used. To find out, I went back to my first love, my old standby: books.

I bought success formula and books like an alcoholic buys six-packs. For years, on a weekly basis, I had traveled my small group of book stores on a regular route to check out the latest pop psychology, self help books available. Now the new age section could gather dust and get eaten by moths for all I cared because I was going to get rich!

I read *Think and Grow Rich, The Magic of Thinking Big* by David Swartz, M.D., *Psycho-Cybernetics* by Maxwell Malty, M.D., *The Magic of Believing* by Claude Bristol, the biorhythm books by George T. Thommen so I could hit my stride on the right day. And hundreds more. Then I was ready for action.

I sent for a course on Import/Export by the Mellinger Company from California and started getting merchandise from around the world to be used as samples to show my friends. I learned how to start a mail order business and run it out of my house—I just needed the right product to sell!

The trouble was the samples looked too cheap to sell, and besides I didn't want anyone to know what I was getting into (in case I failed, you see). With an outlook like that, there was nothing I could do but fail!

Finally my brother, who had a small neighborhood store, agreed to place ten watches in his showcase that I bought direct from Hong Kong for nine dollars each and sell them for twenty-five dollars each.

These were magnificent watches in appearance. They looked like the hundred dollar watches shown in uptown jewelers' showcases. The trouble was, though, instead of having jeweled movements there must have been fleas or something pushing the gears around, because within a week I had all the watches back: they wouldn't run.

I took one to a jeweler who also was a watch repairman, for an estimate on how much it would cost to repair it. He opened the back of the case as I watched. I guess I can take a smart sarcastic word or two as well as anyone because I was so good at giving out one line zingers myself, but the sort of bugeyed look on his face as he put on his black one-eyed magnifying glass and peered inside my magnificent nine dollar watch from Hong Kong really got to me.

Like I said, I could have taken a good one shot zinger, but... laughter... I mean he didn't have to laugh, did he? So what if there were fleas pushing the gears around instead of a Swiss spring set in a jeweled movement.

That ended my import/export business.

Next I was introduced into the wonderful world of multilevel franchising. I met Amway!

A friend, Bob, phoned and wanted to know if I was interested in going into business with him. If so, a business plan was going to be presented at his house the following week— it would be good if my wife came, too. I was thinking, synchronicity.

When we got there, Bob introduced us to Ralph, a nice looking young man in a business suit. Soon other couples arrived, until the living room was full, and Ralph began explaining the Amway Business Plan.

He set up a portable blackboard as he talked. Soon he began to draw circles on it which symbolized business partners. If there was anything I now understood in life, it was symbols.

As Ralph drew more circles, the concept behind "The Amway Marketing Plan" became instantly clear to me. "Why," I thought to myself as I watched, "I could get rich doing this!" I was hooked. It was now only a matter of waiting to be reeled in.

At the end of his talk Ralph asked for questions. There were a few polite, halfhearted queries, then silence. He waited a few minutes, then said, "Thank you for coming. There are soft drinks and cookies if you would like some." Then, like a magician had waved a wand, the room cleared instantly. One second the room was full of people, then... gone, everyone was gone. I didn't think people could clear out of a room so fast without knocking over chairs and falling over each other. Maybe the others couldn't see anything in those circles, but I could.

I walked up to Ralph and said, "I can see these people are serious when it comes to leaving." I asked more questions and he gave me three or four audio cassette tapes with the stories of several who had made it big in Amway.

As we rode home I asked my wife what she thought about Amway, and the circles. Verda is a practical, feet on the ground, what you see and what you hear is what you get, kind of person.

Whenever I spoke of my search Verda would just look at me—her face that of an actress looking at the most incredible sight they have ever seen, that they don't believe, and that is funny because it can't be real. Her lips would open wide with surprise, clamp shut with disbelief, then go into a half smile.

As the half smile appeared, she spoke. "Never work!"

I could feel my own face turning bright red. "Never work? Never *work*? What do you mean, never work? That's not even a sentence!"

My voice had gotten louder than the radio, so she reached over and shut it off. The half smile stayed. "It means that it will never work, that's what it means." Then she said it again. "Never work."

I braked because my foot had pressed the gas feed harder and I was now speeding. As I slowed I bit my lower lip in a half pout and asked again. "I'm serious, what do you think?"

She realized that I had apparently liked what I had seen. She said, "What do you think?"

After twenty years of marriage, I should have seen through this parry. Instead I rose to the bait and with considerable elegance explained why this was the greatest money making venture I had ever seen in my life.

She wasn't impressed. "Never work," was her reply after I had finished.

"Fine," I answered, red faced again. "I'll do it myself."

"Go ahead," she said, half smiling. "I've never stopped you from trying anything yet."

"Yeah," I answered back, still hot. "You never stop me, but you never help me, either."

Well, I did try Amway. I tried and tried and then tried some more. I stayed with it for eighteen months. To get started, I booked business meetings in my home; Verda even invited many of her own family and relatives. The trouble was that the people who came seemed to leave after the meeting even faster than they had at my friend's home. There was coffee and soft drinks, but except for a few times when they were drunk before the meeting started, few were used. I thought about getting some of the plastic cookies and pastries that restaurants display in their windows so I didn't have to keep buying new ones.

After I'd run through my and also Verda's list of friends, neighbors, and relatives, whose opinion of what I was doing didn't bother me much now for some reason, I floundered. Dead in the water. I had hundreds of names written down, but when it was time to call and invite them to the meeting, I choked up. I'd look at a name and think, "No, he wouldn't be interested," or "what will he think when he finds out it's a soap selling business called Amway?" Also, I didn't want any of the people I knew whose opinions I really respected to know what I was doing(just in case I failed). Also, I didn't want my good friends and relatives to feel like I was using them.

What the Amway business was achieving was to make me see deep inside myself all the flaws that were keeping me from becoming rich and successful. It wasn't the Amway Plan that was flawed—lots of people made a lot of money in that business and still do—it was me that was flawed. And I didn't like it at all when I realized this.

To my surprise and embarrassment, I was finding that I had, deep inside, a *fear of success* problem. I was lucky to have identified it, but had no idea how I could ever remove it.

The discovery of this new hangup traumatized me so badly I became physically sick. To overcome the fear, I decided I just had to push myself harder. I listened to the audio tapes of others who had become successful in Amway so many times I could lip sync the words as they spoke. By now I now wanted to be rich more than I wanted to be a Seeker.

Still, I couldn't break the ice; I just couldn't invite another person to my house to hear a business pitch. I spoke to the friend who'd sponsored me in the business and he said Amway was having a huge rally; why didn't I come down to Seven Springs, a ski resort outside Pittsburgh. Maybe that would help.

So I did, and my wife came too. Seven Springs is a place of great beauty and it is expensive. As I listened to the success stories of all the featured speakers, I just knew in my heart I could do it the same as they had.

After the rally finished on Sunday, Verda and I got in my worn out car to drive the sixty miles back home. As soon as I started up I heard a grinding, rattling noise in the engine. I got out and opened up the hood, and saw antifreeze dripping from under the fan. I decided I better get it checked and pulled into the nearest service station.

"Yup, it's the water pump," the attendant said.

"How about putting in a new one?" I asked.

"Don't have one and the parts store won't open till tomorrow. Better get a motel room, you won't get a mile before it blows."

"Then what?" I asked.

"Then all the water goes on the ground, that's what! How you going to run a car with no water?"

"Thanks," I said. I got back in the car.

"What are you going to do?" Verda asked, thinking of the kids at home, being watched by our teenage son.

"Drive home," I replied. I said nothing more, but I started to think. I knew my car was made out of steel parts; I also knew from the Search that God can do anything, theoretically.

So in my mind I said, "God, I know you exist. I know you can do all things. God, I'm asking you to keep this water pump going till I get home." I didn't pray; I didn't get mushy or flowery by making grandiose statements like "Oh, Mighty and gracious Father, your humble servant beseeches you to help me in this, my hour of need," etc. I always talked to God simply as if God were my creator good friend. "God, I'm asking you to keep this water pump running till I get home." No big deal, I figured. God *could* do it, the question was *would* God do it? Or did God even hear me?

I kept listening to the water pump noise and watching the temperature gauge. After about thirty miles, it started to climb higher, so I pulled into the first service station I could, waited till the engine cooled enough, and re-filled the radiator.

Each mile we went, the water pump got louder. "Will we make it home?" Verda kept asking.

About a mile from home the temperature gauge started creeping up again. I increased speed, hoping to air cool the engine. Finally I slowed to pull into the driveway, and as soon as the rear bumper cleared the main road there was a big "clunk" from the water pump. I put on the brakes and watched a cloud of steam rise up from under the hood. Then a big stream of water ran away from the car towards our house.

You could say the moment my car was completely off the main road was the exact moment I arrived home. I had asked God to keep the pump running till I got home, and as soon as I did it blew apart. I don't know what anyone else would make of this, but for me, at that instant, I believed God heard my simple request and kept the pump running. I felt humble, proud, and awed by the realization God knew I existed and would do physical phenomenon things as an answer to a simple request.

The thing I've always noticed is that God doesn't advertise and doesn't brag. Therefore, when God really does listen and answer my prayers, I'm not always sure if God got the job done for me or it was just luck or a coincidence.

If, as soon as my water pump blew apart, a huge bolt of lightning had flashed across the sky, I would have said, "Aha, that's God punctuating the good deed it just did for me. God's doing a little bragging!" But that's not God's style. As soon as my car cleared the main road and I was completely home, the pump blew; it blew with a big bang and a huge cloud of steam.

I had the car towed to a garage the next day and the mechanic said he'd never seen one blow apart like mine had; I was lucky I made it home. I said, "Yeah."

With the pump replaced and the car running again, my attention returned to Amway. I had left the rally all psyched up by the success stories and was eager to apply what I'd learned.

I made up a new list, practiced a new phone routine, and went to the phone to dial the first name on my list and. And... I couldn't do it. I just couldn't. Right there, by the phone, I just fizzled out like a carbonated soft drink and went flat. My enthusiastic drive to be a great success drained away like the water leaving my radiator.

I hung up the phone and slumped in my chair. I must have sat there for half an hour. Finally my wife came by. She wanted to know what the problem was. I stood up. I said, "Amway. That thing will never work." I meant *I* couldn't make it work because of some strange hangup inside me. "Don't say it," I added, "don't say it!"

Verda's half grin turned into a wide smile and she shook her head. I turned and just before I got out of the room I heard her whisper, just loud enough so she knew I would hear it, the four little words that always made her day. "I told you so!"

I pretended I didn't hear a thing.

For yet another time in my life, I went into a deep depression. I agonized over my failure of not being able to do so simple a business as Amway. I knew people were getting rich in that business; I had met them, and I had listened to their success stories on tape. Yet I could not do the same.

Now here again was a mental phenomenon that puzzled me each time I got trapped in it: the dilemma of having a strong desire to take a certain course of action, but when I would accept the urge to do it and start to run with it, almost immediately another urge, the complete opposite of the first, would appear.

This had happened many times on The Path. I would seek out and pray to have some truth revealed to me. Then, when it was revealed, I couldn't believe it. It was like what happened with the water pump. I asked God to keep the pump running until I got home, which it did. Then I didn't want to accept this as a real answer from God to a request of mine.

Now it was happening again with Amway. I had the desire and urge to do this business because I could see it would work; and I had a conflicting feeling that it was wrong. And then another strong desire rose up as I was still struggling with myself about Amway. I was having dreams about becoming a writer, showing me I should start to write. So, while I was still trying to make Amway work, I sent for a course on how to be a writer. I also did my usual research and read all about book writing.

Then, to get away from the guilt trip I was on because I couldn't do Amway, I started writing the Great American Novel. I figured I would do as the training books suggested and write about something I was familiar with, so I wrote a novel about a steel worker. I just knew this would make me even richer than I could have gotten in Amway.

When I had my novel finished and typed up, I wasn't sure what to do next. My older brother was visiting at the time. He lived in California where he was a full professor at a state university. He had always given me the impression he didn't like me being "just" a steel worker, but I never told him of my Search, my journey on the path to find God, because with his new education and sophistication he had outgrown God.

He had written one scholarly book that fit his field, or his "discipline" as he liked to call it. Somehow, during our week long conversation, I announced that I, too, had authored a book. My brother has a lot of psychology degrees and is sure he knows the world inside out, and that he knows what makes people tick. He looked at me as if I had just "tocked" when I should have "ticked".

He got really upset. "All you are trying to do is imitate me!" he screamed. I denied it! We argued some more and then, as if remembering himself and the fact that he was a professor and had studied a lot of psychology, he calmed down. He suggested he take my manuscript with him back to California and read it.

I guess that's what I had been hoping he would say when I brought up the topic, although the bit about me wanting to imitate him hadn't really crossed my mind. I wrote the book to get rich, not to imitate him. Besides that, it was a thing my dreams had repeatedly shown me, as a recurring dream, that I should do.

About six weeks later I got the manuscript back by mail. I quickly opened it. My brother said he had read through it and then had decided that maybe it would be better if a colleague he knew reviewed it. He said this colleague was a fellow that liked to read colloquial writing. (I went to the dictionary for this one—I took it to mean a kind of writing by hillbillies, which is what some college Californians seem to think live in Western Pennsylvania.)

In his reply to my brother the colleague wrote that I appeared to have some primitive writing skills, but if I was really serious about writing I should go to the public library and check out the one hundred greatest books ever written and study them. Then I should take some writing classes at a local community college. The letter then went on to comment that right now I was just an amateur trying to write. I was stunned, then embarrassed. Talk about breaking someone's bubble! I was devastated; I was wiped out.

My wife asked what my brother, the professor, thought of my book and I showed her both letters. She got both mad and defensive for me. "Those people are ignorant... they have no right to say those things to you." She was fuming and her voice was loud.

"No, they're right. It was an amateur effort." I re-read the novel. I had already read thousands of books, so I could tell when I re-read my own that it wasn't very good. I took the typewritten manuscript, still in its mailing box, down to my basement and never looked at it again or even attempted to write anything else for the next fifteen years.

It wasn't just the fact that I hadn't succeeded. Worse was the fact that I wasn't good enough to do it, I couldn't get the job done—not as an import/export salesman, not in Amway, and now I was also a flop as a writer.

I had followed the careers of high school friends who had gone on to college and were now becoming captains and majors in the military. I could follow their successes, because with each promotion, either in business or in the military, their mothers would put their picture and an article describing their sons' latest success in the business pages of our local newspaper. I had one older brother who had started in the army as a private and was now a warrant officer. My other brother had started college at age twenty-eight and had kept going until he became a full professor. And me? I was still just a steel worker!

"What are you doing now?" my high school friends would ask me, and I'd say, "Oh, a little of this, a little of that." I wouldn't even admit I still worked in a steel mill!

My depression got deeper; I was in agony. "Good God," I thought, "am I never to amount to anything more in this life than to be a mill worker? How can I have this intense desire rise up inside of me so strong I feel I'll burst if I don't give it expression and then the moment I try to fulfill the desire, an opposite emotion comes upon me that effectively kills my first desire dead!

I felt like a rag doll with no stuffing left inside of it. I was being torn apart, threshed and drained by the excesses of my own personality. I began to analyze my emotions and my thoughts, to try to find the origins of my desires. I wondered why it was that just when I would be on the edge of a breakthrough, at the high tide, with success in my grasp, at that very instant, a feeling of procrastination would descend over me like the weight of a ten ton truck and would anchor me so I *could not* advance any further, not even a step.

This wasn't a one-time thing; it was a recurring theme that now defined my life—get almost to the top, then stop and roll back down.

And it was this recurring theme that had started me studying my own consciousness—to see if I could change it.

Then I realized that this had also been happening in my search for the meaning of life. First I would have a desire to know more about God. Because I had this internal desire surface in my consciousness, it became the force, the strength that would motivate me to once again get on the path and continue my search.

Then, after I had read and studied for maybe a year or more, I would have a desire surface to change the mental knowledge I had accumulated into the physical action that I wanted to do—for instance soul travel, or Amway, or writing a book. I had accumulated all of the theory—now could I physically do it? As you remember, the answer was "No".

THE SEEKER STUDIES SUCCESS PATTERNS

Years before when I vowed that I would start down a path to find God, I hadn't expected to find only the chaos of my own consciousness. Like an animal trapped in a closed room, my mind kept running around going this way, then that way, then circling back.

Earlier, when my periods of prayer and meditation had "worked", I had felt complete and whole inside of myself; I had felt satisfied and that deep down I had finally found God. Then a week or so later, I would wake up to find that during the night, in some strange way like the action of a high tide washing a beach clean, all the spirituality had been washed out of my consciousness. Depression and frustration once again filled my life. I had ebbed back once again into a black sea of anxiety, fear, and lost hope. I had no one to turn to.

As I continued to fail in my secret life, I had a hard time not allowing it to affect my work at the steel mill. I would think back over my failed attempts to be a mail order saint, my disappointment with the Catholic Church. And now my failure to succeed in becoming rich, the final straw.

I didn't understand how this desire to be rich had anything to do with the spiritual path I wanted to travel. But I had learned to trust my inner instincts and my own inner desires. If I had a desire to be rich, then there had to be a God given reason for that desire.

One day as I was doing a mental review of my life up to that point, I started to think about where the desire to get rich had come from. I knew that what I did in my physical life had to first be modeled out in my mental life. So what was it that I had been thinking about which would create an inner desire to become rich? I wrote out all my reasons for wanting material wealth just as I did a dream interpretation. What was the spiritual equivalent of the physical state called being rich?

Then, as an awareness, it came to me. I was spending almost all my waking hours reading about and thinking about spiritual matters. I was still on the path, still searching. What I was actually doing was making myself spiritually richer each day. And the physical equivalent of being spiritually rich was transformed into a mental and emotional desire to be physically rich as well, rich in money and material possessions.

After thinking all this through for a week or so, I realized how I'd created this desire to become rich. I had to make a free will choice as to whether it was a false desire that should be suppressed or a desire that should be brought to fruition by making the mental model become physical.

Well, I didn't have too much of a problem deciding which way to go. Obviously the answer was rich, because riches and material possessions can make a human life more pleasant and easy.

I had been poor, and I had already learned all the lessons I needed to learn from that experience. I wanted to learn rich lessons now.

I remembered all the Amway success audio tapes that I had bought and decided to replay them, sometimes for hours at a time. I reread the biographies of people who had become successful after overcoming great obstacles in their lives.

As I listened to the tapes and re-read these books over a period of weeks, I slowly realized there was a familiar theme that ran through all of these success stories. At first I couldn't identify it; it was like the feeling I get when I catch a whiff of some new scent in the air. I can recognize the familiarity of the scent, but can't identify it.

What was this scent, this underlying theme I found in every success story I read or heard, that seemed so familiar? I could think of nothing but this problem, while I was at work or at home. Then one day I discovered a part of the underlying theme—tests: I saw that all the people I'd studied who had become successful in life had found themselves in situations that had no apparent solutions. At this point, they had the choice to either quit or to look for ways around the roadblock. Then they had had to fight their way through those obstacles— the obstacles became the tests on their path that had to be passed.

Because of the failures they were experiencing as their plan of action fell apart, their own personal consciousness would be thrown into the fiery pit of their own fears, frustrations, and anger. This would be the *fiery hell* into which their own minds would descend.

If they could pull themselves out of the fire of negative emotion and personal passion that had ignited their own mind or consciousness, then by fighting it off they could again start moving forward with their life's work.

But if they stopped or hesitated, they became lost. There could be no turning back or looking back if they were in fact to succeed. If they hesitated, they could become like Lot's wife: unable to ever move forward again because the act of continually looking back at their own past froze them into place. Their consciousness became like a solid block of salt that paralyzed them.

One of the reasons I was unable to obtain success myself was because I kept looking back at my own poor childhood and average education. Instead of leaving my past behind me, it froze me in place just as effectively as if I had turned into a pillar of salt, like Lot's wife in the Bible. Only after my dreams showed me I had to learn to give myself absolution, to forgive myself, was I able to move forward again.

This is what happens with things that keep recycling, reappearing in your life—if you don't master the problem then it returns again and again until, hopefully, you do.

What I was discovering was a double pattern. The first part was that everyone has to first make a mental commitment to do those things necessary to become a success. This is called *getting on the path*. It didn't seem to make any difference what field of endeavor they finally found their success in, or what particular path they were on, and this surprised me.

The second part was that each person, in roughly the same order, encounters a series of obstacles or tests that try to force him or her off the path.

I found this same pattern of success could also be found in the lives of saints. They would fight great inner battles, and sometimes outer ones as well, as they worked to master their human nature to become more holy and find God.

Some people would have fewer tests along the way while others might have more. And some people never experience even one failure in their climb to success, while for others the path is so littered by the debris and mental agonies of their many failures that their paths look more like a tornado of destruction than the path of a seeker of success.

But what was it about the double pattern of success that seemed so familiar? Then suddenly I had the flash of inspiration that always brings a new awareness into my life. I knew where I had seen this double pattern before—it was in the Bible. It was the pattern that Jesus had enacted in his own life culminating in the Last Supper, the agony in the Garden, then the fourteen steps called the Stations of the Cross which ended with Jesus' crucifixion and the Resurrection.

I realized that all modern successful people have their "Agony in the Garden", that dark night of the soul experience. They have been nailed to their cross of personal beliefs where they died. Then, unless they give up, they have all had a resurrection and a new life for them begins.

Some people have two or three success/failure cycles as recurring patterns where they obtain great success, then that success dies and they become failures. Then, sometimes years later, they again get reborn with a new success period even greater than the old. Often people's lives are like a close score basketball game where the last one to score before the final bell is declared the winner. What cycle they are in when they die determines whether their lives are declared those of winners or losers.

I could see the correspondence between the pattern of the life of Jesus and the success stories of modern men and women, but I didn't understand it, nor could I quite believe what my inner intuition was showing me.

I noticed that everyone who has ever had great success in their life will at some point acknowledge that "I didn't get a free ride from life and it wasn't always easy. I deserve what I got because I paid my dues."

This was also what my own dreams were telling me: I didn't want to pay my dues; I didn't want to pay the high price that success cost. I wanted instant riches and instant stardom, and it never happened because I would not walk through my baptism of fire. I would always quit!

Well, I finally admitted to myself that I just couldn't do the Amway business. In the next few years I was introduced to other multilevel business plans. I never got seriously interested in any of them, but I did get involved for a short while in a motor oil additive multilevel plan.

Then I dreamed I was in a back alley near a local book store, taking a sip from a can of a popular soft drink that I had quit drinking because it gave me a headache and sore bone joint pain. I was alternating between taking a drink from this soft drink can and from a bottle of the motor oil additive. On both of the containers was a label that said "Poison".

The book store location was a place where by the act of reading, other people's ideas could be digested. Back alley is a slang phrase for something that isn't quite legal or on the up and up. My dream was clearly a warning not to swallow or assimilate any more of this business because it was a back alley shady operation and it would be like poison to me.

Needless to say, I got out of that one immediately. A few years later, law suits about the motor oil additive were flying around like model airplanes at a hobby show. I was glad I wasn't into this so deep that I, too, might have been sued for misrepresenting a product. I was also thankful I had a good paying steel mill job, because I sure wasn't making any money out of my "get rich quick" schemes.

I didn't know where I should go next in order to get rich, however. Finally I decided to pray and meditate with the idea of trying to get some kind of guidance from my dreams. So for more than a week I prayed and meditated for an answer as to how and in what way I could get rich.

I had no problem seeking guidance from God, even though I had been off the pure spiritual search for more than a year and a half, from 1981 to 1983. And after a week of prayer and meditation, it happened. The dream was short but it was sure a sweet one. And it contained a truth, a gem of wisdom, that I have continued to use all the rest of my life.

THE DREAM

I am standing bewildered and lost on a concrete road that passes in front of the fertilizer plant which is operating near the old neighborhood where I grew up.

As I stand there in front of the plant, I look up at the heavy cloud cover above. Suddenly from out of the clouds, a voice speaks. The voice says, "Peter, don't you understand that you must *Act As If!*"

End of Dream.

Well, I want to tell you I woke up excited. It had been years and years since I had been spoken to in a dream. It's impossible to describe the feeling of joy and happiness that comes over me when this happens. It's as if the voice speaking and the joy and happiness are given to me together, the emotions simultaneous with the speaking voice.

It's such a satisfying and pleasurable feeling that my immediate reaction is always that it was God speaking to me in this way.

The problem with answers from God is that there may be a considerable time lapse between the time of the prayer and the day the answer comes back. Often, after weeks or months had passed, I would forget about the prayer when the answer did appear in my life. But when a voice speaks to me in a dream from out of a cloud in the same time frame when I am meditating and praying for an answer to something, that really gets my attention.

This dream was very easy for me to interpret. The setting symbolized me standing on my own road or path of life, confused and bewildered. I knew that fertilizer from the fertilizer plant was used by local farmers to stimulate new and healthy growth in the crops they planted each spring.

Therefore, *Just As* a chemical plant can produce a fertilizer that stimulates new and healthy growth in newly planted seeds, *so also* was I now standing at a place in my life near a place (my fertilizer plant) where I could go to get something that would create tremendous growth in my own life. The new seeds I had planted were the new beliefs I was planting as seeds in my own consciousness.

What was this great fertilizer I was to use that would produce such spectacular growth in my newly planted beliefs and in my own life? What was it that would act on my own consciousness in the same way that fertilizer works its wonders on soil and seeds?

It was to *Act As If.*

I had read a book about this idea a year or so before, describing how we role play many different character parts in our lifetime. We also, each one of us, carry around with us a *self image* of who we are as total human beings. This self image of who we are is also the total composite of our belief system.

And, our belief system is the myth we live by.

And, what we really and absolutely believe in our own mind includes the beliefs we have about ourselves.

Now this comes to the heart of the matter. *How could I do the things that were necessary and needed to bring change into my life if I believed that I could not do these things?* What I had to do now was to learn how to take the theories that I had read in books, plus theories I got from dreams, and make them into a practical, physical working model in my own life.

If I succeeded, I would create a new belief system within myself. *This is an important point*—because humans need an actual physical model of a theory before they can accept it as a new belief system to guide their lives. This idea that a physical model must come before belief is the basis for modern science, and it is also the basis for superstition.

Superstition is a false belief that when a physical model is experienced at more or less the same time as a daily life event, the physical model is the *cause* of that life event.

For example, take a professional baseball player who has two pairs of tight fitting leather gloves that he wears when he is at bat. One pair is black and the other is white, but they are otherwise identical—one is not more worn than the other, etc. Throughout his career, this player has always been a good hitter, alternating in no apparent pattern between wearing the white gloves and the black ones. But one week he realizes that every time he has the white gloves on he has an especially good hitting day. So from that day on he wears nothing but white gloves when he is at bat.

In this example, the physical model is the white gloves; the event is a good hitting streak. The new belief adopted is that it was the white gloves (his coincidental physical model) worn while having good hitting streaks (the event), and not his natural hitting ability, that caused the hitting streaks. This belief that white gloves make him a better hitter is now a superstition that will start to dominate his natural hitting ability—if he doesn't have white gloves on, he won't hit well.

I realized that just this sort of thing was a problem in my own life. I had adopted a lot of false beliefs, and I didn't know how to break their hold over me.

God's spoken answer while I was in a dream state of consciousness was: "Peter, don't you realize you must *Act As If!*" I had to start acting as if *I had already become* what I was seeking so hard to be. Why? Because the way I act in a physical lifetime is what I really believe.

How could the professional baseball player break his superstition about white gloves being the *cause* of a good hitting streak rather than his own natural physical abilities? By throwing the white gloves away and continuing to play ball and hit pitches without them.

He has to *Act As If* the white gloves are meaningless when it comes to hitting a baseball. On the other hand, if he continues to *Act As If* the white gloves are a *cause* of good hitting, then because he isn't wearing them, he will fail to get a hit. He will become his own self fulfilling prophecy because of the way he is *acting*.

In my own case, the way to overcome the personal fears that were holding me back, that were keeping me from becoming rich and successful, was to first *Act As If* I was already rich and successful. Why? Because the way I act is truly the way I believe.

No man, no woman, can ever become greater than their own self image.

How can a person change a poor self image? By *Acting As If* they are greater than they perceive themselves to be in their mind.

It took me a lot of thinking before I understood why either God or my own higher self would give me a positive desire for growth in some field of endeavor which I would recognize and nurture in my own consciousness, only to see it killed by a negative fear of the same attainment.

I would realize years later that these are the tests between mind and matter, or the consciousness of a spirit soul versus the consciousness of a human mind and body, tests that have to be passed before success can be obtained.

These negative conflicts produced by our human mind are the devil within that tempts us and to which we have to say, as Jesus did after forty days in the desert when his own human ego tempted him, "Get thee behind me, Satan!"

THE SEEKER'S NEW IDEA TO GET RICH

The realization that I couldn't do multilevel marketing, along with the new *Act As If* dream revelation, decided me that if I wanted to get rich I should concentrate on my strengths.

I was good with my hands. I could do carpentry and plumbing, electrical wiring—actually, there wasn't anything in a house I couldn't fix. I decided the best way for me to become rich was to buy old houses, remodel them, and then either rent them out or resell them at a profit. Satisfied that I now had a workable, realistic plan to get rich based on my own proven abilities, I felt excited once again! It was 1984 and I was fifty years old, but felt thirty. I had been working in the steel mill for twenty-eight years, but I was still full of energy and ambition.

I bought books on real estate investing, appraisals, how to operate a rental business, how to re-sell real estate.

I learned how property could be bought in Pennsylvania by using a contract called an "Article of Agreement" between the buyer and the seller. Sometimes, if the buyer has a good credit history, no down payment is needed. The buyer just makes monthly payments to the seller, particularly if the property is run down. Since there is usually no realtor involved, there are no selling commission fees that have to be paid.

As soon as this all became clear to me, I bought an old three-story brick house that was so large I decided to convert it into a duplex. The owner lived out of state and because the property needed a lot of repair work, I was in a better bargaining position as a buyer than he was as a seller.

The roof had leaked badly for some time, and since the house had plaster ceilings, much of the plaster had fallen and only the old fashioned wood lathing was left exposed on the ceiling. The roof was covered with slate, and I had no idea how to repair a slate roof.

This leaking slate roof was the major repair item that had kept the more professional contractors from grabbing the property—but I chose to ignore this defect because I somehow believed there had to be a cheap way of getting the roof fixed. I didn't know what this might be, I just accepted the idea that the leaking slate roof was no big deal.

Unworried about the roof, I began the remodeling process by moving all the junk and debris in the house out onto the front porch. I figured I'd just call a junk man or rubbish hauler and for a few bucks get it hauled away.

The first rubbish hauler said, "Five hundred dollars." I said I had thought it would be more like fifty or sixty. He laughed and asked what planet I had come from—his dumping fee for a truck would be that much at the local landfill. I told him I'd let him know. Finally I found someone to take it away for two fifty.

This was two to four times over my estimate, and unfortunately that same ratio between estimated and actual costs continued throughout my whole remodeling project.

I began inside the house by rewiring it. I did this myself and then had it inspected.

Everything passed and I got a certified wiring inspection sticker on my new two, one hundred amp electrical boxes.

Then I was ready to start replumbing, but was informed I needed a building permit, which had to be posted where it could be seen from the street. When I applied for the permit, I was informed that I had to get a registered plumber to do the work. Then this work had to be inspected.

I told the building inspector I could do my own plumbing, I'd been plumbing houses for years. "Not inside the city limits," he said, "we have a city ordinance against people doing their own plumbing work." So I had to hire a registered plumber for three times what I could have done the job for myself.

I had learned how to buy property, but not how to estimate costs. My nest egg was going down much faster than I had anticipated—but then another bit of synchronicity came into my life. A neighbor strolled over to talk one day as I was working outside. He said my remodeling efforts were making the property look better and they, the neighbors, appreciated what I was doing because it made the whole neighborhood look better.

Then, out of the blue, he asked me if the slate roof leaked and I admitted that it did. He gave me the name and phone number of a local man who repaired slate roofs on the side. This man turned out to be a high school friend of mine and he went all over the slate roof and repaired or replaced over fifty individual slates for only ten dollars a slate, or five hundred dollars. That was a bill I was happy to pay.

I wondered about the synchronicity. With no effort on my part, something that I needed appeared. But this event with the leaking slate roof being repaired because of a chance question by a stranger didn't seem to me to be anything spiritual; what I was involved in was anything but spiritual—I was the old fashioned capitalist wanting to make a profit on an investment.

I put the remodeling job on hold a day or so and took some walks in the woods, thinking the thing through. Part of my deep personal belief system that I had so long ago accepted was that God, or some higher intelligence, was helping me. This was especially true when I was traveling the purely spiritual path.

What I hadn't realized was that *it was the belief that I would somehow be helped that was causing the synchronicity event to happen.* When I bought the old house with a leaking slate roof, I had automatically accepted as true the idea that I could get the roof fixed cheaply and that, therefore, I shouldn't even worry about it—it would just happen.

Then I realized something else. When I accepted this belief that somehow my slate roof would be repaired, I was *Acting As If*—just as my dream had told me to do. What I had been doing as I worked on other things inside the house, without concentrating on the roof first, was *Acting As If* the roof problem had already been solved.

I got excited as I realized I had found out the secret reason synchronicity was happening so easily and fluidly in my life. Then I realized that there is also a Biblical term for *Acting As If*. In the Bible, it is called *Faith*.

Acting As If is the physical application of the mental concept of *Faith*.

I thought of the many times Jesus spoke of the need for humans to act with faith in all they did in their lives. He said things about mountains being moved and cast into the sea and that if one would just believe, then all those things would come to pass (Mark 11:23).

But, I reasoned, if I had faith from the day I was born to the day I died that a huge mountain would move—it wouldn't. So it wasn't physical mountains Jesus was talking about, it was what the mountain symbolized, an impassable, insurmountable mental obstacle in our life path. And the sea was the sea of our own mental emotions. If I would *Act As If* the obstacle would be overcome by me, then somehow, in an act of synchronicity, a way around or through the mountain obstacle would appear. *Act As If* also was about expectations—the way I expected things to occur was based on what I believed.

What I expected to happen would always become a self fulfilling prophecy because we always get in this life what we expect because... this is really what we believe! We constantly live out our internal self image of ourselves, and if our self image is false, full of superstition,

70

then the life we lead is false. Most humans live a false life while their higher self and God are trying to guide them by dreams, inner desires, hunches, and intuition to change their lives.

With this new awareness glowing inside of me, I went back to work remodeling the house with renewed vigor.

But... bad times were coming. I had estimated it would take only six months to remodel the house into a duplex. Then, in my projected plan, just as the mortgage payments would begin (I had gotten the seller to agree to a six month deferred payment), I would have renters in both the upstairs and the downstairs apartments. Their rent would then cover the mortgage payment, plus enough left over to begin to recover my up front remodeling expenses.

But at the end of the six months, the remodeling was only eighty percent completed. This meant I had to start making mortgage payments, which was a problem since I needed my savings to complete the remodeling, so the mortgage payments would have to come out of my weekly paycheck; this wasn't something I had put into the equation when I was doing my dollar-in/dollar-out work sheet before I bought the unit.

I could see now that my two plus two arithmetic wasn't adding up the way it was supposed to, so I made a complete list of everything I needed in materials to complete the remodeling job. Then I took the list to the lumber yard and got an actual cost figure. When I looked at the new actual cost figure, I swallowed hard because I knew I was in deep trouble.

The figure the lumber yard gave me was three thousand dollars more than I had left in my savings. And this didn't include the monthly mortgage due. I truly knew now what the expression "between a rock and a hard place" meant. I had more than a brief moment of panic as I struggled for a solution.

I wished with all my heart I could go back in time and forget the nightmare that my dream duplex, my get rich quick scheme, had gotten me into. But I couldn't go back to the way it had been—not having an old house to remodel and my nice nest egg safely intact in the bank, with no worries or headaches.

That left another option—I could just quit! I could walk away from the remodeling job, sell it for whatever I could get, and write the whole thing off as another dumb mistake. Then I realized I couldn't do that either, because I was still legally obligated to make the monthly payments.

I couldn't go back, I couldn't stop, and I didn't have enough money left to go forward.

One of the abilities I have always had is an active, fertile imagination. This has often been a real plus when I am trying to analyze a problem but don't have enough pieces to make the pattern whole. I then use my imagination to jump over the fragmented pattern and try to imagine it as a whole—and I most often succeed.

When I was at work in the mill and had free time, or when I was at home, I re-assembled the duplex in my mind in a room by room, wall by wall sequence. It was just as if my mind was a computer monitor and on its screen I could arrange and re-arrange walls and rooms like I was moving a mouse to create computer graphics. I could lay out all the wiring and plumbing schematics in my mind, then overlay the drywall and the paint, so that I had a complete visual image of how the rooms and the whole house would look when it was completed.

This created image was imprinted so strongly in my memory banks that I could return to it just as a computer user could request a computer image of a room in a house that was stored in its memory.

Mental image recall and a good active imagination are great things to have when on a pure spiritual path. However, a fertile imagination applied to a purely material problem can be a blessing or it can be a curse.

It is a blessing if the mind and the attitude can be kept positive, but it can be a curse if it becomes negative. In this case my imagination went negative—it went south in a big hurry because being negative was my natural state of mind and I constantly had to use will power to keep myself positive. It was my black dog that I fought off each day.

I have always envied the "up" people, the Pollyannas of the world. They always wake with a smile on their faces and a song in their hearts, and I would want to rap them with something each time I saw them whistling or humming their way into work when I was in one of my black moods.

After I did my re-evaluation of the remaining costs, I went negative big time. I have this Irish ability to spin grandiose dreams of fame and great success in my imagination, so I can't or won't see the small problems ahead. What I saw now, with my active Irish imagination, was a disaster of horrendous proportions. I could see a complete, total financial collapse coming into my life with the speed of a runaway freight train. It would be so complete, so final, so devastating, that I would never be able to recover in this lifetime. I got physically sick at my stomach; the outside of my body seemed to quiver.

That night I dreamed that black storm clouds were forming and I took this to be the *worst omen of all.* I was done! I was financially ruined! Here I was, already into my fifties, and I was going to be completely, totally wiped out financially. Everything I had sacrificed for, had worked so hard to bring to completion in my life, would be gone! Gone, swept away by my own stupidity. I would probably lose our new home I had helped build; my wife would leave me; my children would have to live with relatives or friends. It was over. "The end was near!"

I could imagine the guys I worked with whispering, "Did you hear what a dumb thing Pete did?" after they saw the bankruptcy proceeding against me posted in the local newspaper and my "get rich" story became public knowledge. As I thought of these things, I would slap my forehead with the heel of my hand and mumble to myself, "Dumb, dumb, what a dumb thing to do!"

I knew I had to somehow become mentally positive, but it seemed impossible. I come from a long line of wish dreamers who could weave both verbal and imaginary spells as easily as a Russian rug maker can weave a wall tapestry or a spider can spin a beautiful web. My own father's imagination wove him a false life dream that caught him up in its web of negative emotions and superstitious beliefs so tightly that he was never able to break free.

I knew if I continued to let my imagination have free rein, I would just run away. I could dream up disaster scenarios as fast as I could think, and I was now thinking with a full head of steam. I was really chugging down those railroad tracks toward complete ruin. Unusual images of doom and disaster were coming into my consciousness so fast they seemed blurry and meaningless as I sought to slow down and reorganize my thoughts and emotions.

This was not the way I had imagined the path of success or even the tests within the path. I had visualized a nice relaxed stroll through the park, and what I'd found instead was a jungle path leading me through my most primitive emotions: fear of failure, fear of ridicule, fear of being poor, fear of being alone, fear of loss of family and home.

Against this jungle of negative fears and emotions, I had only one weapon—my own conscious choice of free will.

I couldn't go forward, I couldn't go back, and I couldn't stop. "Wait a minute," I thought. "What did I just think?" I repeated it out loud. "*I can't go forward and I can't stop!*" Where had I heard those words before?

Then I remembered. They were part of the steps that people who are on a chosen path have to go through before they become successful. This awareness came to me with a suddenness, with such a quickness, it almost seemed to ring in my mind.

"That's it," I thought, getting excited. "I'm in the middle of the first few steps on the success path. I have just fallen and my own mind, my Judas, has betrayed me by going negative, and for the last few days I have been experiencing my agony in the garden, my dark night of the soul."

"Hey," I thought, "I finally got what I asked for." I was always bitching when I woke up and a dream had shown me I was being given tests in life and failing them when I didn't even know they were tests that I was taking!

Now, here was a real life physical test where I *realized* I was in the middle of it and I also knew the solution: "Ask and you shall receive" was a thought that suddenly rushed into my consciousness. I could never solve the mystery about the origin of thoughts, but I *could* solve my house problem. All I had to do was apply what my studies of success stories and my dream teachings had taught me, and that was to *Act As If.*

With my gift of being able to create mental images of great beauty, I visualized my mind as a beautiful spider with my individual conscious thoughts the silk threads flowing endlessly from my mind as streams of conscious thought. It is my personal beliefs that form the pattern, the design, of my web of consciousness, while my individual thoughts are the silk thread used to create this pattern of belief.

And if my belief system is always open and truthful, this web of consciousness will expand endlessly outward into a beautiful web of intricate single and composite patterns so beautiful that they defy description. (Is this the ever expanding universe that scientists see?)

But if my beliefs become untruthful and my emotions negative, then as I become more conservative, more restrictive, my endlessly flowing and spinning web of personal consciousness begins to bend the pattern back towards myself. As I become more self centered, more negative, more self destructive, then the outward flow is stopped. Then my pattern of consciousness, my endless spinning web of intricate beauty, will begin to wrap around itself tighter and tighter. The silk threads of thought that had been an ever expanding web of belief will become the prison that holds me—the spinner and the mind spider—tightly bound in an impersonal cocoon of my own spinning.

Trapped then in a cocoon of my own making, I must await the day when the *veil of false beliefs*, this web of consciousness that has self contained me, is split apart so I am free to fly again. To do this, I must change while in this self constructed cocoon, from an ugly worm of false beliefs and deceit into a beautiful butterfly of optimism and change.

To succeed in changing myself while still trapped in my own cocoon web, I must use, exactly as a worm would, something that is part of the individual DNA pattern that I was programmed with by God when I was born.

This is *free will choice.* I have always had and will forever have the ability to make free will choices that can create change within my life. In order to create change in my life, I would have to do three things.

1. Make a mental free will decision that I wanted this new change in my life.
2. Begin to expect this change to come.
3. Physically and mentally *Act As If* this change had already occurred by doing the physical and mental things that proved it a fact.

I had to get hold of myself and, with the use of my own will power, force myself to become positive in both my thoughts and expectations. Because it was in my *expectations* that I would be able to make the application of *Act As If.*

I now knew what I had to do. I would just keep going forward and not look back. I would continue to do the remodeling on the duplex and just *Act As If* everything would turn out fine. "Piece of cake," I thought to myself as I started to hum and whistle.

I soon found, however, that it wasn't going to be that easy—it's one thing to dream up a sequence of physical events in your mind and quite another to turn the mental dream into physical reality.

I realized I had to quit working on both apartments. I had to concentrate my efforts and finish first one, then the other. Since the upstairs apartment was the closest to being completed, I should finish it first. Then I would rent it out and use the rental money to pay most of the monthly mortgage payment. With the problem of where to get the mortgage money mostly solved, I could then concentrate all my efforts on the downstairs apartment.

Happy that I had a workable solution, I started back to work. To speed up the process, I got my son and some of his high school friends to help. I explained I couldn't pay them for a while, but I would just as soon as possible and they accepted the conditions. I completed the upstairs apartment in a room by room sequence. As I finished a room, the boys would come in after school or on weekends and do the painting. After a month of these faster paced remodeling efforts, I was done with the second floor apartment—just when I went completely broke!

I rented the apartment within a week to a young architect, and started on the downstairs. I now had to come up with a sizeable mortgage payment in a few more days. "What to do?... What should I do next?" I was again beside myself with worry and anxiety.

I started to pace the floor and my mind filled once again with fear and frustration. I was getting into screaming matches with my fellow workers and with my sons and other family members as my worry over being broke and being behind schedule boiled over into my private life.

I had learned from my boa constrictor dream that when a desire or emotion surfaced into my consciousness, I had only two real choices. I could use my free will to choose to indulge in the emotion or desire, or I could choose not to indulge in it. What I couldn't do was ignore it in the hope that it would go away: to ignore a desire or emotion is actually to tell yourself that maybe you will indulge it sometime in the future, but not right now.

In my fight with the desire for alcohol, I'd had to consciously say to my inner self that I wasn't going to drink anymore, and know deep inside that I meant it, before the snake of temptation would shrink and then die.

So until I made the decision as to which way I wanted to go, I would be constantly hounded by stray emotions and desires. They would chase me, wanting a decision one way or another, like a dog chasing a rabbit.

If you think you don't have to consciously give yourself permission to indulge or not indulge in each thing you do each day as an habitual occurrence, then you are not friends with your own thoughts, desires, and emotions. We can't control things we don't understand. When we don't understand ourselves, then we can't control ourselves and are instead controlled by our random thoughts, desires, and emotions.

If an alcoholic refused to open his mouth to drink, or a drug addict refused to inject himself, then from that moment on they would be cured. They would still have to go through the withdrawal symptoms, but the addiction would be broken. Instead, addicts, at some point in their past have consciously told themselves, "I can't fight this desire any longer; I'll just indulge." This, in effect, gives them blanket permission to do alcohol or drugs until they die.

But the world is also full of people who at some point in their lives made a free will choice to stop indulging. Maybe they did it themselves "cold turkey" or maybe they asked God for help or sincerely participated in AA or a drug rehab program. Either way, there is a day in their lives, a story they will always remember and can tell: the day they shined up their rusty free will and made the choice.

As memories of my own acts of free will flashed through my mind, I could see that the whole load, the whole show, was sitting firmly on my own two shoulders.

The remodeling project was a "path" I personally chose to travel because of the free will choices I had made in the past. Here I would meet my own devils and angels, and no one else's. I had never quite been able to understand, before this happened to me, how billions of people could live on Earth at the same time and yet each would always be traveling their own personal path, meeting their own devils and their own angels as they passed or failed the tests that they, themselves, created.

I now realized that what was creating the personal paths and the tests for each person was each individual's belief system, which in turn created their own expectations. *My expectations for the future became my own self fulfilling prophesy.* I would, through time, become exactly what I expected I would become.

I could say something in my thoughts, say in words that I was going to become successful and rich, but unless I actually accepted this as a *belief*, deep inside, it would never happen. Why? Because deep inside, I *didn't* believe it—I expected to fail. And did I always fail? Yes. I became my expectation.

I was now broke, and had no more money to complete the downstairs apartment. What could I do?

I could start to *Act As If* a large flow of money was entering into my life.

Now if you or I knew that soon we would win some prize or receive a large sum of money, what would we do? We would start to buy what we needed on credit, knowing full well that soon the money would come. So, that's what I did. I went to our steel company credit union and borrowed as much as I could—maybe twelve hundred dollars.

With that money I went back to complete the downstairs apartment—but the money only lasted about a month and then I was broke again. No problem! *Acting As If* a large flow of money was soon to be mine, that Friday, I stopped on my way home to play the state lottery. I gave the number to the clerk and when she handed me the ticket I saw she'd made a mistake. She said she'd take it back and give me the numbers I wanted. "No," I said, "it only cost me a dollar; I'll just keep it and get another one, too."

That evening the number the clerk gave me by mistake hit straight and I won five hundred dollars. I immediately said, "Thank you, God," rushed to the place where I had bought the lottery ticket and cashed it in.

In two weeks the lottery money ran out and I was broke again. I still was only about ninety percent finished, so I got out my Mastercard and my Sears charge card. I used the Sears charge to get the gallons and gallons of paint I still needed, and the Mastercard at the lumber yard and hardware stores.

It took six more weeks and about fifteen hundred dollars in charges on the cards to get enough material to complete the downstairs. It was now nine months since I had started, three months longer and three thousand seven hundred dollars more than I had planned on. But within a week I had the downstairs apartment rented to a young working couple. Now I finally had a positive cash flow coming out of my duplex.

But what about my *Act As If* theory that was supposed to generate the cash I needed? Outside of the five hundred dollars I won on the state lottery, I had received nothing! What I had instead was an empty nest egg, a twelve hundred dollar loan at the credit union, and almost two thousand dollars owed on my credit cards.

I just couldn't understand it! According to the success stories I had read about, and according to my *Act As If* dream, I should be on money road. I had done everything by the book, so to speak, in an effort to put the theory into action, but all I had gotten out of it was a great big debt!

I didn't know what to make of this apparent collapse of my *Act As If* theory. However, there was nothing I could do about it now. The remodeling was done, the apartments were both rented, and in five years the short term mortgage would be paid off and I would own the property free and clear. I sat back and collected the rent payments.

A month passed and I was half way into the second month, robbing Peter to pay Paul in order to get all my bills paid on time each month. And I still owed my sons and their school buddies for the work they'd done and they were becoming impatient and verbal about it as teenagers do.

One night when I was working the three to eleven shift, I came home about 11:30 p.m. and my wife and all her card club friends were waiting for me. I mean to tell you, when I opened the front door and saw my wife and all her girl friends smiling and laughing as they looked at me, I felt a little spooked. What was going on?

Then Verda burst out with a shout. "You won! They just called and you won!"

"Who called?" I asked.

"The fire company! You won their five thousand dollar drawing!"

"I did!" I hollered, running up the steps toward her and all her smiling, laughing card club girl friends.

And I had. I had actually won a huge 50/50 drawing that was held each month. The next day my brother picked up the money for me because I was at work again on the three to eleven shift, and the money could only be paid during the evening because the treasurer worked daytimes, also.

As soon as I got the money I put three thousand dollars in my checking account and started writing out checks. I called up my son's friends and paid them off. I paid off all my charge cards and, with a smile on my face, I walked into the credit union office and handed them a check that paid them in full.

Then I took my wife and family out to a huge "get anything you want" dinner at a good restaurant. As I sat back, after eating so much I felt stuffed, I looked over my family as they talked among themselves and ate. I thought to myself, "Ah, how sweet it is!"

I thought about the events of the last nine months and of the intense agony I had been through that no one in my family knew anything about because to share my thoughts and my troubles with them, when it looked like my world had collapsed, was something I had been ashamed to do. I hadn't wanted them to know what a mess I was in for fear they would think I was just a fool for ever attempting such a dumb thing. To completely remodel a three story brick house and turn it into a duplex, when I was already working turns and overtime in a steel mill and was fifty years old, wouldn't have seemed too bright a thing for their old man to be doing.

Now, in the secret glow of my own satisfaction, I was basking in the sweet taste of success. I was grinning from ear to ear and encouraging everyone to get second helpings of dessert or anything else that pleased them.

I thought, as I have so often in my life, "Thank you, God. Many times I have failed myself and others, but *You* have never failed me!" As I sat there and listened to my family chitchat and nodded and smiled at them when appropriate, my mind was really on the fact that my theory, my *Act As If* strategy, had actually worked. *I had finally had a success in my life*! (Actually I had great success in my steelmill job, but I always looked down on that and didn't think it counted.)

That night as I lay in bed ready to go to sleep I again thanked God, then gradually fell asleep and had the following dream.

THE DREAM

I was in the steel mill, but not in my own department. I was in the one that rolls steel down to its correct gauge and shape while it is cold, the cold rolling department.

I went toward one of the large twenty foot high mills with rolls sixty inches wide and two feet in diameter and jumped onto the conveyor approach tables which were running into the mill.

I let myself go head first into the mill. I could feel the pressure on my head and body as I got squeezed. As soon as I was completely through, I stood up and went back around to the front of the mill, jumped back onto the approach table and went head first into the mill, to get squeezed down and be made longer again.

As you can do in dreams, I was also standing back watching myself do this. As I watched, I thought, "That's really a hard way to be doing it."

End of Dream

I woke up and looked at the clock: 4 a.m., and reached for my spiral notebook.

My hands and body were still feeling funny and kind of trembling, remembering the sensation of having my head and body squeezed and stretched while going through the steel rolling mill. It hadn't been a pleasant thing to experience or watch.

I wrote the dream down, and re-read it. I paused over what I'd been thinking as I watched myself put myself into the mill over and over: "That is really a hard way to be doing it!"

I knew this meant my own higher self was watching me and thinking, "That is really a hard way for him to be doing it." I thought about the mill and I recognized what kind of a mill it was. *It was a tempering mill.*

As a young man of eighteen I had worked at that mill as a feeder. Along with another man I would take a stack of two or three hundred flat steel sheets, three feet wide and nine feet long, and in a one by one sequence we would keep lifting the top sheet off the pile. Then, in a synchronized motion, we would take that sheet and throw it onto a moving conveyor chain that carried it into the temper rolling mill. This process is called tempering cold steel. Reducing the thickness gauge of the steel sheet, while also slightly elongating it, causes the steel to become harder and flatter.

Then I knew what the dream meant.

It was an evaluation by my own higher self of what I, as a conscious human, had been doing as I remodeled the duplex and went through all the agony, pain, and doubt, to finally *Act As If* and succeed.

I had been expecting a dream where I was being congratulated as a hero for finally passing some life tests, but that wasn't what my higher self was showing me.

My higher self was showing me that yes, I was actually tempering myself by using this process, but it was sure a tough way to do it.

That got my attention! I realized the dream symbols were showing me that *Just As* steel can be tempered by going through a tempering mill, *so also* was I trying to temper my own spiritual and mental consciousnesses by putting them through a tempering process.

But... it was a process that didn't fit me, as a human being. Therefore, it was a tough way for me to be tempering myself. Well, I had to admit this dream took the wind out of my sails and the smug smile of satisfaction off my face.

You see, I not only evaluated my dream, but with my active Irish imagination I tried to put myself in the place of the intelligence that was giving me these dreams as a form of personal guidance. Hey, something has to make up or create the dream images we get each night, so why not put myself in its place?

I knew I was only spoken to in dreams in times of dire emergency when a quick, severe warning was needed before I fatally screwed up and got caught in a web I couldn't get out of. Or else, as in the *Act As If* dream, when I was so completely lost on the path I didn't know which way to turn or even how to get restarted.

I began to think about why this higher intelligence overseeing my human progress didn't think too much of the physical success I'd just had remodeling the duplex and using the *Act As If* advice.

I thought back over the last nine months. I realized that I had never taken a day off, with a few exceptions when I got puzzled by what was taking place and went off to walk in the woods to think about it. I had been physically working fourteen to sixteen hours a day, seven days a week, for nine straight months, and I had thrived on it—I was in better physical shape now than when I had started the remodeling.

I had given up being an alcoholic to *become a workaholic*.

Because of my intense spiritual drive that wasn't being satisfied, I had transferred my spiritual drive into a physical work drive. I mean, I could work with a vengeance. I was still overweight, but I had moved through that old house like a man possessed, in a whirlwind, a human dynamo, in perpetual motion. From the time I'd walk through the door of the duplex in the morning until I left in late afternoon to get ready to go to work on my three to eleven shift at the mill, I never stopped moving—and I loved it.

I justified being away from my wife and my family so much by telling myself I was really doing it for *them*. But actually I was only doing it for myself.

So, as my own higher intelligence, my oversoul, appraised the last nine months so it could give me a "wrap up" dream, it could do no more than concede that I was, indeed, tempering myself, but... "it was a tough way to do it!"

And I could see that, whether I liked it or not, the dream was the truth.

This concept of putting myself into the place of my own higher self, of looking at myself as the intelligence that is feeding the dreams to me each night, can be most revealing and unsettling. When I changed my perspective from myself to that of an impartial observer of myself, as my higher consciousness is, then I began to see myself in quite a different way.

As I changed the perspective from looking at myself as a human on earth to that of an intelligent form of energy floating up in the sky watching me as a human being on earth known as Pete, then by analyzing my dreams in this imaginary transference, I could understand how I must look to it. It also made it easier for me to understand the dream symbols.

The dream made me realize I should stop my workaholic ways, and gradually I did. But it was hard to do because I'm like the line I read somewhere in the Bible: "Whatever ye do, do it with all thy heart". That was me; I never did anything in a normal way; I was an extremist. I either went at it at 110% of capacity, or I just quit completely. Moderation still wasn't a part of life that I had mastered.

But because of my extremist trait, I noticed something else about humans. And that was that often their emotional, physical, and intellectual excesses will push them higher and further than they could ever have hoped to go by having moderation as one of their strong points. In their search for the center, for the balance necessary for a normal life, they keep swinging to the opposite extremes of their own personalities; these extremes will eventually destroy them if they don't get centered and stay balanced.

In my life as an extremist, I had gone from extreme introvert to extreme extrovert, for example. But I realized that without the ability to allow myself to indulge freely in the extremes of my personality, I would never have discovered the truths I had uncovered so far in my search. In the strange way of our human world, my weakness was both my strength and a weakness that could destroy me.

So it was with my work habits. I was so far off center as a workaholic that my return to the center would take some time to accomplish.

The next year I helped my son completely remodel the older home he and his wife had bought. We stripped off all the old plaster board and uncovered the 2 x 4 walls. Then I completely rewired and replumbed the whole house and put on new doors, windows, and insulation. I even installed a new oil furnace for them, complete with new ready-made duct work and floor registers. Then new vinyl siding was put on to finish the outside,

Perhaps I loved doing this because at the same time I was also remodeling myself—from a human being tied down by negative beliefs into a new-belief butterfly ready to burst free from my cocoon of ancient, self woven limitations.

As I reexamined the life I had lived, I realized my physical life always resembled my mental life. As I had an inner desire as a Seeker to remodel my mental and spiritual life, *so also* did I have a physical desire to remodel physical houses. As I became spiritually richer, I also had a desire to become physically richer.

I bought another old house—even though I knew better. I got it so cheap it was too good a deal to turn down.

I played at remodeling this one in a more relaxed way, often taking off weeks at a time. When I did complete it after a year's work and got it rented, I discovered all the fun had gone out of remodeling old houses. It was as if a cycle had been completed and I had no more things to learn from it or to prove to myself.

After I rented the remodeled houses for a few years, and had the misfortune of getting renters who enjoyed destroying my old houses with the same enthusiasm as I had remodeled them, I decided to get out of this get rich scheme, too. I was now in my middle fifties and realized that working turns in a steel mill and remodeling houses on the side was a young man's game. The real money to be had by remodeling old houses was in renting them for twenty years or so and then selling them as clear profit. But I was now too old to wait twenty years before cashing out; I had started too late in life, with too little money and too big an idea. All I was left holding now was a sore back and a flat wallet.

I sold the houses and got back my original nest egg plus a small profit. I probably would have made more money by investing the nest egg in an aggressive, no load mutual stock fund and forgetting about it.

But if I had done that, I would never have gotten all those valuable insights into myself. I wondered, after all the houses were sold, if that latest get rich scheme wasn't just another guidance lesson given me by my own higher self under the guise of an intense desire to get rich, just so those lessons could be learned.

CHAPTER

THE SEEKER'S LAST ATTEMPT TO GET RICH

I had read several books on creative visualization, and after my *Act As If* dream and re-modeling the old houses, I came up with a new plan. I would use all the knowledge I'd accumulated so far in my life and use it mentally and emotionally, rather than physically, as a means to get rich.

What I had in mind was to use my newly acquired mental skills as a way to win the Pennsylvania State Lottery. I figured there was no sense getting greedy the first time out because this was going to be like dipping water out of a well with a bucket—when I needed more money I would just dip into the state lottery. I would then pay the appropriate federal income taxes and have all the extra money I needed.

I decided I would first go for one hundred thousand dollars. With that sum in mind, I set a goal some six months in advance to give me plenty of time to visualize myself winning a big jackpot. I realized that six months ahead would be close to the Fourth of July, and I felt that would be nice and symbolic. *Just As* America became politically free on a Fourth of July, *so also* was I going to be financially free on the coming Fourth of July.

I did visualizations until I could see the check being handed to me, the great Fourth of July lottery winner. I worked out a scenario in my mind of me receiving and depositing the money. I wasn't sure just how I would win the money, I knew that somehow on the Fourth of July a synchronicity would occur in my life that would culminate with me being a one hundred thousand dollar lottery winner.

I had no moral problem with this gambling fantasy—after all, my *tough way to temper myself* dream had already made clear that physical hard work was too tough a path to travel. And my *Act As If* dream didn't seem to have any stipulations attached. Furthermore, at least once a week someone became a millionaire by winning the lottery while I was merely trying for a conservative one hundred thousand dollars.

Keeping these rationalizations firmly in mind, along with another that "If God didn't want me to be rich, then God wouldn't have given me a *get rich desire*", I began my last great attempt to become rich.

As the Fourth of July came close I worked myself into a frenzy, filling my mind with positive mantras and bright mental pictures of the expected wealth within my grasp. The night before the big day, I dreamed I had taken the top half of my skull off and was looking at the full top half of my exposed brain. It was an inflamed bright red color; it looked so hot it appeared ready to burst into flames. I had gambling fever.

When I woke up, I was alarmed because I knew my brain symbolized that part of my body where thought originated. I realized my brain looked like other parts of my body when they are infected. If my brain was red and inflamed, it must be seriously ill.

I transferred this body symbol by saying to myself that *Just As* my brain is the source of all my human thought and if it is seriously diseased and inflamed, *so also* are my own spiritual thoughts and emotions seriously diseased and inflamed.

I had bought hundreds of dollars worth of lottery combinations and tickets the day before. As I had done this, I had mentally congratulated myself for having such splendid foresight. "The mark of a true winner—be prepared for any eventuality," I had thought. "I'll succeed for sure this time."

Well, 7 p.m. came on the Fourth of July and the lottery ping pong balls did their pinging and ponging and I, with great expectation, recorded each number on my white scratch pad. Then I went to my study to see which of my tickets was the winner.

The fact that I was already one hundred thousand dollars richer was, in my mind, a given fact. I had, months ago, accepted this as part of my belief system. It was now just a matter of seeing which ticket was the carrier of my new found fortune.

I checked, one, then two, then all of the tickets. I checked them again. I reread the numbers on my scratch pad to see if I could possibly have missed one or two but the sad truth was, *I wasn't even close*!

My great Fourth of July grand finale, the greatest of all my "get rich quick" schemes—was a flat bust. I had won *nothing*! I hadn't even won enough to get back the price of the tickets!

I was stunned! How could this be? I knew how the *Act As If* game was played; I had done my part; I had visualized, believed, expected... yet... *Nothing*!

I had put so much emotion and belief and thought into making the lottery dream come true I just couldn't accept the fact that I was wrong and that I had, in fact, lost hundreds of dollars. For four hours, from a little after seven until eleven, I could think of nothing but the fact that I had been *totally wrong again*. How could I have been so dumb as to believe this would really work? I was in my middle fifties and prided myself on having finally reached some semblance of maturity and clarity of thought even if I never had become a saint, mail order or otherwise. I began hitting my forehead with the palm of my hand, muttering, "Dumb, dumb, what a dumb thing to do to myself."

Then I remembered my dream of the night before and I realized that my desire, my passion, to get rich quick had infected my thinking. My brain, my thoughts, were so over heated by the frantic desire to be rich that my very brain was inflamed.

When I finally came up the steps from my basement study, my wife had already gone to bed. I went into the bedroom, but wasn't sure I could sleep.

I didn't know what to think or do so, as I have done all my life, I turned inward and prayed: "God, what I did today was lay my whole belief system on the line. I don't know if it's right or wrong to gamble, but I do know I believed with every bone in my body that my premise about *Act As If* and my expectations and beliefs form the structure of my human consciousness. If I'm wrong about these three things, then I'm wrong in all the beliefs and conclusions I've formed so far in my life. This means my whole belief structure is wrong! I need an answer, God, as to what I did wrong or else I'm shattered. *I'll never know what to believe in again for the rest of my life.*"

That night I had the following dream.

THE DREAM

I was lying on my back on a bed, fully clothed. I looked down across my stomach. My legs were spread wide apart and from out of my groin area was coming a great stream of gold forms and statues. Some were all kinds of animals, some were small buildings, some were like models of skyscrapers, and some were statues of men and women. All were pure solid gold.

As I watched this endless stream of gold animal forms, buildings, and people, I noticed that many of them were only half or just partially formed. Yet they were still flowing out of my groin to join in the flow of the finished golden statues and animals.

End of Dream

As I awakened, I knew this dream was a direct answer to my prayer to God for an explanation of how and why I had erred. I had literally put my whole belief system and personal value system on the line and... *it hadn't worked*!

Therefore, the conclusion that I, or any Seeker of the truth would come to, was that my whole belief system, which was the skeleton on which I hung my consciousness *was wrong*!

Now it was up to me to correctly interpret the dream, so I got started. I knew the man lying on the bed was me and that from my groin, my place of physical creativity, came an outpouring of golden statues of men, women, other animals, and buildings.

This meant to me that *Just As* a female gives birth to new life, a baby from her groin area, *so also* was I giving birth to new creations from my area of creativity. I was seeing, in symbolic form, my own stream of consciousness that had creative ability and was giving birth to golden forms in an endless, never stopping stream or flow.

The golden creations which were only half formed were not yet completely developed enough to survive on their own. Yet I was expelling them along with the fully developed statues in a continuous birthing process.

I knew that animals almost always represent an emotion, so I knew my dream meant that some parts of my human emotions were being born before they had fully developed. I was giving birth to them before their gestation period in my own consciousness had been completed. Therefore, some of them were shown as being half formed and stillborn.

The golden statues of men and women represented human states of consciousness that I role play each day. Since some of these also were only half formed or developed, this must mean I was giving birth to some states of consciousness which hadn't had a full period of gestation.

The golden buildings were states of consciousness I had built for myself, and some of these were shown as fully developed at birth, while others were incomplete.

The color gold, or gold itself, is a metal that will never tarnish even if buried deep underground or deep in water. Therefore, gold has always been a symbol for truth that can never be tarnished.

Since all of the creations I was giving birth to, whether fully formed or incomplete, were made of gold in the form of statues, this meant my own stream of conscious thought was giving birth to untarnished truths. This birthing process was never ending and flowed out in a stream ahead of me as far as I could see.

As I rolled all the symbols over and over in my mind, I realized that what I had been shown was that my own consciousness, made up of thoughts, emotions, and belief patterns, did indeed have creative abilities because they were shown as having gestated or formed in my groin, my physical area of creativity. They were pure gold or pure and untarnished truths, emotions, and beliefs. If not, then some would have been rusty and tarnished.

My prayer had been a request to God that I be shown why my belief system and creative visualizations, my *Acting As If*, had not on the Fourth of July created and brought to gestation my desire for the hundred thousand dollars as a physical reality on Earth.

God's answer showed me that yes, my beliefs could create untarnished truths in the form of golden statues or matrixes of gold, and I could, indeed, give birth to these golden matrixes, but first they had to be brought to a full term of gestation or else they would be born only half formed or stillborn.

I was also having a problem by creating an endless stream of these golden images and that, too, was not correct.

If I wanted to give birth to full healthy creations, then I should slow down the process enough for nature to take its course, which meant they would be born when they were fully formed thoughts and emotions.

Once I had this interpretation clear, I felt better and again in awe that I could pray directly to God and receive a beautiful vision as an almost instant explanation.

For weeks I thought of nothing but this dream. Once satisfied that my belief system and consciousness had actual creative abilities, I couldn't have cared less whether or not I had won the lottery. I had been given something more holy, more valuable, than money.

After my gambling episode and this vision, I lost my intense desire to become rich. I even changed my whole attitude about money because I knew that if God thought enough of me to directly answer my prayer, then if I ever really needed anything it would be available. I remembered Jesus' comments about the lilies of the field; this was now my attitude toward money.

From that day to this, I have always had enough money to meet all my physical needs. Years later, when I would need money, I would win tens of thousands of dollars at a time; then I would spend it quickly on the needs of myself and those around me. I became more free with the money I had and freer in my attitude toward it. As I became more balanced in my personal life over the years, my financial life also came into balance.

As I gave money away, it always seemed to come back with interest. One time I used up all my savings to purchase my son a nice car and he wrecked it without insurance coverage, so that I had neither my money nor he the car. Then I won a new Ford Escort, a door prize at an Iron and Steel Exposition in Pittsburgh. I simply said, "Thank you, God!"

CHAPTER

THE SEEKER RETIRES AND QUITS THE SEARCH

Unless one has experienced a direct or almost instant response to a prayer directed to God, then one cannot know the deep feeling of calm and release from all earthly fears that such an answer produces in a human being.

When this kind of answer comes to me a feeling of contentment, of an inner satisfaction like a deep inner knowledge of truth, permeates all my consciousness in a saturation effect, and it lasts for weeks.

For over forty years now I had read, dreamed, and struggled to stay on the path. I had gained deep spiritual insights about human life and about myself, but I had also been badly bruised and abused by myself in the process. My dreams, revelations, visions, and mind awarenesses had taught me well, but in the process they had also exposed me.

I seemed naked now, unable even to white lie to myself so I could masturbate my own ego just for the pleasure it gave me. I seemed destined to be the type of human who would always have to learn wisdom from his own mistakes, because there had been no major successes. I had accomplishments, but never that white flash of instant stardom, of instant success that I both craved and feared. As I looked at myself in the mirror of my mind, I didn't see one of life's great successes, what I still saw was one of life's great failures.

"Oh, God... Oh, God," I would cry out in my thoughts. "I know you are real; I know you have comforted me in the past when no one else cared, but why, oh why, can't I ever see or touch you? Why can't I really know you, know your secrets?

One day when I was in my late fifties, still wondering, still going ahead three steps and back two—I simply stopped. I stopped the endless struggle of the past forty years.

On that day I simply said, "I damn well quit! I'm getting old and I'm tired." I had reached the realization that the pleasure of success would never be worth the pain of attainment. I mumbled softly to myself as sadness fell over me, "I quit... I give up... this time I'll really do it—I quit the Search!"

I felt I was doing this because even though I knew of God, I had never really found why God lived. All I had were smoke wisps of God's presence which would come upon me like a scent in a breeze. At this time I also gave up all my dreams of fabulous success, of great attainment, of being rich, of being somehow a great leader among men. The dreams drained away and faded. In a lifetime of work I had accomplished nothing. The fire went out; the dream died; the Search ended. I'd just wait for death, I decided.

Disappointment at a lost life of seeking and wandering from one religious theory to another hung over me, and I lived always in the shadow of this defeat.

In 1993, at the age of fifty-nine, I took early retirement from the mill. I could easily have worked till I was seventy, but the endless shift changes were bringing out a resentment in me. I had almost thirty-seven continuous years of service in a specialty steel plant, plus another three years that didn't count for retirement purposes because I had once quit for nine months which broke the continuous seniority count. A total of forty years of shift work in a steel mill. So I retired. I'd had enough of the steel mill, too.

83

I now had plenty of free time, and I began to run across America like a water bug skipping over a pond. I did physically what I had been doing mentally all my life—seeking and wandering but not finding.

After a year I stopped all the wanderings, stopped them cold! I stayed home day after day, took long walks in the woods in the rural area of western Pennsylvania where I live. I would get up in time to see the sunrise and set all in the same day. I shifted gears down; I slowed.

I waited and I thought about the strange life I had spent as a Seeker who had found nothing. "A useless life by a worthless person on a dumb planet where God never visited, but once sent his son only that was two thousand years ago. Ten years or so and it will be over: I'll be dead."

Sometimes (just between you and me), I thought, "the sooner, the better; this world, this thing called life, is the most screwed up mess I ever saw." And from everything I'd read, nobody else could make any sense of it either. "Yeah, the sooner, the better."

Yet, I still believed. I meditated daily, prayed daily, and asked for help for my children so their lives would be better (they weren't). I thought constantly about God and life as I had known it for the last forty years. In the end, what did it amount to? Nothing.

So I would sit down and think about it all some more, and then I'd get up and walk in the forest some more. I always loved walking in the coolness of woods, stopping to lean on a tree, seeing shafts of sunlight come through the tree tops and reach down like a flashlight beam to brighten up a single flower or a bush of thick green leaves, thinking strange thoughts like, "Why would that ray of light pick out that individual flower just when I'm leaning against a tree looking at it."

I knew it was a random act of nature, on a random day, in a random place, but I always liked to believe that everything I saw in nature was done just for me, that the bird I heard singing and the answering song from another part of the woods was for me... me alone! It's funny, I thought, how I like to personalize everything I see in nature. Then I'd go back to my screened-in porch that faced south into the trees, and sit down. From that porch I had seen the sun rise that morning, and I would see it set that evening.

When I am sick or depressed, I instinctively go to nature for a connection with the deeper meaning of life. I like to look for faces and shapes in white clouds. I like to see the instant brilliance of the sun coming from behind a dark cloud after it has first painted on a silver lining. Just as in nature the silver lining fades and the cloud passes, again becoming ordinary, this also happens to humans. We have our moments of glory while we are in the light, then we, too, become ordinary as our own inner light passes us by.

When I am out in the woods, I see the sunshine with its shafts of light coming through the trees making shiny paths to the ground. Insects and dust float into these streams of light, then out again. Sometimes, out of the corner of my eye, I see something dart through the sunbeams with such a quickness I wonder if it could have been a wood fairy. Then I smile at myself because of the silliness of the thought.

All of these experiences of nature seem to go inside me and permanently reside in my heart. As I think about them later, with my imagination I can experience the scenes again. A scene from the natural world will come alive in my mind with all its vibrant colors and pure, fresh smells. If I am upset, I can become peaceful again just by thinking about them.

What is it about nature and her wild creatures that can always touch something so deep inside of us? Does this built-in affinity we humans have with nature have a deeper meaning in some mysterious spiritual way? Maybe, just as cures for many of humans' physical illnesses can be found in the plants of the natural world, so, too, can a deeper meaning for our spiritual lives be found in nature and the animals, plants, and oceans she contains.

As I slowed down my life, as my desires drained away, I began to feel lighter and cleaner. As the lust for fame, riches, attainment, and success faded away, I didn't feel like I was carrying the weight of the whole world anymore. When I watched the birds, saw the chipmunks and squirrels play, watched deer and turkey come out of the woods, I wondered about this strange world I had fought so hard to gain supremacy of, but failed.

"How," I wondered, "could I be *feeling better by doing less?*"

I thought of a person covered with mud jumping into a stream and, with no effort on his or her part, being cleaned by the passing water. "Maybe that's my problem," I thought, "I was struggling in the mud and getting dirtier when I should have been doing nothing and getting cleaner. Odd metaphor," I thought.

I still visited the old occult sections of book stores now called "The New Age" section—whatever that means. I would do a quick run through of this and the religious section but seldom saw anything I wanted, mostly it was all just a rehash of old ideas I'd already assimilated. After a quick review of the current best sellers, I would leave.

If I went on vacation or to a new town, I would make a quick check of the local book stores to see if they had anything new or different, but then I stopped doing this after all the Mom and Pop stores disappeared and big chain stores took over. I can't wait until the Mom and Pop stores, with their warmth and individuality, make a comeback. *And they will!*

If I could find something new, I told myself, I'd read it and study it—but I couldn't seem to find the right chemistry, the catalyst that would make all I had stored in my mind come together as one composite picture. If only I could make this happen, I thought, then I still have a chance at finding God and the meaning of life.

I was unwilling to ever join another organized religion or any other type of organization because I didn't want to follow their "Apostles Creed", but I stayed with the A.R.E. as an associate member.

I thought about how fast the years of my life had flown by.

I reread many of my old favorite books; I studied the dream records I'd made over more than forty years as a whole package; I continued to meditate each day. Then one night I had a most interesting dream.

THE DREAM

I dreamed that as I lay in bed, a man in a white robe and a great white beard came into my bedroom. I somehow knew he was St. John of the Revelation. He came over to where I was lying and placed his thumb on a spot between my eyes.

Instantly little postage stamp images began to float into my mind. I knew that I had been blessed or given some valuable thing. Then St. John went away.

End of Dream.

As I woke up, I knew immediately this was another particularly significant dream. And from that night until the present day, I often have periods during meditation or during my waking hours when this spot between my eyes starts to tingle so strongly that I have to massage it with a finger to get the vibration sensation to stop.

Sometimes when I meet complete strangers and we're having a conversation, this sensation starts. At other times, when I'm in a book store, I need only look at the various titles and wait for the tingling to begin as an indication of which book I should buy. I have learned that this tingling starts whenever I am reading, hearing, or seeing some truth about life or people. Even if I'm just thinking, sometimes it starts up and I use it as a guide as to which stream of thought to follow.

As I said, I continued to read, think, and meditate, and about six months later I had another very significant dream:

THE DREAM

I was looking at my face in a mirror. As I looked, I could see that the skin on my face was starting to slide off. As this transparent human facial skin slid away, I could see that underneath it my skin had a diamond shaped pattern appearing on it just like the pattern I had seen on the faces of large snakes.

I had shed my human skin and underneath it had the skin of a snake. As I continued to look at myself, my head and face gradually changed, in that delightful way possible in dreams, into the shape of a very beautiful snake.

I still seemed to be myself; it was just that I had the facial features and skin markings and coloring of a snake.

End of Dream.

I woke up and immediately wrote down the dream. What did it mean? Was I now turning into an evil tempter? No, I knew that wasn't what it meant because I had felt happy and pleased with the change. And, I had a feeling of great satisfaction and contentment when I woke up.

I thought about how I had been praying, meditating, and studying lately, and became aware that snakes also have another symbolic meaning. Then I knew what the dream meant.

It was the great snake of wisdom that I changed into as I looked at myself in the mirror. I had absorbed great wisdom from the books, meditation, and experiences I had passed through in my life, and ever since the dream where St. John touched my forehead, things that I read or thought about were becoming clearer and more meaningful to me.

My own past life, with all its awful mistakes, was being shown to me in a different light so that I now better understood the path I had traveled as a Seeker.

The head of a snake, especially a hooded one like a cobra reared up, ready to strike, has been a human mythological symbol for wisdom as far back as humans have been recording their thoughts and observations. It symbolized that once wisdom strikes you, your old conscious state of mind will die just as your human body will die if a snake bites you.

I knew now why I felt so comfortable and satisfied as I woke up. I was becoming so well versed in symbols after reading so many mythology books and exploring and interpreting my own dreams for so many years, that I, too, had finally started to gain deep wisdom.

My snake dream was showing me I was shedding my old skin of human consciousness and putting on the skin and face of spiritual wisdom.

A month or so later, I had what I call a verification dream.

THE DREAM

I was in a public library and asked the librarian if she would bring me a book on mythology and symbolism so I could study it. She just looked at me and said, "I don't know why you want to read any more of those books, you could now write one yourself!"

End of Dream.

After that dream, I lost the desire to read any more books on the occult or on metaphysical theories. From that day on I knew my own higher consciousness had verified to me that my interpretations of mythology and dream symbols were correct and I no longer needed to read other people's interpretations.

I also realized that while after forty years of study I hadn't found God, I had found out a lot about myself; I had discovered my many weaknesses and had struggled hard to strengthen them. I had also fought my strengths, because my strengths brought out the arrogance and pride which, if not tempered, would make me weak.

What a strange world I had uncovered: weaknesses grew into strengths, strengths turned into weaknesses. Too much gentleness and humility got me trampled on by the more ruthless parts of my own personality, yet aggressiveness and pride were needed to fight off the strengths and weaknesses that would also destroy me. When I was weak, I was rewarded with fear, and when I was strong, I was given arrogance and pride. I found I could not be too strong or too weak, so I became more centered. In forty years I had gone from a shy, quiet introvert into a loud, domineering extrovert; from a young man torn apart by fear and indecision to an old man filled with self confidence. My life became balanced, and peace and contentment were my rewards.

I had been tempered by the fires of time and experience, but they had left me scarred inside and old outside. In my youth I had read about the ecstasy of the saints, but for myself I had only found the pain of the struggle.

As my retirement continued, as I sat on my back porch, I began to ponder and reflect back on the way things were instead of how I'd dreamed they would be. The young man yearning and struggling to be a saint ended up an old man still fighting his own humanity.

At night my dreams were upsetting me, because they showed me killing off old friends, and I was doing this without any remorse or anger. I would wake up horrified at what I'd done. Then I would calm myself and do a verbatim interpretation and realize that the dream meant that I had only succeeded in killing off a character, role played back to me as a dream symbol, of an emotion or mental attitude that had to die if I were to have more growth in my life.

Sometimes I would really be sad to see these people die—my male symbol of aggression or my female symbol of someone with not enough compassion and tenderness—we had been friends for so long.

I started to meet again old high school friends in my dreams, friends whose company I had really enjoyed, and I knew that positive character traits that had been hidden behind the ones I killed were coming forth into my life once again.

CHAPTER

14

THE THIRST RETURNS

I rested, soothing my inner wounds, for almost a year and a half. Then, as had happened so many times before, the old thirst came back.

My desire to drink once more from the fountain of God's wisdom began to tease, then haunt, then to obsess me. *I had to find God*! I just had to. I knew it wasn't a rational desire, and after the beating I had taken as a three times failed Seeker, it wasn't even good common sense.

Still, I couldn't help myself. I had to give it one more try before I died. If I didn't find God this time, then I would concede that my brother and other atheists I knew were right: man is nothing more than an accident in the evolutionary pattern of plants and animals and God is an invention of the conscious mind, a salve to soothe the weak.

Jesus had made the unusual statement that the Kingdom of God is within. I knew this meant that it was inside myself that I should look to find the kingdom of God and therefore God himself.

My plan this time was to complete the journey one hundred percent inwardly. I no longer had to join organized religions or the occult or even a cult. In some strange way, by discovering more clearly who I was, with each passing year I had also been discovering God. As I learned how I myself operated, spiritually, mentally, and physically, I had also been finding out these same things about God.

I became more interested in how my body acted and reacted to food, to mental images, to scents and sounds. I gradually quit watching TV shows and movies because their grossness and violence would instantly give me a negative feedback like the portrayed emotion I was watching. I began to watch only public television with its wealth of nature programs and got a feedback sense of calm and pleasure. I started going to natural scenic places such as mountains, seas, lakes, and wooded areas, whenever I could.

I sent for videos of our great National Parks and of other scenic wonders of the world, and enjoyed watching them. I found I now had a desire to listen to light classical music, and bought these kinds of cassette tapes to listen to in the car if my wife wasn't along (this wasn't her musical preference).

I realized that God could have created the Earth and all its life forms in any manner it chose. What was the reason God created things as it did? What was the pattern of God's creation that existed in plants, in planets, in humans, and in the other animals of Earth?

I really never thought about animals having emotions just as we do until I saw a TV story of how the movies with the little dog Benji were made. It is incredible, but this dog could produce a whole range of emotions by using body and facial expressions on cue.

Then I watched our collie, Taffy, who would grin and wag her tail when she was happy; Taffy would pull her lips back like dogs do when they snarl, except she would be grinning. Our pet cat would rub against my leg and I knew this was contentment personified.

Fascinated, I started to watch the wild animals on PBS programs, even bees and insects. I started to see bits of my own and others' personalities in wild animals. This wasn't the Dr.

88

Jekyll and Mr. Hyde thing—it was little subtle things that animals do instinctively which are the same as mental traits that I and other human animals have.

For instance, I have a tendency to keep things forever that are half worn out or that I don't need in case I might be able to use them "some day". In a film clip about pack rats, I saw how they gather and store things they will never be able to use and I thought, "That's me; I'm a pack rat; I do that. But what is that about—that I, a human, and a pack rat have the same instinct to save? This is really strange."

As I was coming home from work one warm, dark summer night, my headlights caught the shining eyes of an animal in the middle of the road. I go to great lengths, as do most people, to keep from hitting animals, so I slowed down. As I crept up on the animal, waiting for it to dart off the road, my headlights illuminated a scene that haunts me even today.

I saw a pair of raccoons in the middle of the road. One was on its hind legs, hunkered over a fallen raccoon. I pulled over to the right side of the road to go around the animals and when I was about three feet away, I saw a fallen raccoon, covered with blood, twitching and thrashing. It had been hit by a car and was dying. As I got nearer, the uninjured raccoon sat up, and with its front paws grasped together, looked right into my eyes. Then it let out the most agonizing sound I have ever heard a wild animal make, rolling its head as it screamed. I shivered because I knew I was hearing an animal crying over its lost mate.

That raccoon had the saddest, most agonized look on its face I have ever seen. It was a look of terror, hurt, bewilderment, and heartbreak. It looked at me as if to ask, "Why?" In that brief instant of agony, as I was eye locked with a supposedly "dumb animal", I felt the pain, the torment, of every living thing that has just lost its mate.

The scene so jarred my mind that I shuddered and got chills as I drove past the poor animal to go home to my wife and children. The look on the raccoon's face was the same crying look of terror and agony one sees in the faces of women on TV news shows when they have just learned that a child or husband has been killed.

For days afterward, I would get mind flashes of that raccoon on its hind legs crying over its dead mate and screaming its agony to me. I don't know how or why it should be, but I knew from that night on the other animals have emotions just as we do, and get lonely and scared and heartbroken when a mate was gone. What I saw that night in a wild animal was a human look of sadness, anger, and terror, and I never forgot it.

If God was the creator of all these things, then it would make sense that God would create in a flowing, smooth pattern of evolution and design. Created physical things would all be designed differently, but still they would fit the pattern of the overall design that was "Creation by God".

What *was* this pattern of God's creation that I was seeing in animals and so many other things?

As I looked back over my life, I could see the recurring themes and patterns that I had kept repeating over and over. I could also see recurring patterns in nature.

Just As there was a physical evolution of plants and animals, *so also* could I see a mental and spiritual evolution of ideas and ideals within myself.

Then all of a sudden, in my nice laid-back relaxed retirement world, I began to get nightly dreams with a recurring theme: I was told to learn how to type, to pick up my pen and begin writing.

It was the same during my waking hours; I kept having a recurring desire to start writing again. I remembered the novel I had written, and my brother's scathing criticism. After he and his friend were done with me, I had never written again. I had little appetite for getting emotionally beaten up again because of poor writing skills, so I tried hard to ignore this new desire. But as always happens when I try to ignore a strong inward drive, I found that the attention given by me to myself in trying to ignore the drive only intensified its strength.

From my much earlier snake dream about alcohol temptation, I knew that a desire had to be dealt with decisively one way or another. Because I didn't seem able to make a free will yes or no decision whether to write again, the desire kept striking at me. I started to physically imitate the inside of my mind by becoming restless and uncomfortable on the outside, in my body, during the day.

Finally I made the decision to obey my dreams and my own desire to write. I vowed that *soon* I would begin. A week came and went and still I procrastinated. The memory of my past writing failure kept coming back into my mind in vivid recreations of the embarrassment I had felt as I'd read my brother's and his colleague's words of condemnation.

I should have remembered what I had learned about Lot's wife and what happened to her as she looked back at her past: it turned her into a pillar of salt, a symbol of being frozen in one place. If I didn't quit looking back at my own past failures, I, too, would stay frozen in place.

As I drifted off to sleep one Thursday night I said to my higher self and to God, "Tomorrow, I promise I will start to write." Friday came and all day I fidgeted around and found all kinds of house chores to do to prove to myself that I was too busy to begin writing just yet. That night as I went to sleep, I suddenly remembered I had faithfully promised God and my own higher self that on Friday I would begin writing.

Friday had now come and gone and I hadn't even picked up a pen.

I fell asleep. I woke up suddenly at 2:30 a.m., totally, vividly awake—as wide awake as if I had just had eight hours' sleep. I tossed and turned for a few moments, I didn't want to get up. Then I suddenly remembered what I had been dreaming.

THE DREAM

I was back working in the steel mill where I had been employed for a lifetime (my life's work). It was the daylight shift and I had only been at work for two hours or so when I decided to sneak out the gate and go home without completing a full day's work.

The plant manager met me at the main gate and he was furious, livid with anger, because I would dare try to sneak out without doing a full day's work. He then screamed out to me, "You are fired!"

End of Dream.

Needless to say, this really got my attention—one thing I had always prided myself on was that I was a hard worker who needed no supervision in order to get an assigned job done. Now I had tried to sneak away without doing the work—*and I had been fired*!

As the dream came back, so did a horrible realization: *I could not feel the inside of my body.* I had never had this sensation before and I didn't like it.

Frightened, I quickly got out of bed, went to the kitchen and sat down at the table. Try as I might, I still could not feel the inside of my body. I thought I might have had a stroke, but I knew that wasn't right because I'd been moving and walking all right from the bedroom to the kitchen. I felt the outside of my body and I could feel the skin on my face, arms, stomach, and legs, but I had this inner sensation of an empty loss; I no longer had an inside. It was as if I were hollow, as if I were made up out of mere hollow tubes.

"*What is wrong with me?*" I thought, really alarmed. Then suddenly an awareness came over me that yesterday I had faithfully promised God and my own higher self that I would begin to write.

And I hadn't done it.

Now I knew why my dream had shown me I was symbolically fired from my life's work; now I knew why I felt as if I were made out of hollow tubes.

The night before, I remembered, I'd been thinking that if I had this strong a desire to write pounding at me without letup, then there had to be a reason why God wanted me to write.

As I sat there at the kitchen table at 2:45 a.m. with no inner feeling left in my body, I decided that there still might be time. Very scared, I got a ballpoint pen and a spiral notebook, and began writing. I wrote quickly for the next two and a half hours as thoughts raced into my mind as fast as I could get them on paper. After an hour or so I began to gradually get feeling back in my inner body. At about 5 a.m. and ten pages later, I could feel myself again inwardly as a total person; the empty body sensation that had lasted for more than two and a half hours was gone.

Because I had a lifetime of experience working with dream symbols, I knew that I had been shown by my own higher self, or God, that promises made to it by me were not to be taken lightly. To demonstrate how serious a violation this was, my own inner physical awareness was taken away, I became hollow inside. And I also knew what this meant. *Just As* my body's physical inner awareness can be taken away from me, *so also* could all my spiritual inner awareness be taken from me unless I physically applied the inner knowledge I had been given—because spiritual knowledge doesn't become wisdom until it is physically applied. My book would be that physical application.

I wondered what it was that I knew or had stumbled onto that was considered important enough by my own higher consciousness or God itself that it had to be put into book form for others. I didn't feel either worthy enough or qualified for the job.

I knew one thing, though: I could feel myself again inside, and that feeling only returned after I started doing the writing. Before I fell asleep again, I made one sure decision. I vowed to myself I would never again make a promise to my own higher self or God and not keep it.

"No, sir... one time like this is enough! Never again... never again," I mumbled as I went back to sleep.

To begin to write again after fifteen years was a hard thing to do. I told my wife I felt I had to write a book about the things I believed I had learned about life.

She simply said, "Go ahead, I won't stop you, but I'm not going to help you and I don't want to read it. I don't believe in those things!"

I wrote in longhand with a ballpoint pen because I liked the smooth flow in my hand better than a scratchy pencil. I asked my daughter-in-law if she would type the pages for me.

I asked how much she wanted. She said a dollar a page. That was as cheap as I could get it done anywhere and I wasn't much worried about the cost anyway. After the "loss of my inner awareness" episode, I felt willing to pay any amount to get the book completed.

My daughter-in-law offered the comment, "Well... if that's what you want to do...!" After my oldest son read the first draft, he offered the observation that it all seemed weird to him.

With my family support group firmly in place as opposed to my book writing attempts, I began.

Once I had made the mental commitment by the use of my free will, the writing started to flow easier. Since I was retired, I could now write all day long, and I did. I wrote a "throw in." I threw in all my great thoughts and what I perceived to be wisdom in bits and pieces just as they flowed into my mind in a stream of consciousness sequence. Some of these random thoughts were a paragraph long; others ran on for many pages. By the end of the first month, I had over three hundred pages in my spiral notebook. At that point I stopped for a week just to give the book and myself a rest. Then I reviewed what I'd written.

Uh, oh. As I read the whole thing in one sitting, I felt sick. My book of great thoughts and pure-gold wisdom was awful! Not only was the sentence structure bad, but the transition from thought to thought, idea to idea, was fragmented and disjointed. I would begin a thought, develop it for a page, and then jump to a second and even a third thought, only to go back three pages later and pick up and complete (or at least continue) the first thought. What I had just written was not just bad—it was incomprehensible.

I set the spiral notebook aside and said, "God, I need help. If you want me to write this book then I have to be taught how to write it".

I put the pages I'd written aside and turned on the TV to watch a public broadcast station, but I could think of nothing the whole evening except how badly written my book was.

What was really going on in my life? I was retired, and should be taking life easy as my wife and kids kept insisting. But instead I was having dreams telling me to write—and I lost my body sensations if I didn't. Before I went to sleep I again asked for guidance—and had the following dream.

THE DREAM

I was standing inside a big computer room, just like the one that controlled all the hot mill department's individual computers. As I watched, the whole place, with all its giant computers, was shut down. Then it was started back up again in a process called rebooting or reprogramming the system. As I stood there watching this happening, I knew that somehow this was my own consciousness that was being reprogrammed.

End of Dream.

I knew what this dream meant as soon as I wrote it down: *Just As* there is a room that controls all the computers that run the hot mill department (the place where I did my physical life's work), *So Also* is there a mental room within my own consciousness that controls all of the different states of consciousness that are within me. I had long before realized that an almost step by step correspondence exists between computers and the human mind or human consciousness. What I had not realized, however, was that the human mind can in some way be similarly reprogrammed. If this is so, then the key question is: "Who is doing the reprogramming?"

I thought I knew the answer: my own oversoul or superconsciousness, *a totally different thing* than my human consciousness or human ego. But at the same time, like a river connecting to the sea, because I am a part of my own oversoul I can give myself permission to reprogram or guide myself. As an answer to my prayer to God for help in writing the book, I had somehow been given free will permission to allow my own consciousness to be reprogrammed.

I had by now reached an awareness in my thinking that there was only one form of creation and that everything— physical, mental, and spiritual—evolved in compliance with this pattern which I called First Creation.

If *everything* complied with this pattern, then everything I had found to be true in my mental and spiritual life should have a *physical counterpart* here on Earth. Therefore, if I was ever to show to others what I'd learned about God and God's First Creation, I first had to show that a physical model existed.

I wasn't too well grounded in the theories of physical matter or solid state physics, so I put the writing aside for a while and went back to my old stock in trade—books. At the library I checked out physics books four and five at a time. Since I was now retired, it was now easier to read all day and all evening than when I'd had to take time off to go to work for eight hours. My wife had long ago adjusted to my strange ways, so this didn't concern her.

As I read, I made notes. Gradually I became acquainted with Newton, Galileo, Hubble and others. I read books like *How the World Works*, *Tesla*, *Perfect Symmetry*, *Solid Clues*, *The First Three Minutes*.

After that I moved over to the behavioral sciences with books like *What B. F. Skinner was Really Saying*, *Human Aggression*, *Beast and Man*, *Seasons of Life*.

Then I went back to the physics books and studied about inertia, acceleration, action and reaction, and gravity. I got into atoms, electrons, protons, neutrons, quarks, and haydons, leptons, gluons, and the world of solid state physics. These physicists seemed to have everything figured out except force.

I learned of the physical law which implies that an object with no external energy source tends to approach a state of equilibrium as time passes. These objects' energy must constantly be replenished from outside, or they die. But they can sometimes learn how to recycle their own energy and sustain life this way. I remembered that back when I was doing my research on how to become successful in Amway, I'd read that most businesses only have a life span of some seventy or eighty years—the same general life span as a human—and that had surprised me.

Most businesses are only successful as long as the original founder or creator is alive. After he or she dies, the business stagnates and usually within twenty or thirty years it folds up and dies also.

The exception to this rule is when new management breathes new life and new ideas into the business. If this happens, then a rebirth of the business occurs. As with the law of physics, the business has learned how to become self sustaining by creating a new internal energy source after the original external energy source—the founder—has died. The business has taken on a life of its own. (For example, Ford, DuPont, Sandoz, Krupp Industries, Rolls Royce, etc.) I could see this same correspondence in my own consciousness. An idea or an emotion that I create lives only as long as I keep thinking about it; when I ignore it, then it, too, dies. My thinking was the idea's or emotion's energy source.

As I got older I could see that I had distinct seasons in my life: childhood, young adulthood, mature adulthood, and old adulthood. And I could see that everything around me seemed to cycle, as well. So I began reading books about the Earth and the cycles of nature.

The work with cycles was begun at the University of Pittsburgh by Edward R. Dewey, who had once been chief economic analyst to President Herbert Hoover. President Hoover wanted a study of cycles done so that the Great Depression, the economic collapse that started during his time in office, might be better understood.

This work on cycles is presently being compiled by the Foundation for the Study of Cycles, Inc. at Wayne, Pennsylvania. So far the group has identified over four thousand individual cycles which they follow and collect data on. This includes the stock market.

It wasn't just in books that I was seeing patterns and cycles, but also all around me. When I was flying across the United States to visit my brother in California and the plane was at 33,000 feet, I noticed how the tops of cloud formations are shaped differently than the bottoms. On a cloudy day, from the ground the cloud cover looks flat and a bit bumpy, but from above I could see that those clouds contained huge canyons, great mountain ranges and series of hills and valleys like the mountain ranges on Earth. Clouds are light and fluffy, turbulent and moving—yet they are shaped exactly like the mountain ranges that are solid and still. I had recently read that when silicon crystals are magnified under a high-powered electronic microscope, a pattern of design that looks exactly like the Grand Canyon can be seen in them.

The crystal and the Grand Canyon are solids and the clouds are vapor; the clouds took hours to form, the crystal months, and the Grand Canyon millions of years. Yet they all have the same design—on a different *size* scale and also on a different *time* scale.

"Hmmm," I thought, "same pattern but using different scales of measurement." I wondered what force there could be in the world that would give a shape or design to something I consider a vapor—clouds—and do the exact same thing to something I consider solid— rock. Whatever this force was, it was operating on a scale and with a power that defied my imagination—and as you will probably remember, I have a good one.

I remembered that when I'd read the novel *Jurassic Park*, the author spent some time explaining the new "chaos theory" that modern mathematicians had recently developed. Chaos is a part of nature which science does not really understand—in its very essence it *cannot* be understood in terms of basic scientific methodology such as predictability, repeatability, etc. Chaos is a part of nature which seems to have no order and no definable borders.

I went back to the library and checked out everything they had on chaos theory.

CHAPTER

15

FRACTAL PATTERNS

One October day in 1994 as I was sitting on my back porch reading, I came across a reference to the discovery of fractal patterns by the great modern mathematician and physicist Benoit Mandelbrot.

On my next trip to the library I looked for books that explained his work. I couldn't find his original book on *Fractals*, written in 1975, but I did find another book.

In this book were a few black and white pictures that showed a *Mandelbrot Set*, or Mandelbrot's Gingerbread Man because of its obvious resemblance to that cookie design. Here is a black and white picture of a Mandelbrot Gingerbread Man (Picture 1)

A series of colored pictures showed closeups of parts of this gingerbread design.

When I looked at these pictures for the first time, the spot between my eyes began to pulsate and get warm.

An awareness came over me that after forty years of searching I had finally found how God created the world. It was a feeling that went through my body like of shock of electricity—that jolt of instant awareness one gets when a great truth becomes so apparent to them that it forever changes their belief system. And it had just happened to me. I had an inward sense of totally knowing and absolutely believing that what I had been seeking for so long was finally found.

All the floating pieces from forty years of study and learning from life's hard experiences raced around my mind. Finally they slowed and formed into a single comprehensible pattern that I could visualize as a whole instead of in its many parts.

I was seeing, in these computer pictures of a fractal pattern generated by the insertion of a mathematical formula, something in *symbolic form* that no one else was seeing.

I went into my house so excited I was out of breath. I found my wife, got her attention, and said, "I found it... I finally found out how God created the universe and the world we live in. It's all falling into place now!"

"I'm glad for you," she said. And that was it!

I looked at her in amazement. "Don't you want to know what it is I found?" I asked, thinking it incredible that she displayed no curiosity at all.

"No, you know I don't believe in those things!" was her reply.

I went back out to the porch and looked again at those beautiful, fascinating pictures of Mandelbrot's fractal patterns—ever-evolving patterns made up of smaller patterns that look similar to the large or complete pattern. Evolving, they keep changing back to a pattern within, and self similar to, the original pattern.

It wasn't primarily the pictures *per se*, nor the beautiful colors and designs that had grabbed my attention, but what those fractal designs could represent or symbolize. Fractal patterns seemed to reproduce *symbolically* for me because this type of reproduction imitates the design of living organisms when they are in a birth to maturity growth period: fractal patterns are an imitation of physical evolution. By discovering the mathematical formula of fractal patterns, Benoit Mandelbrot proved that they exist.

This design of living, expanding growth can be reproduced in a series of self-similar patterns which can now be duplicated in computers, because of Mandelbrot's discovery—a mathematical formula that can duplicate creation.

It can now be proved, and duplicated by computers, that a single cloud, and clouds that cover an entire sky, are similar in design. They are self-similar. Only the dimension size or scale of the dimension is different. A huge cloud is nothing more than a series of individual miniature clouds pushed together to form a new pattern.

In the same way, huge mountains are nothing more than a series of individual small hills piled one on top of the other, getting higher and higher until they appear as a mountain range, a new design. A tree can start out as a single shoot coming out of the ground from its source, the split seed. Then small limbs sprout out from this main stem. Soon, even smaller limbs sprout out from the larger twigs, growing and evolving the tree until it reaches its full height and maturity as a fractal design concept of one large tree trunk that has a series of self-similar limbs attached to it.

The only thing that varies in the design is the size and number of the individual clouds, the individual branches of the tree, or the individual hills in a mountain range. A single hill can be five hundred feet high and a single mountain five thousand feet high, yet both have the same design.

This is called *a change in the measurement scale within a design or pattern*. It is a *renormalization* of a design within a design. Renormalization means that when a design starts to evolve into a new design, then within this evolving bigger design an exact miniature version of the master design reappears. This miniature reproduction of the macro design is the design becoming normal again, or a renormalization.

Many people have seen the photographic laser image of Abraham Lincoln that is on a stage in Disneyland. Instead of a flat, two dimensional image which has just a height and a width dimension, this image of Lincoln also has the third dimension of depth.

A three dimensional laser picture is called a hologram. The way holograms are made is of interest to us here because it is an example of the renormalization process that characterizes fractal designs. A hologram is actually made up of millions of exact replicas of the whole—if it is a laser hologram of Lincoln, one can see by closely examining the hologram that it is actually made up of millions of little Abraham Lincolns. Imagine that Lincoln's fingers are actually made up of little, whole, Abraham Lincolns.

All holograms are comprised this way, regardless of the subject. A hologram is actually a fractal pattern—a *self-similar design that has renormalized* as one whole pattern.

As I mentioned earlier, I had long ago come to the conclusion that if there was indeed a God, and this God created the universe, the Earth, and all that lived upon it including myself, then God could have done this in any manner it chose. Therefore, the specific patterns God created had to have meaning; there had to be a reason why the Earth, plants, people, and the other animals are created the way they are. The Universe has order, form, and balance, with very, very precise and enduring laws.

And the fractal patterns finally showed me a definite, precise, orderly pattern which creation follows as a master design pattern. Now, suddenly, the answer was right in front of me. It was in an easy to understand form as pictures, and best of all for me because I'm lousy at math, the mathematics had already been worked out.

I had long noticed these self-similar patterns in the different disciplines of learning such as psychology, physics, and astronomy. I could see from my studies that there were self-similar patterns everywhere. The movements of planets in the universe, for example, are strangely similar to the movements of atoms, electrons, and sub-atomic particles found in solid state physics.

The great Swiss psychiatrist and scholar Carl Jung noticed that there was a pattern in the way the human mind operated which correlates with certain other consciousness found in humans—and in astronomy. He saw that a black hole in space which was drawing into itself, for instance, was self-similar to a catatonic mental state where a human's consciousness seemed to be drawing into itself.

Long before I came across Mandelbrot's patterns, I had wondered if there was only one pattern for all of creation and whether all of these "coincidences" were self-similar patterns within a bigger pattern that seemed to be always evolving. Because today was never exactly like yesterday.

Chaos theory proves that chaos has both a measurable part and a part that cannot be measured. Fractal patterns are the part of chaos that can be measured.

Mandelbrot wanted to split chaos from its unmanageable part and then study only that part of chaos that produced rough self-similar patterns that could be measured. He wanted to study the self-similar part of chaos because of the innumerable occurrences of self-similar patterns he kept finding in nature.

Chaos is made up of *non-linear* forms which in turn are always made up of *curved lines*. In chaos, for example in clouds, there are no straight lines because a chaos shape by definition is always made up of non-linear or curved lines, or circles. These curved lines within a chaotic shape can be thought of as being a *fractional dimension* for measurement purposes because a section of a curve or circle cannot be called *one whole dimension* by itself: a section of a curved line can be part of the height, part of the width, and part of the length of the form. So, in effect, a curved line is never whole but is only a *fraction* of certain of these dimensions.

These *fractional dimensions* of chaos forms, or rough self-similar shapes which Mandelbrot called fractals, were what he wanted to measure. How he accomplished this feat is explained by him in a contributing paper on fractals included in *The Beauty of Fractals* by Peitgen and Richter.

This *concept of self-similar fractal patterns is so important to the understanding of my own findings* that I will include a few examples of just what fractal patterns are. I'll do this in a layman's way so there can be no misunderstanding.

The pictures on the following page are examples of a colored fractal design that is evolving, a design with no straight lines, only curves and swirls. This concept is important to keep in mind because it is the basic, most important truth that I have found as to the pattern of creation and the meaning of life.

To sum up, a fractal pattern is a pattern of chaos or curved forms that reproduces or evolves into a new larger design which will always carry all parts of the design it originated out of within the evolving design, as can be seen in a three dimensional hologram, in cloud formations, etc.

If a smaller design within the original design is evolving, then it, too, carries all parts of *the design* within itself internally (just like Lincoln's hologram), and if this smaller design is allowed to continue to evolve, then it will eventually renormalize as an exact replica of the original pattern.

When Mandelbrot's formula was fed into a computer and allowed to generate into a graphic picture form, a form of Pictures 3 and 4 appeared (see following page). Actually the first image, generated in 1980 on a computer much less powerful than today's models, had more side detail than is shown in Picture 1. This side detail was described as "fractal dust" because the mathematical formula used needed to be cleaned up a bit.

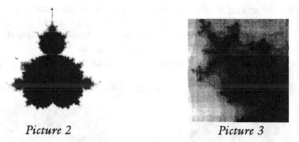

Picture 2

Picture 3

Pictures 2 and 3 are simple and easy to look at as they represent a single unit or symbol. On the next pages, in a sequence progression, are pictures of new computer images of this same gingerbread man. These images have been made by a computer that has the ability to "zoom in" on one particular square of the gingerbread man and produce an enlargement of that square. This computer enlargement shows what the fractal pattern that evolved inside of the larger original symbol looks like.

It is a remarkable thing to witness the unfolding of a fractal pattern, and we can only do it because with our late 20th century computers and Mandelbrot's mathematical formula we can now explore a fractal pattern as a picture design.

As we progress from picture to picture, I will use a large arrow to show where the square in the original gingerbread man symbol is located, the square that is going to be enlarged next. Then, of course, the next picture will be the enlargement of the area within that square. These pictures are shown and numbered in the same step by step order in which they were generated by the computer.

I hope these pictures will allow you to see how a fractal pattern evolves and how, inside of the design, it keeps renormalizing into self-similar patterns.

By the use of "zoom in" enlargements, new computer images will emerge. This allows us to see "inside" the design of a computer generated fractal pattern as shown in Picture 3.

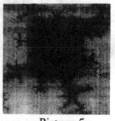

Picture 4

Picture 5

Picture 4 is the gingerbread man; on the right side is an arrow pointing to the square that will be enlarged.

Picture 5 is an enlargement of the square shown on picture 4, showing a little gingerbread man within the larger gingerbread man pattern. This is a good example of what is meant when a fractal pattern is described as being *self-similar* on *different size scales* or *measurement scales*. Remember a small cloud and a large cloud or a small hill and a large mountain?

It is also a good example of what is called *renormalization*, which means that as the larger gingerbread man evolves, smaller gingerbread men appear within this pattern of evolution. It is like the example of the mountain range being a series of single mountains evolving over and over to produce a mountain range. The larger mountain range is still designed by evolving the separate hills. Or one can say that within the design of the complete mountain range there are three hills that look exactly like the *normal* three hills that started to originally grow or evolve into the mountain range. These three hills are a renormalization of the original design.

Picture 6

Picture 7

The arrow in Picture 6 shows the next area of the original gingerbread man that will be zoomed into.

Picture 7 shows a zoom in of Picture 6. It can be seen that more miniature gingerbread men are appearing around the edges of the larger gingerbread man. This shows that in a fractal design, the original design keeps reproducing or renormalizing (gingerbread men keep re-appearing).

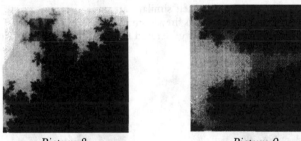

Picture 8   *Picture 9*

Picture 8 shows the original gingerbread man, with the arrow indicating which part will be zoomed in on next.

Picture 9 shows the zoomed-in area of Picture 8 enlarged. The arrow shows what portion of this enlargement will be zoomed in on next.

As I studied the fractal design pictures, new ideas raced through my mind. It was falling dominoes time again because I have always had this strange way of mixing up material things of nature with my own mental activities.

Perhaps because of my long study of dream symbols and practice of dream interpretation, it had seemed to me for a long time as if nature was symbolic of different states of mental activities. Now, as I sat looking again at the set of fractal pictures, my mind shifted from low gear to overdrive in an instant; an incredible excitement raced through me.

At last I was looking at the answer to the questions I had so long been asking.

Why did mystics and religious leaders keep saying that we were made in the image of God? How did God create the universe? What was the master plan, the master pattern?

I did more research on fractal patterns, and found that all modern physicists have accepted the concept as being valid. Furthermore, new pure scientific research work has to include this new discovery before it, too, can be considered valid. I got even more excited.

Now I knew what this self-similar pattern was that I had always seen in nature, in the design of my own body, and in the way my mind worked—it was the pattern of creation. I could see fractal patterns everywhere. And if there was a self-similar pattern to creation, then it could be followed backward as easily as it could be extended forward into the future.

Why could I track such a pattern backward or forward? Because it always evolves in self-similar steps. Therefore, things of creation that exist today have a self-similar correspondence to the way they were made in First Creation.

This is a hard concept to understand from reading these written words, but in my mind it is all clear as a bell tone on a crisp winter morning.

If I am made in the image of God, this has to mean that I have self-similar features that are the same as God, only on a different scale. If God is the original gingerbread man, in other words, then in some mysterious way I am a miniature replica, a miniature gingerbread man or... a miniature God?... Or, more likely: *the potential to be a miniature God!*

What was the *scale difference,* and what was *self-similar*?

Long before I had come to the conclusion that a human life is lived more as a mental experience than a physical one. I had also noticed that plants, the Earth, and even the other animals seem to have characteristics that fit the mental traits of humans. I thought of how hard foxes are to catch, how they often will double back to watch their hunters and pursue them, so that the *hunter* becomes the *hunted.* When a human has an agile, mentally tricky mind, that person is said to be foxy and crafty, as is a fox—they both share this quality. Jackals look, act, and are sneaky, and share this with the sneaky trait that some humans have.

Sometimes then, one wonders if the animal is imitating humans or if it is man who is imitating the other animals. What if the right answer is *neither*?

Humans and the other animals have many similar body traits and instincts. The major difference between them is in their conscious awareness. Perhaps both the other animals and humans are personifications of a trait of some other consciousness?

The next question would then be: What consciousness is being duplicated by both the other animals and humans? My mind jumped to another possibility. *What if the fractal pattern of creation being duplicated isn't physical matter?* What if some kind of *consciousness* actually *becomes* physical matter? What if it is this *consciousness,* and not matter, that is evolving as a fractal pattern form?

Who or what is this consciousness? And why did dream symbols seem to be a necessary form of communication between my human mind and my higher self?

I thought long and hard about each of my dream symbols that I had identified through the years. I wondered again how it could possibly be that animals, birds, the Earth itself, parts of the Earth as locations, and also other people, could represent, as symbols, human mental traits, mental traits that I needed to change, encourage, or eliminate within myself so I could have spiritual growth.

I decided to use a new approach, the same technique used in solving algebra problems—to substitute or invert the answer so that the answer becomes the first part of the problem. I had kept getting feedback from my higher self to learn symbols; now I realized that when one understands the symbols of nature and the surrounding world, and also understands the symbols of his or her own dreams, *then one begins to understand the consciousness of self—and the consciousness of God!* Since physical symbols in dreams always represented mental traits in myself, then it could be possible for physical things to have first been mental or consciousness concepts.

An awareness came over me instantly: *this was the key thought I had been searching for.* Finally I had it! I had found out where God had been hiding! It was the same truth that Jesus had spoken twenty centuries before: "The kingdom of God is within." It was my own consciousness that I had to clean, understand, and perfect before I could find God, because as I did these things by learning dream symbols so I could understand my dreams, and understanding how my own mind worked, only then could I understand how the mind of God works: *the mind of God is made as a fractal designed consciousness.* This is the way physical matter grows and evolves. The physical duplicates the spiritual consciousness.

Just as God's mind is the macro gingerbread man, *so also* is my mind the micro gingerbread man. My own consciousness is an exact miniature replica of the consciousness of God! As above, so below! And not only my mind, but matter too conformed to the pattern of First Creation: an evolving fractal pattern. Finally I understood what all the mystics had meant.

So what was First Creation? It was the new birth of the consciousness of God. How do I know the consciousness of God had to have had a new birth? Because of the discovery of fractal patterns—whatever is being duplicated has to be a micro pattern to the original. And birth is a pattern found in all nature.

A birth is part of the consciousness of God, and everything found in the universe of matter is a fractal pattern duplication of God's consciousness as it is today. Therefore all things in matter—insects, plants, humans, the other animals, even planets, stars, and solar systems—have a birth.

There has to have been a death of God's consciousness at one time because death, too, is a pattern found in all matter. The death of God's old consciousness happened at the very instant that his *new* consciousness was born. (Does this sound like the Big Bang theory?) This death/new birth created the fractal pattern that is First Creation.

My deepest desire during my long years of study was to find lost or hidden secrets about God. Most of those ancient secrets were hidden in symbolic form in the different mythologies I explored. So for these reasons, it was natural for my mind to be full of esoteric thoughts. As I wrote the following section of this book, which is presented in the form of an allegory, I became concerned that it was becoming too abstract, esoteric, and metaphysical. I had known going in that writing about esoteric and metaphysical things would be a tough write because it was all mental *theory* and not physical *fact*.

As I wrote, I sometimes wasn't sure if I was being guided or if I was just writing down things that were a by-product of too much reading and an overactive imagination. Over the years I had run across some really crazy "off the wall" books that went too far in their reach for answers. *I did not want to write one of those books!* One day as I was writing in my glassed-in back porch, I paused as these fears once again came into my mind. Then I became aware that an easy way to solve this self doubt would be for me to get a verification that didn't come from my own thoughts or even as a dream while I slept.

I asked God to give me a *sign in the sky*. I asked that this sign be designed in such a way that I could not misunderstand or misinterpret it. It occurred to me that if I photographed it, then I could study it at my convenience, plus I would have the photographs as a record. When self doubt again recycled into my life, I could look at the photographs to dispel the doubts. So I loaded up film in my camera and kept it on the writing desk in front of me, ready to photograph my *sign in the sky* when it appeared.

A week or so passed. I used the loaded camera to take a picture of my grandson and the first buck deer he got during deer hunting season. But I had seen nothing that I could consider to be a *sign in the sky*.

A day or so later, as I was again writing on the porch, for some reason I looked up and glanced out the window to the right of my desk. There was a small up and down rainbow in a mostly blue sky with a few white clouds. I thought that if this was my *sign in the sky*, it sure didn't amount to much! Then I noticed a cloud to the left of the rainbow, went outside, and took my first picture. I decided to walk closer so that the edge of a nearby tree wouldn't be so dominant in the next shot.

I took the picture and then went back inside the porch. I took one more picture from where I sat at the table because the rainbow was still there, although the cloud seemed to be dissipating somewhat. Very quickly, the rainbow also disappeared.

After I finished writing that day I thought about how quickly the little up and down rainbow, in an almost cloudless sky, had appeared and then disappeared. I took the roll to a local one-hour photo developing machine and got it printed.

When I picked up the developed film, first I saw the picture of my grandson and his deer. It had come out well. Then I saw the first photo of the rainbow—it was a clear picture but didn't really amount to anything, just a cloud and a rainbow in the sky.

This is the first picture I took when I went outside. Notice how the cloud has no apparent shape but the rainbow is clearly visible.

Then I looked at the next photograph and I was absolutely stunned! I couldn't believe what I was seeing. I didn't remember seeing it when I took the shot.

But... I was looking at what I had asked for. I examined the picture more closely. I could still see the rainbow, but to the left and on top of it was a cloud that had assembled itself into the form of a white lamb lying at rest. And no matter how I moved the photograph—up, down, left, or right—the eyes of the lamb were always looking directly at me.

I stared and stared at the photograph (Picture No. 11 below) which was taken sometime in the first week of December, 1994.

This is the last of the three pictures. Notice how the rainbow is rapidly fading and the lamb cloud image is now almost gone.

After I looked at the third picture of the fading cloud and rainbow, I went again to Picture 11 of the lamb/cloud/ rainbow and pondered its symbolic meaning, both as to the symbol of the lamb and of the rainbow.

I knew the lamb symbolized the Lamb of God who would come as a savior to the world. I remembered vaguely that the rainbow was a sign God had placed in the sky after God destroyed the Earth by a flood.

I have both a Catholic Bible and a King James version. Since the King James was the closest I grabbed it, and found what I was looking for in Genesis 9:12-16. It reads as follows:

Genesis 9:12   "And God said, This is the token of the covenant which I make between *me* and *you* and every living creature that is with you, for perpetual generations.

Genesis 9:13   I do set my bow in the cloud, and it shall be a token of a covenant between me and the earth,

Genesis 9:14   And it shall come to pass, when I bring a cloud over the earth, that the bow shall be seen in the clouds,

Genesis 9:15   And I will remember my covenant, which is between *me* and *you* and every living creature of all flesh; and the waters shall no more become a flood to destroy all flesh.

Genesis 9:16   And the bow shall be in the clouds; and I will look upon it, that I may remember the everlasting covenant between God and every living creature of all flesh that is upon the earth."

Edgar Cayce was once asked about the significance and symbolism of this passage in Genesis and his answer, in reading (1436-2), is as follows:

> *"... the promises of the Divine that were and are written in the rainbow of the sky, when the cloud has passed, are the same as written in the lives of individuals that they too, who are in a closer walk with the Creative Forces, may see their sign, their colors and know whereunto they have attained in their relationship with Creative Energies or God."*

I hadn't known this Cayce reading even existed until months after I'd asked for the sign, when I ran across it in another book I was reading.

Was the cloud/rainbow scene in the sky my sign, my colors, given so I could know that I had attained a relationship with Creative Energies or God?

Was this cloud/rainbow/sky scene given me as a verification that my book did indeed contain information I was to share with others? Or was it a coincidence?

What was the meaning of having both the *Lamb of God*, or the *Christ Symbol*, and the rainbow that represented God's covenant with mankind, as a *sign in the sky* symbol for me?

Did this mean that the promise of God to set a bow in the clouds as a sign that a covenant existed between God and man which was personalized in Genesis 9:15 as being between *me* and *you* could also be interpreted as a sign between God and myself, as Edgar Cayce implied was so in reading 1436-2?

Could the cloud image of the Lamb of God mean that in addition to God's covenant with me and all mankind shown in the rainbow, that the sign of his son was also included to show me that the Christ or Savior consciousness was also looking over me, to sort of guide and protect me as I wrote?

Well, I know what I did after the lamb/cloud/rainbow sign in the sky. I picked up my pen and began writing with a new confidence, sure now that I was writing the book I should be writing. The self doubt had vanished.

In addition to the sign in the sky I had other guidance dreams as I continued to write. I had many cave dreams, a symbol of my own unconscious mind. In one of these, I was in a cave and no matter how hard I tried, I could only dig loose, with a pick, an occasional nugget of gold. I knew this symbolized a nugget of pure untarnished truth I was occasionally digging up as I explored different topics to write about in my unconscious mind.

My dream was telling me to get out of the current topic because it had already been worked over before and there were few nuggets of truth left to be found. So I'd throw what I had written on that subject away and continue to search for the mother lode, that seam of pure truth that was still hidden—it was there and I must dig.

I had a dream of rewiring my inner electrical circuits so I could re-energize myself. Another time I dreamed I opened an electrical box and all the fuses and connections were burned out; I had to rewire the circuit board. This meant I was burned out, from thinking about all of this too much.

Then I had dreams where I was stringing out a heavier communication wire, or setting up a new TV antenna, and I knew that these symbolized my attempts to more directly hook up my own inner self, my unconscious mind, to my own oversoul and to God.

When I wrote about the esoteric things that are in the allegorical section of this book, I dreamed that I was talking all night long with angels.

The next guidance dream I had related to the deep concern I felt about quoting God in the allegorical section. I thought it was all right for me to put down my viewpoint of how I thought esoteric things might have happened some time in the past, because I could validate my statements, either from the books I had been studying or from some of my own life experiences. However it seemed quite another thing to be writing that God said this or God said that.

On the night of January 8, 1995, I had the following dream, and it eliminated those concerns.

THE DREAM

The Catholic Pope, John Paul, has just entered my house. He sees me and tells me he wants to talk to my wife, he has something he wants to show her.

The Pope and I go into the kitchen where my wife is. As she looks up at Pope John Paul, he removes from under his garment something that is wrapped in silk. Then he asks my wife to go to the refrigerator and get out the quarter pound of butter that's shaped like a long bar and give it to him.

My wife does this. Pope John Paul takes the butter and puts in on the kitchen table. Then he puts the package he is carrying beside it on the table. Both the butter and the Pope's package are still wrapped.

The Pope unwraps the silk covering from his package and shows my wife that it is a bar of pure gold. Then he unwraps the quarter pound of butter and lays it beside the bar of gold and tells my wife to come over and look at both of them.

I come over with my wife and we look at the bar of gold and the bar of butter which are identical in size, shape, and color.

The Pope tells my wife to look at the top of each bar and see how they are marked. All this time, the Pope talks only to my wife, not to me. He points out that the markings on both the bar of gold and the bar of butter are exactly the same.

On the table, side by side, the two bars look like this:

They each have nine marks that appear to be an identifying code of some sort, short lines in groups of three's.

My wife and I can see that the markings on both the gold and the butter are the same and this really puzzles us because we know that butter is never marked this way. So how did those identical markings get on the bar of butter?

Then Pope John Paul points at the bar of gold and says, *"This bar of gold came straight from God!"* This really surprises me.

Then he tells my wife he wants her to leave the house and travel with him, the Pope. I can't believe he wants my wife to travel with him, nor does my wife.

Then the Pope, my wife, my brother, and I sit down at the kitchen table and the Pope begins to play cards with us for a short period of time. Then the Pope leaves, taking my wife with him.

End of Dream.

I knew immediately that this dream was especially important. I wrote it out in my spiral notebook, then began a symbol-by-symbol interpretation. Remember, as I did, that this dream is a direct answer to the deep concern I had the day before about quoting God in my writing.

THE DREAM

Symbols in Dream	*Meaning of Dream Symbols*
My House	This symbolizes my own human state of consciousness in which I now live.
Pope John Paul	The Pope is the direct descendant of Saint Peter, appointed by Christ to be *God's personal representative* on Earth. Therefore, *Just As* the Pope is the Catholic Church's personal representative for God, *so also* do I have a part of my spiritual consciousness that can come to me *as a personal representative of God*.
Gold Bar that was sent from God	The symbol of gold represents pure truth that can never be tarnished. God's pure truth is being carried by the Pope to show to my wife and me.
Refrigerator	This symbolizes a place where food for the body can be stored *unspoiled* until it is time to eat. Therefore, *Just As* I have a place in my physical life where I can store food unspoiled for my human body, *so also* is there a place inside of my own consciousness where I can store *unspoiled* food for thought, my memory.
Quarter Pound Bar of Gold Colored Butter	This is a symbol of pure truth that is stored in my memory just as butter is stored in a refrigerator.
My Wife	This symbolizes the feminine side of me which is my

own inner awareness of my own consciousness. *Just As* I am married to a female human, *so also* am I married in my consciousness to my (female) own inner awareness.

Identical Markings on the Bar of Gold and the Bar of Butter	These marks symbolize a code that is exactly the same on the bars. It is also a play on words—these markings are *bar codes*. So *Just As* there is a bar code on both the bar of gold and the bar of butter that shows they are exactly the same, *so also* is the gold truth from God and the gold truth (the butter) I have stored in my memory exactly the same.
Wife to Go with the Pope	This is a symbol of both my own inner awareness (my wife) and a part of my own consciousness that can represent or meet with God (The Pope). Therefore, *Just As* I have a wife and a pope in my house, *so also* do I have an inner awareness and a higher spiritual self that can communicate directly to and even represent God inside my own human consciousness, and this inner awareness will travel with the Pope.
Playing Cards with the Pope	The kitchen table is a symbol of the place in my consciousness where food for thought can be eaten. The playing of cards is a symbol for a saying that I have often repeated: *You have to play the game of life with the cards you are dealt!*

Therefore, *Just As* I play the game of life, *so also* will the Pope or my highest spiritual self sit with me a while and play the game of life with me.

MEANING OF DREAM

My own highest spiritual part (the Pope) has come to visit me in my own human consciousness (my house) and tells me and my own inner awareness or intuitive self, the feminine part of my consciousness (my wife) that what I have stored in my own memory (the refrigerator) can be used as a golden spread of truth (butter)—the gold bar of truth from God and the bar of truth (butter) from my own memory are exactly the same (the identical bar code markings).

For a while, my own highest spiritual self will stay with me to play a few hands of the game of life (the playing cards) and then my own inner awareness will leave me to travel with my own highest spiritual consciousness.

Connecting my dream to the events of the day before, I could conclude that what I had written, which had come from the storage place of my own memory, was a wisdom or truth that was exactly the same as the pure truth of God.

I was very happy with this dream, and now felt satisfied that what I was quoting as the pure wisdom or word of God was acceptable.

I should have trusted my inner self more, because I had been aware as I worked that the spot between my eyes was tingling, which has always been a sign for me of the presence of truth.

With the blown up picture of the lamb cloud over a rainbow in front of me, and a copy of this dream nearby, I began to write again free of the worries and fears that had been plaguing me.

As I wrote I realized that each beginning is an ending and each ending is a beginning is an enigma which describes God and God's evolution as a living Consciousness. It is a riddle within the pattern of the evolving, fractal gingerbread man that continuously makes tiny gingerbread reproductions of itself.

How did God have a beginning? If God's consciousness is the pattern that all of creation duplicates, evolving into new beginnings that end, then how did God have an ending?

Was there a death of God?

Why are humans living on Earth? Why do humans have souls? Why do humans have religion and what does religion teach them?

How did I reach the conclusion that the Earth, man's consciousness and physical body and soul are all formed as micro fractal patterns of God's own evolving Consciousness?

It is difficult to explain spiritual concepts in physical terms because an exact correspondence is not really possible. Consider the difference between the written word and the spoken word: the spoken word is round, full, and three dimensional, while the written word is flat and two dimensional.

Esoteric findings fall flat and become less appealing to the mind when presented in written form rather than in a spoken or visual form of communication.

Since this is a written rather than spoken account, I decided to present the following chapters in an allegorical visual form of communication.

This is the definition of allegory as found in *The New Merriam-Webster Dictionary*.

Allegory (ál-a-gör-ë) n., pl. -ries.   The expression through symbolic figures and actions of truths or generalizations about human conduct or experience. Al-le-gor-i-cal (al-a-gor-i-kal) Adj.

PART II
CREATION
AN ALLEGORICAL PRESENTATION

IN THE BEGINNING

A long, long time ago, before stars shone with mysterious wonder in a dark sky, before a sun made hard daylight for work and a moon created a soft, gentle light, before birds sang their songs of early morning greeting to a new day and a new beginning, there existed only one life.

This was a *passive consciousness* without form, without name, which lived in eternal space. This consciousness, which we call God, was the sum total of everything that had ever existed, and it appeared to be in eternal meditation. It showed no activity, no outer feeling, it felt no sensations. It just stayed calm and in a state of inner peace. It had been this way for all of time—but there is really no way of telling how long that was, for time did not exist.

This consciousness, or God, had only two aspects or dimensions: space and mind. Since God was all things in the beginning, space has to be a part of God. If it was not, then one could say that in the beginning there was God... and also space—which would mean that in the beginning God was living inside of something—of space. But in the beginning, there was only God.

Inside the mind of God were two subdivisions that could be considered as two different awarenesses, one being an inner awareness and the other an outer awareness. You could also call them female and male. So in the beginning, there wasn't just God's consciousness, *per se*, as a single unit. In the beginning and from all time, God's consciousness had an inner, female, and an outer, male, awareness, *and* it had space.

At some given moment—no one knows when, or why—a movement started within this great consciousness called God: it stirred, and trembled awake.

God had just become aware of itself as the sum total of all things.

How do I know this? Because this is similar to what humans still do today as a micro fractal pattern of God's consciousness. When we wake up from sleep, meditation or daydreaming, we shift consciousness and then we become aware of two things: First, that we have been asleep, meditating, or daydreaming, and second, we become aware of ourselves as the sleeper, meditator, or dreamer.

This is what God did. God became aware for the first time that not only could it dream, but that it was the dreamer. This was the awakening of God's consciousness.

As God stirred awake, perhaps God began to think these thoughts: Well... since I am all things, I have no companions, no others to keep me company... I am lonely! How can I ever have another, if I am already all things? If there were another, then I wouldn't be all things, for then there would be myself and this other.

The awakened consciousness thought about this paradox of limitation for further eons. "What should I do?" was the question that cycled endlessly round and round in God's thoughts. "How can I have a companion when I am already everything?" was the question it endlessly could not answer.

"Am I to be alone forever? Am I forever limited to being just me? I want to grow and expand. But how can I grow and expand when I am already fully expanded and fully grown because I am already everything?"

Then God had an instant revelation. "My wholeness is a limitation! Because I am everything, I can be nothing more! This is a strange paradox. I am everything, so how did I become limited?"

On and on, God rolled this thought over and over until suddenly another awareness came over it: "In the beginning I always knew I was limitless, then suddenly I became aware that this business of being everything was a limitation."

Puzzled, God dwelled on this new awareness. "By my own thought I created within myself my own limit! Therefore I created something new, something that was not there before! I created a limit within something that was supposed to be limitless, and I did this by thinking!

For more eons God dwelled on the fact that it had created something new even though it was already everything—it had created the concept that it could place a limit on something limitless. Then another new thought came: "I've been alone *long enough*. I want companionship. But can I create souls, and a universe for them and myself to evolve and grow in, if all there is, is myself?"

Finally God had the idea of doing something to its own consciousness to solve this problem, so it could both create and have material to make creation from.

What material did God have to work with? It had its *own consciousness*, the only thing that existed.

God decided to change from a passive, non-creative consciousness into an active, creative consciousness.

To do this, God willed that its own interconnected female inner awareness, and its male outer awareness, would not be intertwined or connected any more. Instead, they would be parted into two separate units of consciousness.

And by an act of God's will, they were: God's consciousness split in half!

After this separation, God willed that its outer, or male consciousness, penetrate into its own female or inner consciousness. Then, within a millisecond of time, God's inner awareness penetrated God's own outer awareness; for a brief instant of time they were one. After that there was again a separation, except that now the two halves of God's consciousness were different in design. Neither now had a pure identity; one was no longer a pure inner awareness and the other was no longer a pure outer awareness. Although still blended together as both the male and the female awarenesses, they now were split in half so that they were two composite parts that were each male/female.

These parts then reconnected in such a way that each was one half of the other: the male was now half female, and the female half male. Then both again split apart to become separate male and female awarenesses—but each now carried within itself the potential of the other.

When God's two newly formed combined male/female awarenesses split apart, God's consciousness was forever changed. God was now a mother/father composite. God had become an active creative consciousness. This mother/father consciousness is self-similar to two gigantic electromagnetic magnets of different polarities, positive and negative. Now, because of the new interaction of God's own negative and positive polarities of male and female, *God could now generate* or *create* energy.

This act of splitting apart is the Big Bang theory of creation, while the Biblical phrase "Let there be light" is a symbolic explanation of the beginning of the flow of the new energy of God. This energy can also be thought of as *life*, in the sense that *life* disappears when energy leaves a living object.

It could also be said that the *old passive consciousness* of God had just died, and that at this exact same instant God, as a creative consciousness, was born. These events began the fractal pattern of creation. With the newly created energy coming from itself that was actually a part of itself, God had the building blocks needed to begin creating companions and a physical universe, i.e., more energy.

110

As God's consciousness expanded, the design of that expansion was in the form of four fractal patterns co-existing as one good design: God created miniature patterns of itself which were self-similar in appearance. Then God gave those patterns a spark of its own life essence, or energy, so that those patterns became alive and moved freely on their own, just as God did. In this way souls were created, patterns of consciousness exact replicas of the consciousness of God.

The souls had their own forms, or space, and their own energy as their spark of life. They were androgynous spirits made in the image of God the Father and Mother of Creation. Energy was be the Holy Spirit or Holy Ghost which would animate the new creations so that lessons could be learned and consciousness expanded. Therefore souls have a double consciousness, or mind—they have a mind of their own, and they have a seed, a spark, a bit of God's own mind, in them. Along with this bit of their own energy, or spark of life, God also gave the souls free will. Each soul was born as a small virgin consciousnesses that could evolve and grow, by the use of its free will, any way it wanted. It could choose to evolve into an adult consciousness that would be a companion and co-creator with God. But this had to be a free will choice. It could also choose not to grow. However, before a soul was given power that it couldn't handle, it had to prove it was worthy of receiving more power.

Power is an extra awareness of a soul's own unlimited potential, known as wisdom, which can become a permanent part of a soul's makeup.

One reason souls were born as seeds of consciousness, instead of with the whole of God's own consciousness, was because having the whole consciousness of God in an individual soul would have created nothing but a bunch of clones of God. I know the last thing I'd want to live with would be a clone of myself; it's better to meet someone with different experiences and viewpoints.

Apparently God felt this way, too. Souls' experiences and diversities were also a part of God's consciousness which souls would have to develop for themselves, until they finally passed all the tests to become true companions and co-creators with God. This would also, in a subtle way, allow the consciousness of God to grow and expand. After all, that is what creation was all about anyway. God wanted companions, and God itself also wanted to grow.

Acquiring discipline is part of the training and tests each soul must pass. A soul must also learn how new knowledge can help, and how it can hinder, its own progress. When this is understood, knowledge is changed by experience and discipline into wisdom.

In its journey to spiritual perfection, each soul has to master the nine planes of heaven. In heaven, as is the present case on earth, it is necessary to do the actual work required in order to learn any body of knowledge, so that knowledge learned is not misused. Since there is no time in heaven, but only new awarenesses learned as each of the nine planes are mastered, there was no problem in allowing each soul to learn at its own pace.

There was a problem, however. Angels, as teachers, and souls, as students, couldn't understand the consciousness of God because the evolving expanding design of creation was too huge to ever be seen in its entirety.

When the angels went to God and explained their difficulty, God decided to create a new teaching tool for the angels' use. This tool, designed as an exact self-similar pattern in matter of God's own consciousness, was *the planet Earth*.

CHAPTER

THE CREATION OF THE EARTH

God realized that for the physical model of its own consciousness to have meaning as a teaching tool for the angels and souls, it would have to be created with a difference: on Earth, equal emphasis would have to be given to both halves of each separate creation. This difference insured that each opposite half of the new creation could be isolated and studied as a separate unit. God's own consciousness could not be understood unless one first knew of and identified the opposites that comprised the whole and then learned how the interaction of those opposites causes action and reaction.

Dualism would be emphasized in the Earth model so that souls could understand the concept that hot and cold, or day and night, or smooth and rough, etc., are really opposite halves of the same things—temperature, a twenty-four hour period of time, texture, and so forth.

The principle of dualism as a part of all of Earth as a creation meant that nothing would appear on Earth as a complete, whole, self-sufficient unit. Both halves of each micro pattern would have to evolve as separate entities or designs by themselves on Earth. Only by an interaction of both opposite halves could the action of the whole be understood. In plants, insects, and animals the separation into dual opposites would become the male and female sexes; in chemical elements it would become the positive and negative polarities of their electrical charge. The Earth itself would have a positive and a negative pole so that it would be able to generate energy to sustain the energy forms living on it as bits of matter.

The micro pattern in our physical world of how God made thought into energy to create and control a universe can be found in simple bar magnets and in electrical generators. When two magnets can circle or spin around each other and their magnetic force fields intersect, then a flow of electrical current is induced and made to flow. This is the principle of alternating current (A. C.).

The total makeup of God consists of four distinct parts. The first two are space and emotion. The other two parts are those of inner and outer awareness, or mind and energy. Since God is made up of these four forces as part of its design, all things that are created in a fractal design pattern will personify one, two, three, or all four of these forces in the design. The four primary forces flow out into the universe as design concepts and they also return back to God.

The new physical teaching tool, the planet Earth, would be built to correspond to the four forces, known *in matter* as the four basic elements: earth, air, water, and fire. To do this, God took each of the four parts of its own mind and separated them into their dual opposites. This is exactly how God had changed itself in First Creation from a passive consciousness that did not have the ability to create into a consciousness that *could* create because after splitting itself from one into two, it could generate pure energy.

When pure energy slows down, it becomes physical matter. Therefore all God had to do to create the planet Earth was wait until a part of its own multi-fractal pattern which was expanding, or renormalizing, or becoming a miniature self-similar pattern of its own consciousness, formed—and then slow this pattern's energy down until it became physical matter.

Then to make this physical model come to life, God allowed an essence known as God consciousness to flow into everything on Earth.

After God had completed the creation within a creation called Earth, it watched as life grew in the sea and on the land. All of the planet was now bursting with life in billions of forms: microbes and viruses, insects, plants, minerals, and animals, each of which had its own intelligence, its own consciousness which would control it's personal evolution.

Plants sprouted up and bloomed, spreading their seeds and merging into clumps that together were even more beautiful than the initial individual plant. There were flowering shrubs, green trees, green grass, and other lush thick vegetation. There were sparkling clear springs, high mountains capped with glistening white snow, and live volcanoes spewing fiery red lava, smoke and dust.

With its complex ecological system, the new planet was the living matrix of God's consciousness in matter put together in one place where it could be better studied by the angels and souls: a huge living life form capable of perpetually recreating itself, an experimental living laboratory to be used as a living instruction tool.

The new life forms on the planet depicted the billions of physical matrixes used by God to show angels and souls the endless possibilities that exist within God's consciousness. Combinations of these living matter matrixes clustered into groups, so that scenes could be played out corresponding to their dualities: a resting state of consciousness, a violent one, etc.

Animals, for instance, were each given a bit of the emotion of love that God had within itself as whole love. But on earth emotions were always split into their dual opposites, and so with the emotion of love came its opposite: hate. An animal could be mean and ugly or loving and beautiful, or combinations of both. In this way angels and souls could be shown, for example, the gentleness that is part of a soul's consciousness personified as a gentle lamb; they could also see how cunning ambition, personified by a wolf, could attack and destroy the gentleness in the soul's own consciousness.

The angels and souls needed to observe and understand all the endless possibilities so they could intimately understand how the consciousness of God operates. Only when they had fully comprehended this could they take their places as co-creators and companions to God.

God assembled all the souls and angels and issued a very stern warning: under no circumstances were they to actually enter into the living physical matrixes of Earth, because they could become permanently trapped there if they did. This was because none of the earth matrixes were whole—each was only a dual opposite half. A soul's penetration into a single half-matrix would conflict with that living half-matrix because souls' form and energy matrixes were whole.

A soul's spirit energy would therefore overpower the half-matrix energy that was trying to physically evolve as a living, pure, half-form. Worse, the penetration of soul into a living physical matter matrix would also begin to alter the soul's own evolution. This was because a (spiritual) soul would now have an intimate knowledge of (physical) matter, and this knowledge would then become part of the soul's own evolving created pattern of self knowledge. There were no half matter/half spirit fractal patterns created by God that had an evolution which could be imitated. *Therefore, a spiritual soul would eventually become trapped on the Earth or in matter.* And its own evolution as a pure spirit consciousness would be stopped.

With this warning from God firmly in their minds, souls and angels began their observation of the new teaching tool.

Almost spellbound, angels, accompanied by the souls they were training, circled the blue green globe that was Earth, observing each action and interaction of life. The sight of their creator's consciousness moving, acting, and reacting as living physical matrixes enchanted them.

They watched as a light wave of love descended over the Earth, making clouds whiter and grander in pattern, deepening the colors of flowers. The Earth became greener and richer, the evolving forms purer and more beautiful.

They could watch a thought form of God move like a vapor of energy toward the Earth, becoming cloudlike in density, then slow and settle into a solid matrix form that became a new mountain or another animal species.

The angels taught the souls that on Earth, air symbolizes thought, fire symbolizes emotion, and water symbolizes intelligent reasoning. All three of these act and react with each other and also with soil and rock.

Rock or granite is born deep down in the Earth as molten liquid, which is then pushed to the Earth's surface as hot lava. Once on the surface the lava cools, cracks, and with the aid of the action of water, wind, and sometimes fire, is fragmented into small enough pieces for plant life to begin to use as a food source. These primitive life forms start to grow onto and in the lava. The natural death and decay process of the plants creates residue matter which helps build up a thin soil layer on the broken lava. Then the lava and soil combination enters into a mature period of growth. When that phase is completed, the land mass moves toward its descent into death—its ending.

Because in a fractal design all endings are beginnings and all beginnings are endings, this process becomes an endless cycle. The larger self-similar pattern, the whole land mass, moves in the process known as continental drift until it collides with another land mass. Then the outer edge of whichever land mass is smaller slips under the edge of the larger one, and is driven back down toward the center of the earth, where it melts down to lava—a death. It then repeats the birth process as it is ejected as molten rock to become part of a land mass again—a new beginning.

The land mass still on the surface folds and stretches into the chaos pattern of mountains, valleys, and seashores which are fractal patterns or self-similar designs. It takes hundreds of millions of years for large land masses to move through this birth to death cycle, but it does eventually happen.

The same cycle of birth, death, and re-birth is also going on within stars, nebulas, and galaxies. There the time scale is so awesome it's measured in light years—but it's still the same process.

A fractal pattern design is never the same this moment as it was the moment before. This happens with the Earth mass, too: never the same configuration from moment to moment or year to year. Sometimes the changes are minute, caused by the wear of wind and water. Sometimes the changes are gigantic, caused by flood, hurricanes, and volcano eruptions. In this same way conscious patterns are changed by thought, emotion, and intelligence. How did all three—thought, emotion, and intelligence—work on and within the whole of consciousness? How did free will choice affect all of these things?

To explain these concepts to young souls, a teaching angel would show souls a storm rushing with a vengeance over the Earth and the plants and animals upon it, seeking to destroy all that had been created. Lightning struck in tree-shattering bolts that started roaring fires which consumed and destroyed everything in their path. Then rains came and put out the fire so that the cycle could begin anew.

The angel would explain that this was exactly what was happening inside a soul's consciousness when a spark of emotion came alive in its mind. As the soul's consciousness thinks on this emotion, the spark goes from smoldering to a hot flame. If the soul recognizes that the self is getting too hot, or too angry, then its own reasoning process steps in and thinks things like, "Forget it, it's not worth it," and usually the mind cools down just as if water had been thrown on it.

Souls and angels had no time concept, so they were able to watch hundreds of centuries unfold as if they were only moments. They saw that everything on Earth had a beginning called a birth, a growth period toward maturity, a long period of maturing, then a fading into oblivion or death. They saw that all beginnings are endings and all endings are beginnings, flowing and blending together as morning goes to noon and then to evening to die as one day, to be reborn again from the night as another day.

The angels showed the souls that the earth itself had a beginning, a birth, and was in constant change as parts of itself evolved in its birth/death cycle. The earth's four seasons were manifestations of this cyclical process: Spring, the birth process; Summer, the time of growth to maturity; Fall, the long period of maturity; and Winter, the slide into the coldness of death and oblivion from which would arise the new Spring.

The angels showed the souls that even a supposedly inanimate object such as a rock cycled in a birth/death pattern which could only be understood by realizing that its renormalizing process had a longer time span.

CHAPTER

WHEN SOULS CAME TO EARTH

One of the things that especially fascinated the androgynous, male/female souls was observing the living forms of matter which were separated into the dual opposites of male and female. The living matter matrixes formed as animals attracted the most attention from the souls, especially during these animals' mating seasons.

The souls watched with great interest how an attraction formed between male and female during this time, as the first phase of a sexual joining of the two opposite sexes. The souls would watch animals perform the sexual act, then soon would see a miniature replica of the mother or the father being born from the female's body as a baby micro self-similar pattern. This pattern occurred not only in animals, but also in plants, insects, chemical elements, and even in the electromagnetic force that surrounded and permeated the Earth as opposite electric polarities.

The thing that most interested the souls was the *emotions* that could be seen, as an energy wisp, going back and forth between the male and female animals before the sex act even began. They could see that the physical attraction between two opposites, a male and a female, seemed to generate an emotion that was like the love they saw descend from heaven to become form on Earth, but it was different from the way they experienced love in heaven.

In heaven, as whole souls who had never been split into male and female, they knew a constant form of pure love that flowed from God and surrounded them as an energy and light. It was a form of love that held all of the universe together in a spiritual way, the same way that gravity held the physical Earth together, in a self-similar pattern, in a physical way.

Souls could experience the love of God in heaven the way physical life on Earth could experience light. One can't experience a part or parts of light; you get it all at once, and so it was with love in heaven.

All created souls were aware that they were made in the image of God in the same way a drop of water is made in the image of the ocean. But just as a drop of water doesn't know all there is to know about the ocean, so it was that souls didn't know all there was to know about God.

Souls knew that they had the creative power of thought. In heaven, by using the thought process, they could create anything they wanted as an awareness, but not as a physical living creation. Only God had the power and energy to create matter.

In heaven there was a concept that everything that could ever be created had already been made and was just waiting for the souls to become aware of it. In other words, the complete pattern, the whole gingerbread man, already existed.

Remember the problem God had in the beginning when there wasn't God plus the material to create things from, but only God? What God had created in First Creation was a new concept, a new pattern of God's consciousness. So when a soul in heaven created anything by thought, it really just became aware of something already created by God at First Creation—it was really just creating new awarenesses for itself.

116

What a soul can create is a new awareness of its own individuality. To do this, a soul first thinks of something it wants to create and that thought immediately manifests in spirit form. When the new thought form appears, the soul then has an awareness that its creation now exists.

However, it always existed. A soul just didn't have an awareness of it until its thoughts created a desire for the soul's mind to become aware of it. Always, at any given time, God is the sum total of the fractal, ever expanding pattern of its First Creation. When souls had thought of all the things there were in the universe to think of, then they would also have a total awareness of what God is, and would be ready to join God as equal companions.

God had told the souls that they could learn all that was needed to be known by staying *whole* and *spiritual*, not physical—by remaining as they had been created. God repeatedly warned that they were not to get involved in living matter under any circumstances because of the dangers that could be encountered trying to gain knowledge that way.

Unfortunately the young, evolving souls watching Earth didn't have enough awareness yet to make mature judgments. As they observed the fun and play of the animals and saw life flowing into flowers, trees, and rivers, they could clearly see the apparent joy of sex and of living on Earth, and they began to feel dissatisfied with God's warning against entering physical matter.

Groups of souls met and talked of what they had seen. They knew that their training, for those who accepted the challenge to become co-equals with God, would be long and difficult and require much self-discipline before they could hope to succeed.

Watching the evolving fractal pattern of God's consciousness on Earth gave them the idea they might be able to shortcut their long apprenticeships. If they actually entered into the earth plane and projected into plants, animals, and the earth, wouldn't they immediately get a fuller understanding of the consciousness of God by personal experience?

The souls' guardian angels immediately warned them that this was wrong. The angels also reminded them that God itself had specifically warned them never, never to enter into the plane of Earth's duality.

As young souls do, even today, they said, "Yeah, yeah, I hear you!" but secretly, in their hearts, they had already decided to project themselves into the Earth plane so a living God could be experienced in physical form.

To be fair to these young souls, it should be remembered that the new Earth creation, with its colors, light, four basic elements, and four directions in a three dimensional plane, was extremely alluring. Physical life on Earth was such a magnificent spectacle that souls were drawn in by the sheer beauty, sorely tempted to enter, enjoy, and experience it all. They wanted to feel the physical strength of a bull elephant, or what it felt like to run through a forest as light and fleet as a deer. They wanted to feel the thrill a mountain goat experienced as it rushed across rocks and crevices, and they wondered what it would be like to see as an eagle from high on a mountain perch, or to see through the night eyes of an owl.

They watched the flowing, frothing action of falling water as it splashed and fell across rocks rushing down a mountain, gaining speed and volume until it released into a cool, blue lake that looked peaceful and calm.

They saw volcanos erupt and wondered what the hot fluid lava in motion felt like and wanted to experience it. They watched fascinated as a hawk glided and played in swirling heat waves of energy and wind rising from the desert floors spread out in front of hills, and they wanted to glide and soar as the bird did.

They watched creations in the sea and imagined themselves swimming swiftly through blue-green waters, experiencing the smooth tantalizing softness of the water against their new physical bodies. In sea plants they saw an underwater forest equal to those on the surface, and the desire to experience, to flow into and out of a physical God became more and more intense.

What was the final motivation that made them simply forget, for an instant, God's commandment *never* to enter the Earth plane or physical matter? It was the desire to be part of God's creation in a personal intimate way. The souls understood that what lived and moved was actually a part of God's consciousness made physical and alive, and reasoned that if they projected themselves into the living, moving matter, they would be experiencing a living God.

They knew that an accumulation of facts was called knowledge, but that knowledge lived as experience would become wisdom. And wisdom, lots and lots of wisdom, was what the souls needed to become companions and co-creators with God.

And so it came about that thousands of souls descended, like wisps of ghostly vapor, down onto the strange and beautiful planet called Earth.

Once they entered, they wanted to experience it all. As a ghost vapor mist a soul would go up to a flower, look deeply inside its blossom, and then, by the power of its free will imagination, project into the flower. Ahhh... it was a beautiful experience to feel the heat of the sun on the flower petals and to feel sap moving up one's stem. To feel the contrast of having roots in cool ground while the leaves and flowers soaked up sun rays was pure bliss. A soft breeze made one sway softly in a rhythm with surrounding plants, a soothing harmony of joy personified, a soft gentle feeling of life at peace with itself. Bees and insects would buzz by, and some would stop and remove nectar and bring male pollen with them from another plant so the fertilization process became complete. It was a giving, sharing concept for creating new life that souls had never experienced before—could never have experienced, they believed, as long as they remained in spirit form and were whole rather than divided.

With the inexperience of youth and the recklessness of beginners, the souls explored their new paradise.

At first they were satisfied to simply project into a mountain and feel and sense its great weight and majesty; to feel the coolness of its interior and the warmth of the sun baking its southern side. They felt water seeping and flowing through their cracks and crevices not unlike the action of sap flowing in plants and blood flowing in animals. At night, their exterior would get cool and their insides warm because of the temperature contrast.

Souls had no concept of time, only of awareness, so they sometimes stayed so long they felt a mountain's outer skin being shed, not unlike the action of a snake shedding its skin. Wind and rain would play on and weaken an outer rock layer, and it would fall away to reveal fresh new unblemished layers.

Some rock formations had great veins and capillaries which went almost to the center of molten fluid that gave them the nourishment they needed to continue to grow higher and higher. Molten, red hot lava filled these tunnels and in a pulsating motion, not unlike blood being pumped from a heart, a flow bubbled and burst free from atop the living mountains that was a joy to be a part of and experience.

When it tired of this sensation, a soul would project its *spirit body* out of whatever living form it was in by an act of will, and because it was a higher frequency than any living matrix then existing on Earth, the soul could do this.

Floating in the sky, looking for new pleasures, new experiences, a soul could plunge into an ocean and feel the liquid, fluid, constant motion of water that moved in the sea as air moves in the sky. Sometimes opposite currents of water would pass by and give the soul an instant direction change as it jumped into the different current flow.

Sharks especially fascinated them because their nature was violent and swift, whereby souls had gentle, soothing, slowed-down rhythms. Souls moved the way the sun slides from high noon to sunset, everything a gentle gradual slide, a peaceful observant pace that allows for endless possibilities of action.

The injection of a soul into a shark was like being suddenly transformed into turbulence and chaos, a joining into the shark's sensation of endless seeking for the next prey. When prey was sensed, a chemical reaction, an adrenaline type of excitement, would fill every cell of the soul's shark body. It was like every fiber of the soul's being was participating in the chase. The thrill of the hunt would climax with a blood lust lunge that would take a huge gaping hole out of a victim's side; the victim would then start a death thrashing that excited the devouring shark even more. The flow of blood would attract more sharks, who joined in to devour the kill.

The soul felt the powerful lunges as the shark attacked its prey again and again, thrashing around, rolling over, its huge head ripping in sideways movements, flesh coming away in large bloody pieces. The soul felt the power of the great fish's jaws ripping apart flesh and experienced the sensation of huge chunks of the kill sliding down the shark's throat. It was like experiencing an electrical charge as the excitement mounted, a feeling of being part of raw energy. The soul loved the thrill, the anticipation, the hunt and the kill that the mighty ocean beast went through daily to survive and live.

When the fish pulled away from its kill, the soul could feel the shark glide, then move its tail in powerful motions as it picked up speed and flowed along, at one with the entire ocean.

The soul then projected into another shark—and had the second worst experience it would ever have projecting in and out of animals. It had no sooner projected into the great fish when it was suddenly attacked and a huge, searing hole was ripped from the shark's side and sea water poured in. The initial hit and bite were so great that the soul knew the shark was mortally wounded. This was a new experience! Always before, the soul had projected in and out of living animals—it had never anticipated being inside a *dying* animal.

The soul could feel the muscles in the shark start to weaken and its heartbeat flutter, then slow; life was starting to leave and death was moments away.

Suddenly, the soul felt something tug at its own energy field, a sucking sensation that was drawing and pulling it. The life essence of the sea animal was somehow wrapped around and intermingled with the soul's own life essences and, together, they were being drawn out of the flesh of the shark!

The soul could feel tiny bits of its energy feed into and go after the living vortex that was leaving the shark!

The soul knew, instinctively, that it had to somehow stop this drain and it panicked and tried hard to draw back as the sucking pull got stronger.

From far, far away, the soul heard a distant cry of alarm, then a soft voice saying, "Quickly, quickly... you must use your gift of free will and the power of your imagination! Image yourself somewhere else!" It was the voice of the soul's guardian angel, heard almost as a thought.

The soul had been so scared it had forgotten how to project back out of the dying sea animal but in an instant it shot out, and went up high into the sky before it finally stopped.

The soul was shaken to its very core. Its vital energy had almost been drained away with the dying energy of the shark. It had seemed like the sucking action was coming from the end of a vortex spinning violently like the end of a tornado tail, a whirling and sucking force that pulled up physical energy, then destroyed it from inside its turbulent chaotic mass.

Apparently when something was ready to die on Earth, this swirling mass sensed it and sent a whirling finger of energy to seek and then suck up the vital energy that had been a life essence.

The soul had almost died. Its individuality would have been lost, completely and entirely lost, *forever*. Now it understood death! It had seen it, had almost experienced it. "Too close," the soul shivered aloud, "that was too close."

But the soul now clearly understood that death was an energy transition, an end that became another beginning. Understood completely that life was an energy force of God in three dimensional matter that got drained away when death occurred.

The nearly killed and still shaken soul, hovering above Earth, was in a state of shock. It had almost died, an awareness that lingered as a memory thought form, flowing in and out of its consciousness, wrapping and folding itself in and around the soul like scent wraps and folds itself around a rose bush.

The experience became an obsession for the soul: to find out why death and dying had to be a part of Earth creation. All the soul did day after day was watch animals flee, fight, and perish, to be eaten so another would live.

Life drained from a living creature like a black hole drained into another galaxy. Death was old energy going into a newer, larger energy source. When this essence, this life force, was pulled out of the intelligent consciousness that gave the three dimensional form of matter its direction and a reason to exist, it caused the mass of matter to simply collapse into a heap and begin to disintegrate by a decay process.

Before its terrible experience inside the dying shark, the soul had watched the killing and eating compulsion of all Earth life and had been perplexed by the reason for it. Why wasn't life on Earth like that of the souls and angels in heaven, who never had to eat? The energy of a soul in heaven was just... there. Yet on Earth, every living thing constantly, each day, searched for, stalked, killed, and ate other living things in order to live another day to do it again. "Strange creation," the soul thought.

It happens that this particular soul had been thoroughly trained by its angels on the concepts of First Creation and was more evolved and further along in its training than most of the others who had entered the Earth plane. After struggling to understand the complex problem, the answer came as a flash of instant awareness: all the pieces suddenly fell into place. It was all so clear now! All insects, plants, and animals had to be endlessly searching for food to kill and eat, because each living thing is micro, self-similar in pattern to God, the maker of First Creation. Each animal has to create its own energy supply because by doing this, it is self-similar to God.

God, in First Creation, had to die as one whole passive consciousness so it could instantly be reborn as a dual separated male/female awareness that could create energy with which to make a universe. With this newly created energy, God formed and powered the universe. Animals used their newly created energy to form and power their own universe, which was *themselves*. A self-similar pattern.

Because everything on Earth is part of a fractal self-similar evolving pattern of God and God's First Creation, each creature, each living virus, insect, plant, animal, and the Earth itself, had to have a personal system to create its own energy.

Plants feed on sunlight, minerals, and moisture to get the energy they need to live, grow, and reproduce.

Animals feed on other animals, plants, and water, to get the energy they need to live, grow, and reproduce.

Insects feed on other insects, animals, plants, and water to get the energy they need to live, grow, and reproduce.

Earth, the planet, is an organism that feeds on sunlight, insects, plants, and animals that die and decay to make its outer surface live, grow, and reproduce on a different time scale than its center. It also feeds on sunlight, rocks, minerals, and in its center, water, to get the energy to continue to live.

On Earth, the thing to be eaten is captured, killed, and then, in bits, placed inside of the killer to be chewed into pieces and mixed with water before being sent deeper for further digestion. Soil and roots do this for plants; teeth and saliva do it for animals; earthquakes and continental drift chew up rock. Each living thing created its own energy by eating. When it could no longer create personal power or energy, it died.

This is an important concept. It means that every living thing is created as an individual and is meant to be self-sustaining, self-creating, and free. This is the concept of free will expressed in physical matter.

Each tree is a self-sustaining life form. Each insect, each animal is not tied to a universal energy source, but rather has freedom to seek and hunt for its own energy. Everything alive creates its own personal energy, just as God did.

"And therefore," the soul thought, "what does God eat to create energy? Itself?"

This puzzled the soul. Then it remembered the energy vortex that had almost sucked its own energy away. God *recycled* its own energy! When life died and gave up its energy essence, it flowed back to the Universal Consciousness!

The experience of individuality that a tree had, or a canary, or a deer running in a forest, the excitement and thrill of a life lived as a mountain lion, all went back to God to become part of its expanding consciousness. It was one of the main reasons God had split apart and created: so it could have unlimited new experiences.

How did God know how a bluebird feels as it sings in a tree? How did God know what it is to be a plant, a wild animal, a living planet? Because these experiences were cycled back into God's Consciousness. Not only did God recycle its own energy, but also the consciousness of every living thing that had a life span and died. And in a reverse sense this also means that God is the blue bird, the plant, the wild animal, the living planet.

The soul was awed by the enormous potential for never ending creation that this allowed God. Then the soul remembered that God had told it and all the souls that he would share these experiences as wisdom with any soul who, by free will choice, agreed to accept the training needed to become a co-companion with God. It also remembered that it had been warned never to enter the Earth.

SOULS ALTER GOD'S EARTH CREATION AND ARE TRAPPED

The soul decided it had better warn the other souls of the danger of staying too long in a dying life form, and called a meeting. It explained to the others what had happened, and how to avoid having it happen to them. In this way, knowledge of how one could have fun on Earth and still survive began to accumulate.

Individual souls who entered and played on Earth learned more methods for how to survive the experience; they shared these with others by injecting the thought form of the experience into the group consciousness. Whenever souls wanted information, they thought about what they desired to know and it came to them as an awareness.

In ever greater numbers, souls projected their higher frequency energy down onto the Earth and into animals, plants, flowers, trees, the four basic elements of earth, water, fire, and air.

With great glee, in happiness of spirit, the souls played. They romped and frolicked in and out of nature and the Earth. Lying in a field, they didn't just soak up sunlight, they had the ability to do more. They entered into and *became* the field. As a soul quieted into a sort of meditation, it could feel the very movement and growth of the soil, alive with tiny, teeming life, as it expanded and absorbed warmth.

The souls could feel color making a plant or flower flush with heat. The field and its grass, flowers, and insects were a world, a life form, all their own. The whole moved like a wave and rippled when wind blew, like water rippling on a pond. It was a feeling of total serenity and peace.

Earth and its ecology gave the souls a feeling of total togetherness, of being complete— a life form knowing itself to be one with and the same as its creator, God. And why not? Was it all not really God as a physical expression?

In the same instant of knowing their total connection to God, each life form had an additional feeling of individualism that was unique, different, refreshing. When a soul projected into a tree, it could feel as a background sense the joy of total togetherness, but it could also feel the individuality of the tree itself. Oak trees had a different essence, smell, and sense of power than pine trees, for instance.

Souls particularly liked to inhabit the kind of lone pine tree that carved a niche for itself in a rock crevice where wind had blown enough soil so it could take hold and live. These were the trees that were kin to the free spirited souls who didn't care for the rules and regulations other souls lived by. Here, high on a mountain cliff, such a pine seedling blown by the wind would land and find a home. It knew that it would never be a part of some grand forest. It knew there wasn't enough soil for it to become huge, but even so, here it could find a place of its own and find a peace, a solitude, a feeling of overcoming great odds and of survival that the forest pines would never know.

Here the wind challenged it with great storms and gusts, threatening to tear it bodily from its rocky perch and drop it, broken, down onto the valley floor. The wiry scrub pine dug in its roots, wrapping them more and more firmly around rocks and into cracks. It grew scraggly and had a gawky, bend-away-from-the-wind look. It was a survivor, a loner, a conqueror of the untried, and the souls loved it, for they saw in the cliffside pine a tenacity that the souls wanted to copy as a mental character trait.

Inside the pine, the soul who had entered didn't find the soft, lush wood texture it found in valley pines, growing thick and tall. This pine was hard and dense and twisted; it rationed water to itself as if each drop would be the last; it was tough and self sufficient. A soul stayed for so long that it began to see and anticipate the seasons and to wonder how it would react to each weather change. When the soul saw white clouds go black and start to roll, rather than creep, across the sky, it knew another storm was getting ready for a full attack. But the lonely pine had learned to relax and hang loose so the wind would blow freely through its branches; the only permanent damage came from stones falling from the mountain and knocking off limbs.

The soul felt it could fix this by growing new ones, but that thought shook the soul awake and alive! "What am I doing," the soul thought, "I've been here so long I think I'm the tree instead of myself... strange... this is weird... I've never done this before!"

The soul decided immediately to project out of the tree, but just before it broke completely free—it somehow felt that it *couldn't*.

It was like a part of the tree was in the soul and a part of the soul was in the tree.

The soul then did manage to leave the tree, and went back up into the sky and shook itself, the way a dog does after coming out of the water, but it sensed that something was attached to it. The soul shook again, but still didn't feel clean or totally free. It thought about the tree experience that seemed so vivid and clear now that it was over. Over, but yet... the soul couldn't identify why, but somehow an essence of the tree life seemed to be a part of the soul now. It was a strange, uncomfortable feeling.

The soul looked at itself all over; it seemed to be clean and normal, but... it shook itself again and decided to tap into the group consciousness. Had other souls experienced this residual tainted feeling after they came out of life forms? An awareness came back from the group consciousness: no other soul had ever had that feeling. The soul was puzzled, but decided it was nothing to worry about and soon found new adventures.

Souls loved projecting into stones or plants because there was little or no movement; it was an experience of receiving emotions, feelings, scents, and visual sense input while being stationary. One didn't cause action; rather, one reacted. One had a sensation that just by being alive, all kinds of sense inputs would flow towards one as pure pleasure.

To be inside a flower or cluster of flowers in a field of thousands that spread in full glorious color from hillsides down into valleys was especially wonderful. Sometimes it seemed to an observing soul that fellow souls in flower patches outnumbered the bees and insects. If one wanted to find a friendly fellow soul, the first place to look was in the flower patches.

Just as the sun was rising, a soul went into a hillside flower patch and projected into a tall, orange-yellow blossom firmly anchored on a healthy green stalk that was thick with leaves. The soul settled around the plant quickly so that it would be ready when the sun started to send beams into the overhanging clouds, coloring them pink and then mixing in yellows for harmony. The light pinks and blended yellows would then turn to the deeper red hues that preceded a morning sun, as a soft breeze moved and birds sang to greet the new beginning.

Souls loved mornings and new beginnings on Earth. There was excitement in the air as hundreds of thousands of new souls descended, darting in and out of life forms quickly to find out what each form meant and how it fit the total design pattern. Each soul hoped that by getting these tiny awareness, it could blend them together. The result would be the total wisdom of God, arrived at without the need for discipline.

So why had God so emphatically and repeatedly told souls never to enter into this plane of physical, three dimensional life, or matter?

The first realization that came over them was that they were a higher vibration, higher frequency life form than anything they encountered on Earth.

All souls were the same age, since they were all created at once, but some who were younger in Earth experience were more daring and adventurous. These souls wanted to start training and manipulating Earth's animals. This caused concern among the souls older in experience, so before any attempt was made to do this a great meeting of all the Earth souls was called.

The older, wiser souls pointed out that the only reason they had entered Earth was to observe and to project into, and thereby experience, life forms for the knowledge it could give them about God. It was already bad enough that they had come here at all, against God's will. This caused a pause and a murmur of agreement by all. "But," the speaker continued, "if we make animals do our will instead of God's then we are going to violate God's free will plan for all of creation. This is wrong. We should allow a plant to be the plant it was created to be; we should allow animals to act and grow as they were created. It's not right that they be trained and manipulated by us to act out of character."

Most souls agreed, but some of the young adventurous souls simply left the meeting. Those remaining agreed not to interfere with or manipulate Earth life forms in any way, but to just continue observing them.

One soul asked the others if they had ever experienced a feeling that they couldn't completely project back out of a life form as easily as they went in, and other souls realized that they, too, had experienced this strange feeling. But no one had an explanation.

They wondered if they should do anything about the wild young souls who had left, but since souls had the gift of free will, how could anyone stop them?

Angels weren't as disobedient as souls and they wouldn't enter the Earth plane to guide the souls, and therefore the inexperienced group was now totally without guidance. God also decided to leave the wild souls alone and without any form of guidance, because they had free will.

At first, the wild souls used animals as a form of play. Two souls would project into two deer that were grazing in a woods together and give each one a fright jolt awareness that would cause them to spring apart and start running.

At first, the souls were content just to be inside, enjoying the feeling of being a deer running through a forest. Inside the deer, a soul became acutely aware of all the animal's senses. It could see through its eyes as a fallen tree appeared in its path; it could feel the leg muscles tense as it leaped, effortlessly, to land nimbly without missing a stride or decreasing its speed.

The soul sensed the faster heartbeat and could anticipate, then experience, the thrill that the muscles felt when adrenaline entered the bloodstream. It felt the heightened alertness of the deer driven by fright, running and running. When the animal stopped, tongue hanging out, panting for breath, the soul would project out and search for its buddy soul so they could compare notes on their deer-riding adventures.

They would project into turtles and laugh at the slow swaying walk that took forever to get anywhere, then would go into small animals like foxes to feel the delightful, gliding movement of their running. They enjoyed the way their animals went into holes in the earth or into rock dens, then stopped, breathing hard, trying to figure out what had frightened them.

The disobedient souls especially liked being inside mountain goats. When big males, with their sets of inwardly curving horns, would charge each other, it was a double thrill. One felt the adrenaline rush as they reared on their hind legs, then accelerated into a breathtaking charge that climaxed when the great horns hit together with a sound that echoed out of valleys and between mountains.

The souls liked to project into these animals when they were high up a mountainside, when they were attempting a precarious crossing across rock and cliff outcroppings. When a soul found a mountain goat in these circumstances, it quickly projected in and gave the animal a fear jolt to make it start an all out run.

It was the thrill of thrills to look through the mountain goat's eyes as it plunged desperately ahead, jumping from one tiny rock outcropping to another. Often there would be nothing but space for thousands of feet below. When a rock outcropping broke, or a hind foot scrambled to get hold of a place to propel off of, then fear, pure fear, would send a rush of extra adrenalin to the rear leg muscle so it had the extra strength to leap to the next ledge.

Sometimes the place the mountain goats were taunted and forced to run across was so dangerous that one would miss a ledge or it would crumble from the impact of the leap, and a mighty ram would fall down... down... to smash off another rock before sliding to the mountain floor: dead.

When a soul sensed the ledge crumbling, it would quickly project out and, without remorse, watch the animal tumble, then crash. The soul would then see the finger vortex of energy instantly appear to drain away the life essence of the dead mountain goat. Often the soul stayed to watch vultures and other animals devour the animal's body.

Souls older in experience, observing this, sometimes shivered in a reflex action. They didn't know why, but it definitely seemed wrong for souls to cause the death of God's creations. They wondered why God didn't appear and talk to the rebellious souls. They realized they missed the daily meetings with God which they'd had as spirits in heaven. It seemed so long since they had met with God that they couldn't remember what God looked or sounded like.

"That's strange," an older soul thought, "why would I have a hard time remembering? I never did before...."

Puzzled, it quickly went to other souls and asked them to describe God and what the instructions were that God had given them in heaven. The other souls laughed and said, "Sure, here's what God said... " and then realized that they were having the same problem.

They went to a soul who had had training with God's Recording Angel. This soul liked to write things down and project it into the Universal Consciousness, sort of a daily practice lesson so that when it went back to heaven after an Earth experience, it would still know how.

They asked how long they had been away from God. It seemed like only yesterday that they had entered Earth.

"I don't know," the recording soul said, "I'll go to Universal Consciousness to get an answer." Almost instantly, the soul came back. "We have been here for millions of years in Earth time!"

"What does that mean?" the other souls asked, bewildered looks on their faces. "What is millions of years?"

"I don't know... I'm not sure what time is," said the recording soul. "But why can't we remember God's face and all of his instructions anymore?"

No one had an answer. They were alone. They had left their angels, who were their teachers and instructors, behind. They suddenly realized that they missed their angel friends who'd always had the right answer to any question that was ever asked them.

The souls couldn't think of what to do about the problem, other than returning to heaven. But they didn't feel ready to do that yet. So they went back to having fun and discovering more Earth knowledge. They didn't know it, but they were beginning to experience the dual opposite of having memory... lack of memory!

Meanwhile the younger, wilder souls had gotten bored with going in and out of animals to manipulate them, and, with no thought of the consequences, decided to try manipulating them by the use of pure thought.

They went to a field where deer were grazing. One animal stood alone, eating. It was decided to try to make it stop eating and, without reason, start to run. One by one, each soul came forward and gave a mental thought that the deer do these things—but nothing happened. Puzzled, the souls wondered what the problem was.

Then one soul stepped to the front and said, "Let me try!" It looked at the deer, which seemed to get nervous. The soul just stared at it. Then, suddenly, the deer stopped eating, brought its head up, looked around, and took off running.

The soul who had stepped out looked back at the other souls and smiled. "I knew it would work," it said.

"How? How did you do it?" the others asked.

"Simple," the soul said, smiling and enjoying the attention. "I did what we do when we project in and out of things... I just imagined it. I looked at the deer and imagined that it had stopped eating and was starting to run, and it did!"

Soon it became a game to go to a field where animals fed and start moving them around, and it wasn't long before the young souls realized they could make them attack each other. Getting animals to attack and fight each other became their favorite activity.

The souls were now introducing violence into the evolving pattern of animal life. Before, an animal had stalked only for food, and the victim had fought back only in self defense. Now, fighting just for the sake of fighting began to spread among the animals. When the same animal was made to charge and fight other animals, even animals of its own species, time after time during its life span, this behavior became a new imprint in its DNA—a new pattern of aggressiveness used for pleasure.

When the young of these manipulated animals grew to maturity they attacked each other without warning, just for the sport of it. The souls noted this alteration of the animals' genetic makeup and decided to enter the DNA strand to learn how it worked.

When a few young souls did this, they learned how easy it was to genetically alter specific parts of an animal by making just the smallest change in its DNA. Then they watched the newborn to see what the results would be and, when that animal became an adult, they went in again to manipulate its DNA chain, then watched the result in a new generation.

These souls had now been on Earth for so long now that they rarely even thought of God; their only interest was in having more fun and pleasure each day than the day before. One day a group of them decided it would be even more fun to create their own animal species. Before long, the glands of small birds and reptiles were manipulated genetically so that the animals grew larger, faster, and more ferocious both in appearance and in character.

And so, because of the interference of souls, the age of dinosaurs came upon the Earth and gigantic birds and huge reptiles hunted and attacked each other for sport as well as for food.

Wiser souls, who had watched the genetic altering of the animals God had created, were very concerned. Where would this end? When would it stop?

The wild souls showed absolutely no self discipline and no inclination to think about the far reaching consequences of what they were doing. They were like mad scientists and they didn't realize that what they created became part of a living, evolving pattern that was meant to represent God itself. The era of the dinosaurs became increasingly horrible. The very ground trembled as they walked. Their huge appetites were destroying plants and small animal life faster than they could replenish themselves.

The wiser souls looked on in disgust at the way the beautiful world of Earth was being destroyed. They watched helplessly as huge reptiles and dinosaurs tore each other apart in great struggles that shook the ground, as they entered a vegetation patch and stripped it bare almost instantly and then moved on, looking for another.

Sometimes, while other animals were feeding, huge meat eating beasts would savagely attack them, and pitiful cries of hurt and terror filled the air. Animals attacking other animals, plant life being utterly destroyed—the world began to look like a creation of horror and confusion instead of beauty and peace.

The peacefulness, the tranquility, the beauty of the Earth had turned into a nightmare where large monster-type animal forms threatened to destroy the planet. The wiser souls couldn't believe how quickly it had all changed.

Then something that had never happened before occurred, spontaneously, all over the Earth almost at the same instant.

The somewhat wiser souls, playing their games of projecting in and out of life forms just for the fun of it, had made no attempt to genetically alter the animals or life forms they entered. But one day, when a soul felt the desire to experience a tree again, and promptly did so by projecting in, it decided it would enjoy a water experience and started to project out.

But it got only halfway out. And then stopped.

Somehow, for some reason, it was *stuck*. It couldn't move.

It was half in and half out of the tree.

Looking around the forest, it saw it wasn't the only one stuck. Thousands, hundreds of thousands of souls all seemed to have gotten stuck at about the same time. Not only in the little forest where this particular soul was, but all over the Earth, souls suddenly found they couldn't free themselves from the life form they had projected into.

Souls circling the Earth wondering what to do next for excitement heard cries for help coming from the planet's surface. They rushed down to offer assistance. They pulled, they tugged, they pushed, they gave advice. But nothing seemed to help the trapped souls.

They flew around helplessly, bewildered and puzzled. They called a council meeting of the Earth souls who weren't trapped to decide what to do, but they could find no answers. They went into Universal Consciousness for information, but as this had never happened before there were no answers there, either.

An emotion came over the souls: fear. It ran through them like a ripple running through a pond. Real, naked fear! Fear!

They had a feeling of hopelessness, of helplessness, a paralyzing force that made them stop. It was the opposite of courage, which made them move.

The trapped souls looked at each other, confused and terrified by the sudden turn their marvelous Earth adventure had taken. Then they became aware of yet another problem.

Because they were stuck in a tree, a plant, a fish, a horse, or some other type of life form, they had begun to alter their hosts' genetic makeup. This was because their higher soul vibrations overrode the lower life form's DNA vibration.

When an animal or plant reproduced now, it reproduced half and half: half animal, half soul. Half plant, and half soul.

The souls began to wonder why they were on Earth. They wondered what they were supposed to look like. What were they to do next? How had this all come to pass? They couldn't even remember the past anymore.

They had now become trapped in matter.

They began to fear the very plants and animals they had so loved to watch and to experience.

One of the things that had trapped the souls was the law of duality.

Earth had been created as a three dimensional life form: consciousness, physical form, and a life essence. When souls entered the Earth plane they, too, had a three dimensional life form consisting of a consciousness, a vaporous energy body, and a God life essence that made them alive.

Because of the law of duality, everything on Earth, even consciousness, had to be split apart. So now, on Earth, consciousness was no longer a type of total awareness.

One type of conscious awareness is memory and it can be split into two halves, remembering and forgetting. Now that souls had been on Earth for millions of years, their consciousnesses had begun to spontaneously split apart.

What had split apart into opposites was the souls' own personal consciousness. Each soul's consciousness had been separating into an inner awareness and an outer awareness in a very slow, subtle movement that the souls had not noticed as they played and experimented. Instead of remembering, they were stuck in forgetting. When this happened Earth souls suddenly lost all memory of how to project out of the Earth forms they inhabited.

Now, suddenly, all at one time, all over the Earth, panic set in. Souls had no choice now but to conform to the rules of the Earth. Why? Because they could no longer remember anything else. Because they were no longer whole, but split into opposites.

Souls forgot they were souls and started to identify with the Earth. Worst of all, what God feared and knew would happen, did happen. The Earth souls forgot God. they also forgot why they were created, forgot that their purpose for living was to become co-creators and companions to God, using their own free will to make correct choices.

A collective consciousness had spontaneously begun to evolve as a composite of the individual collective thoughts of the disobedient souls on Earth. This first collective consciousness would have to be destroyed, because it had kept evolving after the trapped souls had lost all memory of God.

Souls couldn't project out of plants and animals now, because they had simply forgotten how to do it. And so they trapped themselves on earth, in matter. The only way these lost souls could ever be freed was for God itself to assume the responsibility of intervening into the affairs of these disobedient souls.

GOD'S PLAN TO SAVE THE TRAPPED SOULS

It was the winter of the trapped souls lives, and it would be a long time before their spring. For the end of the souls' freedom to enter and leave the earth plane at will had come.

Now God saw a living physical planet, originally a micro self image of its own consciousness filled with the disobedient souls' thought-form creations which were evolving as half-spirit, half-physical forms. Enormous reptiles, snakes, lizards, savage birds, and lumbering beasts were everywhere on Earth, creating violence in place of peace and harmony. And disobedient souls themselves were trapped in rocks, in trees, in animals.

God said quietly, "I will destroy this ugliness that is now upon the Earth."

The surrounding souls and angels looked worried. "What," they asked, "will happen to the trapped souls?"

"I will destroy them as well," said God. "My souls to whom I gave free will and the power of creation have used those gifts for their own pleasure to desecrate my creation, the model of my consciousness in matter."

God looked at the heavenly souls and angels and continued softly, "I cannot allow this abomination to remain. If I did, it would corrupt the evolution of the entire creation pattern." God turned away and left the group.

The souls and angels felt very bad about their trapped fellow souls. The soul oldest in experience, now fully equal with God, volunteered to go to Earth and study the record of what the wild souls had done. Maybe a way could be found to save them.

The souls and angels went back to God and asked permission. God didn't want its first evolved soul to risk getting trapped like the disobedient ones, but finally relented and gave it and some of the others permission to enter Earth for a short period. Since they were going with God's consent, they wouldn't be tainted by the experience.

The group quickly descended and talked to the trapped souls, who wanted to know who they were and where they came from. Other trapped souls came over and knelt or lay in front of them, crying out, asking if they were gods who could save them.

To have the trapped souls not recognize them as fellow souls from heaven absolutely horrified First Soul and the others. They looked at each other in amazement, and First Soul said, "We'd better leave quickly."

When they were out of the short and limited awareness range of the trapped souls, First Soul said, "I didn't want to give them false hope. I'm afraid they have gone too far and can't be saved! Still, before we leave, let's go to Universal Consciousness and read their records."

The souls read the story of how the Earth adventures had started innocently as a way to know God better and how the souls had quickly become more interested in finding pleasure than in finding truth. When they finished, they realized the problem was so serious they could never solve it alone, so they went back to heaven and reported their findings to God and the others.

A long discussion took place as to whether the wild souls could or even should be saved.

God spoke up and said it had always been its desire that no souls should perish. It agreed to think of a way to save the souls and still not have the evolution pattern violated.

The angels and souls waited, thought, and talked, and waited some more. Finally God summoned them and announced: "I have made seventeen rules that must be obeyed by the trapped souls on Earth so that I may reweave the pattern of Earth's creation. As physical beings, those souls must now do the opposite of each thing that entrapped them. This will eventually balance the entire Earth episode.

"As soon as this happens, an awareness will come over the souls that they have balanced the experience, or the trial of life. The mysteries of matter and consciousness will be changed to an understanding of the wholeness of what they have done, and the souls will then have a new wisdom and a new understanding of the inner working of my consciousness. Which is why Earth was created in the first place.

"Earth will now also be a place where an obedient soul's character and maturity, learned and developed in the spirit life, can be met and tested in a physical form. Souls who master the difficult test of experiencing physical lives will have more knowledge and wisdom of my consciousness than those who merely stay in spirit form because of the principle of duality on Earth. Therefore, it is no longer wrong for any soul who wants to, to enter the Earth.

"The Earth experience will be hard and dangerous, and will require a soul to die and be reborn many, many times. Therefore, no soul who graduates will ever have to return to Earth."

Then God gave a warning. "If those trapped souls won't accept and practice these new guidelines to free themselves, I will destroy them—Earth and the experiment of dual opposites in matter will cease to exist.

"These are the Seventeen Rules:

"Rule 1 - The dualism of opposites that has trapped the souls can now be used to free them. If they are willing to stay on Earth long enough, through as many lifetimes as it takes, then the opposite of forgetting will eventually occur and flashes of themselves as souls from heaven will begin to return. When this happens, they can quickly be retaught what they have forgotten.

"Rule 2 - Souls forgot themselves as being souls and forgot me as their creator. Because souls have free will, each must choose again to know me as its creator. When remembrance comes back to each soul, each must then become its own savior by freeing itself, bit by bit— exactly as it trapped itself, bit by bit.

"Rule 3 - The souls trapped themselves by experiencing pleasure under the guise of learning God's wisdom. Therefore, to become free through the experience of dual opposites, they will have to use their will power and struggle hard, experiencing the opposite of pleasure—pain— in order to learn the wisdom of God. It will always be easier and more pleasurable to do things that are wrong than it will be to do the things that are right.

"Rule 4 - Souls, as spirits in the heavenly plane, can do everything without effort. Souls in physical form will be required to use great effort to do anything on the Earth plane until a balance is reached and that which was difficult becomes easy again.

"Rule 5 - Souls, as spirits, enjoyed on Earth the pleasures of the physical. They will now have to become physical forms over and over again, using the reincarnation principle of rebirth and death, before they can again enjoy the pleasures of being completely spiritual.

"Rule 6 - Souls entered Earth as androgynous spirits, at once male and female, or whole. Now souls on Earth will be split into two parts, male and female, and will spend their Earth time trying to become whole by searching for and mating with their opposite. If a male or female isn't correctly united with another soul, a feeling of loneliness, emptiness, and loss will be a part of its consciousness during that lifetime unless it is able to accomplish the more difficult task of reuniting male/female within itself.

"Rule 7 - Souls entered Earth adult and mature and grew immature. Souls will now enter Earth immature and have to work very hard to gain adult maturity.

"Rule 8 - Souls entered Earth with total consciousness of their past, present, and future, but deteriorated to a low form of consciousness where they forgot everything. Souls must now be born into a low form of consciousness and, with great difficulty, grow to total consciousness where they remember again their past, present, and future as a totality.

"Rule 9 - Souls entered Earth as adult, mature spirits with no guardian angels to guide them and they became trapped. Trapped souls will re-enter Earth as babies that will grow into adults, but with guardian angels to guide them, and will have the *possibility* of becoming free *only as adults*.

"Rule 10 - Souls' inner consciousnesses tempted and led them into Earth against God's will. As an opposite Earth experience, outer awareness will always dominate inner awareness. Inner awareness will be submissive to the demands of outer awareness until the souls come back into balance.

"Rule 11 - Souls, as spirits, have dominated Earth's physical life forms. As an opposite experience, souls' physical forms of life will dominate their spiritual sides until a balance is reached.

"Rule 12 - Souls, as spirits, misused and tormented physical plant and animal life forms on Earth. As an opposite experience, the spirits of plant and animal life forms will become a part of the souls' physical consciousness and will misuse and torment souls until a balance is reached. However, nothing on Earth will be stronger than the souls' free will.

"Rule 13 - Souls entered Earth as spirits not needing earth, water, air, or fire to survive, and proceeded to misuse each one. Now, souls as physical forms will be made from these basic elements and they will have to use them well or die.

"Rule 14 - Souls entered the Earth capable of living forever and so misused this gift that they now are like the dead. As an opposite experience, souls will have to die over and over again until they finally learn how to live forever.

"Rule 15 - Souls entered Earth as Alpha and Omega, the beginning and the end. Now, souls will be born into a physical form, then die as a physical form, to be reborn into spirit. Then they will die as spirit and be reborn into physical form again and again—until they learn once more that they are the Alpha and Omega.

"Rule 16 - In the beginning, souls on Earth could instantly create by using pure thought and imagination to manipulate physical forms; the opposite of this must now occur. On Earth, it will take a long period of time and much physical exertion to make any mental creation become physical and bear fruit.

"Rule 17 - Souls entered Earth and genetically altered animal and plant forms, changing them physically and emotionally. Therefore, as an opposite experience, souls will enter in physical form and will have their genetic and DNA patterns altered by their own thoughts and emotions so they can experience in themselves what they did to others. This will continue until a balance is reached."

God finished speaking, and all were silent. The angels and souls saw that the trapped souls could now be saved, but that it would be a long and difficult struggle.

"Much planning must be done before we can implement this new pattern of creation," God went on. "The good news is that the Earth and the disobedient souls will not be destroyed."

WORKING OUT THE PLAN

Like a breeze sweeping over a blooming field that bends, then stirs the flowers and grass, so did a great excitement ripple through heaven. Because God has created a plan to save their fellow souls from extinction, each individual soul in heaven realized absolutely that it, too, would never be abandoned by its creator. These souls, who had stayed in heaven and never disobeyed God, talked earnestly among themselves and many decided that, with God's new permission for all souls to go to Earth where the most could be learned, it would now be best to have the Earth experience also.

God continued: "It is not yet time for those of you who wish to go to Earth to do so. Much must be accomplished before that happens. Before souls, as a spirit form, can evolve in matter, an animal form now evolving on Earth has to be chosen which will be the mother matrix form best suited for souls to inhabit while living their lifetimes on Earth."

God appointed a group of souls and angels to go to Earth, study the existing life forms, and decide which one would be best.

As all who had gone before, those who went were appalled at the confusion and chaos they saw everywhere. Souls trapped in matter were moving around with tree limbs sticking out, or as half animals and half spirit. Others were half in and half out of rocks, the surface of the Earth, or water. All were crying for help, weeping and screaming as animals do when they are hurt and trapped.

Huge monsters made the earth shake as they ran by swiftly to attack one another, their screams and death cries contributing to the overwhelming sense of confusion, wildness, and savageness.

The heavenly souls quickly projected off the Earth's surface and observed from a distance, so that the sense of chaos that was everywhere wouldn't be such a distraction. They began to look carefully all over the Earth, studying all the life forms. Finally, in the thick warm forests full of huge trees, lush vegetation and vines, they spotted an animal form which they thought would best meet the requirements.

These were the great apes, who had already developed families and social culture, and who stood upright. Because they had developed the use of their front paws into hand and arm combinations, they had a much greater capacity for the manipulation of physical objects than any other life forms on Earth.

The souls and angels went back to report their findings. God agreed the apes were a good choice, and told them that some of the apes must be genetically altered to create a new unique species.

"First, however, all of the half spirit/half matter souls will be removed from inside their physical forms and then temporarily removed from Earth. A new spiritual plane below heaven, called purgatory, which will look and feel like Earth, will be created to receive them. This way, the trapped souls will feel they are in familiar surroundings while they wait for an opportunity to incarnate in the new species on the physical Earth. There will be large learning centers, where angels can continue these souls' training as both spiritual and physical forms. This is necessary because when the trapped souls are freed from physical matter, they will still be impure spirits with no memory of God. The pure DNA pattern of consciousness that these souls carried within themselves now has traces of the DNA patterns of animals, plants, and minerals attached to it."

God then proceeded to free the trapped earth souls from matter, and as they were freed, guides brought them to their new home below heaven.

As the last trapped soul was withdrawn from Earth, the entire planet became dark and cold, with snow and great sheets of ice beginning to cover most of its surface as God withdrew its energy from the plant.

Then this snow and ice was caused to melt, and the moist vapor that resulted caused heavy rains to fall until a great flood covered most, but not all, of the planet's surface. Every single one of the great monstrosities was destroyed, as were all the remaining husks of the physical half spirit/half matter creations.

Also destroyed, actually and symbolically, was the new individual and collective consciousness that the trapped souls had begun to create, which did not remember or even know of God. This separation from God (the original dark night of the soul experience) had to be destroyed. The problem that forgetting God as a creator caused for a newly emerging consciousness was that it left no way for the soul to return back to God, and therefore this first collective consciousness was completely and utterly destroyed in the Great Flood.

The other life forms, including the great apes, were not destroyed in their entirety. Also saved was the concept of duality, because it was needed for the Seventeen Rules. This saving of duality is described symbolically in the Christian Bible as the ark that Noah built and filled with one pair of each kind of animal, thus saving them from the Great Flood. What the ark really symbolized was a safe place inside of God's consciousness where the *concept of duality* (pairs of animals) was placed to safeguard it as a *pattern concept* while the undesirable physical patterns of souls in matter were washed clean and destroyed.

Because the fallen souls could not enter Earth again until their new physical forms were fully evolved, they waited patiently in purgatory while God, angels, and the heavenly souls took groups of the great apes and began to genetically alter their appearance and intelligence by inserting new features into their DNA code.

Before the body changes were begun, they made the brain larger and more active. A more intelligent model, they reasoned, would more easily understand and control the new changes in its body. By altering an adult ape, all its offspring and each succeeding generation would also be changed. Each generation would be gradually altered until the required new species evolved. The changes made followed the normal laws and time scale of the evolution pattern in place on Earth. In this way, the existing pattern needed only a slight altering or reweaving for everything to fit into the larger pattern.

Gradually the apes became taller and walked more upright. They still had the same social behavior they had as apes, but with each generation they shed more hair so that they appeared less like the other animals. Only two *basic instincts* were placed in the DNA code makeup of the physical forms the Earth souls were to inhabit: the instinct of survival and the instinct of propagation of the species, or the sex drive. These instincts were needed for the new species so that the soul could not only survive but also evolve. And each of these two basic instincts could and would be used and misused by the free will of the evolving souls.

Bit by bit God's energy, as a thought form, penetrated the DNA of each succeeding generation. As they became more intelligent, the developing new forms created the ability to use tools, to think, and to speak.

As spirits in heaven, the souls used a form of mental telepathy among themselves and with God. But on Earth, a physical way of communicating had been developed by putting a voice box in an animal's throat where thoughts would be changed to electrical impulses and sent through nerves. The muscles and vocal chords of the voice box would vibrate in certain tones as air moved across them to produce sounds. These sounds would then travel through the air to strike the physical eardrum, which would vibrate and change the sounds back into electrical impulses which nerves would feed into the brain.

This process was much more elaborately developed in the new species, in the form of speech. One brain would be able to understand the speech of another of its species, which was actually thought transferred from one mind to another by physical means.

Hundreds of thousands of years later, the new species would reverse this procedure by speaking into a mechanical vibrating voice box that changed the sound into electrical impulses (a mechanical eardrum) which went over electrical wires (nerves) into another box that converted the electrical impulses back into sound (the receiver). This would be called a telephone.

The angels and souls kept careful watch over the development of this new being. At different states of its evolution, its DNA had completely new additions spliced in so the physical form best suited for a soul to inhabit would come forth. It also had to be genetically altered so the physical form matched the spiritual DNA pattern of the souls who would inhabit it. The soul and the physical form could only be compatible if their DNA matched, yet the DNA of the physical form also had to be similar to other life forms so it would not be a complete alien on Earth. When the ape model was completely evolved, it had to have physical characteristics which would be an exact match or symbolic of a part of the soul in spirit form.

As with the other animals, several of the major organs were two separated halves which were capable of operating alone if necessary. Their electrical polarities were opposite, but they normally operated as one unit. The heart was the energy source, pumping blood through the body in the same way that God pumps energy through the universe. Two lungs pumped air in and out to purify the body and enrich the blood with oxygen while exhaling carbon dioxide.

Air, one of the four elements, would circulate in and out of the bodies of the new species, as it does in the bodies of all animals, for their lifetime. Water would enter pure and, after being used, be expelled as waste through the two kidneys. The body of the new species was of flesh or matter like the Earth. Fire was generated within the body as heat and used by the body for warmth. In this way, the four elements that had been misused by the trapped souls would now be a part of their human/animal body, and if abused could cause death.

The body of the new species would have the five senses all other animals have, to be used to understand the five manifestations of God on the physical plane. Taken all together, souls in their new physical form would learn that Earth is the smell, the touch, the visual beauty, the sound and the taste of God made physical.

There was one last addition that had to be included in the new species before souls in purgatory could enter into the new species: the seven physical/spiritual centers, which correspond to the first seven spiritual levels of awareness in heaven, had to be implanted.

In heaven there are actually nine spiritual planes, or nine types of consciousness. Heavenly souls ascend these levels as they pass their personal tests while on their path to reunite with God, who is the tenth and final level of awareness.

Each level in heaven has a higher vibration frequency than the one below. Before a soul can ascend to the next level, it has to study, master, and pass the requirements of each new level.

Because Earth is a physical form or fractal pattern of God, only the first seven levels of awareness were duplicated in physical matter. There is a great divide between matter and the three higher levels of consciousness: these last three levels can't be duplicated in matter or on Earth because their vibration rates are too high. The new physical form would therefore have only seven spiritual planes of awareness, or vibration frequencies, placed in the body as spiritual centers.

This is not to say that Earth would be the only place where a soul could master the first seven levels of awareness. Many, many souls who had originally chosen not to disobey God never did enter into physical matter and were able to master the seven levels in heaven.

These seven levels of awareness were duplicated within the new species, within the human body, in the seven chakra centers. With this addition, it would become possible for the new species to duplicate the tests and levels of awareness that souls were mastering in heaven. This mastering is a slow gathering of knowledge and wisdom done at the soul's own pace.

With the chakra spiritual centers in place, the new form became a perfect micro pattern to the macro patterns of the universe and the consciousness of God in both a physical and a spiritual sense.

God also chose to give the new species the same two privileges that souls had been given: free will and the power of creation by the use of thought and imagination. Because of these gifts of free will and creation, God itself did not and could not know what direction the free will and creative power of individual earth souls would take.

Only *after* individual and group free will decisions were made could God see to what extent their actions would affect its own evolving pattern of creation. For this reason, the direct intervention by God itself into the lives of all Earth souls, both as individuals and as groups, would be necessary.

CHAPTER

22

HOMO SAPIENS

The new species, known as *homo sapiens*—"man who is wise"—as it rather optimistically named itself—was at last sufficiently evolved to meet the needs of the souls waiting in purgatory. After hundreds of thousands of years, the carefully evolved new physical form could now be the physical manifestation of a soul as a human being: the micro man containing soul, living on a micro earth symbolizing the consciousness of God. The pattern within a pattern.

What had been made into a new physical form on the Earth was the dual consciousness of soul which was now split into two parts, an inner awareness and an outer awareness. This corresponded to its two physical opposite forms of male and female. In the new species the brain was whole, yet divided in half, each side of which could operate separately from the other. This is a micro image of the consciousness of God and the way it is separated.

The male body was created in a straight line design that is a physical personification of the straight-line, linear thinking characteristic of outer awareness. This type of consciousness initiates action, is forceful, aggressive, able to project and to be a doer and a leader. The male body, reflecting this consciousness, is formed bigger than the female, with more hardness, muscle, and strength to carry out force and aggression.

The female body is designed to personify the inner awareness of consciousness, the part that is introspective and learns by internalizing experiences and sense perceptions. When a thought or experience is internalized, it is rolled over, looked at from all points of view in a soft, non-combative, gentle way that looks for the beauty in it. When self-reflective, one becomes more gentle, more passive, more caring.

The human female body mirrors these values with soft curves which symbolize energy flowing in spirals and circles: consciousness that flows back into itself.

But so that a man or a woman would still be a self-similar pattern to their own androgynous soul, a male would have a lesser female potential, and a female would have a lesser male potential, built into their bodies. In this way, the body and mind of the new species were still androgynous, even though physically separated into male and female. Both forms of consciousness were present in each individual.

Because of the rebellious souls' original disobedience, the creative thought process in the new species was reversed. Outer awareness, or male consciousness, would have domination over its inner mind and ignore or override any idea or thought that inner awareness (the unconscious) sent it. The trouble on Earth was that a soul's consciousness was trapped in matter. So now everything that a mind wanted to do as a new creation, or to create as change, had to be pushed into the physical body, and then the body had to do the creating. Outer consciousness would have a tendency to say to each new idea presented by the unconscious: "I can't do that—it's too hard—it will never work—I don't have the training—I'm too old—I'm not old enough," and so on. This part of the mind would fight back all creative impulses and try to kill them with negative thoughts. It would be the same painful creative process for both women and men because women have a male/female consciousness the same as men.

You can see how hard it would be for a soul to create on Earth: it couldn't control the part of its mind that was needed to initiate action. Since, as part of the reweaving of the evolution pattern, the creation process was reversed, the conscious mind would have to go through much pain, agony, and suffering to create anything new. Anyone who is especially creative knows this all too well.

If a part of a fractal pattern is not evolving as an exact micro copy of the original macro design, it is destroyed. It self destructs because it became a pattern that could not re-normalize itself. As we have seen, with the symbolic act of the Great Flood, God had destroyed the earlier form of consciousness that was developing on Earth within the disobedient souls who got trapped in matter.

A long period of time was allowed by God for the new human consciousness to evolve to a point where spiritual training and guidance could begin. This allowing of the new-born Earth consciousness to partially form before training began is still seen on Earth today as a micro pattern within the larger fractal design, where a human infant's mind must have a relatively long period of time before it can begin to be formally trained.

Since this human consciousness never dies, and since all of creation is simply an expansion of God's own consciousness, which of course also never dies, an accommodation between the two forms of permanent evolving consciousnesses had to be made. In order to monitor the evolution of the developing human consciousness, God directly intervenes in human affairs. During the days of mankind's infancy, God intervened many times in the affairs of humans and is still doing so to this day.

As primitive people evolved mentally and physically their thoughts, together, at any given moment, were creating the pattern of a human universal or collective consciousness. This consciousness was a sort of main frame computer that collected all of mankind's thoughts, feelings, impressions, failures, and triumphs as a permanent record. As individual souls grew more mature, they could tap into this larger consciousness for guidance. The collective consciousness also provided feedback information in a mass way to all the souls on Earth.

The design that both the individual human consciousness and the universal or collective consciousness had to follow was the same self-similar pattern that a human experience on Earth had to follow: it had to duplicate the concept of duality and of self-similar fractal patterns, and it had to follow the guidelines of the Seventeen Rules for living in matter which had been given by God.

Using these three guidelines—duality, self-similar patterns, and the Seventeen Rules—a soul could begin a lifetime in matter that would have the same pattern as all other things on Earth. As collective consciousness matured and recycled back to its source, so also would individual human consciousness have a birth, maturity, and recycling pattern within the human as a micro pattern concept.

As souls created their own human consciousness, this was a *new original creation*. The new mind that souls created would give them a conscious awareness of their day by day experiences on Earth and of actually becoming living matter rather than pure spirit. Then, by the training of this new mind as it matured, humans could use their conscious awareness of the Earth to improve their lives.

The mind of the new species, as well as rock, water, air, earth, stars, and the other planets, are all forms of matter and can all be reduced to the same common denominator: *energy*. The only difference between any of them is their vibration frequency and the way they cluster into energy combinations. Collective consciousness is an electromagnetic energy cycling in the same way that energy circles around and through a bar magnet as an electrical force field. Since the brain waves of individuals and of individual thoughts are also electromagnetic energy (though in a weaker form), each individual on Earth is constantly influenced by the collective thoughts of its own mass mind. Therefore, at any given time all humans living on Earth are being guided and influenced by the thoughts and actions of all the humans who have ever existed. Because of this, the affairs of humans are in a constant state of change; the guidance and influence of next week's, next month's, or next year's human collective consciousness will be different from that of the present. Change is guaranteed.

The pattern is for the human body and human consciousness to evolve together. So in essence, when you look at one, you are looking at the other.

The pattern found eons later by human scientists when they explored the universe would be the same pattern which doctors found when they explored the human body, because the fractal design of the human body was simply a micro pattern to the macro, made up like everything else on Earth of air, water, fire, and earth. What made the new species different in design from all other Earth animals was its ability to represent any part of, or all of, the traits of a soul's consciousness and of God's consciousness as a whole. Whatever its human mind could do, its human body could do also in a self-similar physical way. However, the newly developed species had to follow the same pattern of all of Earth's creations: so whatever could possibly happen to any creature on Earth could happen to the body, mind, and/or spirit of a human being: illnesses, emotions such as grief or happiness, evil or holy feelings, low awareness or high awareness, etc.

The ability to continue spiritual evolution while in a physical body as a human being was God's great gift to the disobedient souls. It is why living a human life is as sacred and holy an experience for a soul as living a purely spiritual life in heaven had been before. Through the process of living as many lives as it took until the necessary lessons were learned, called reincarnation, a soul as a human could train, learn, and work itself up through the seven spiritual centers, or chakras, in its own human body by the actual way it lived and thought during its lives on Earth.

The seven spiritual centers, or chakras, are the places where the memories of all past lives' successes and failures are carried within the human body. When a soul enters into a human body to begin another incarnation, its spirit carries the memories of past life patterns, like the memory in a CD. These vibration patterns go into the newly formed seven spiritual centers and reside there. Each center has the ability to influence different parts of the body.

Say, for example, the soul which had just entered a newborn human infant had strong emotional problems not yet resolved. These emotional patterns would be imprinted in the third spiritual center, located in the solar plexus. The result would be a human who, even as a baby, would have a very sensitive stomach; as an adult whenever it became emotional its stomach would seem to tie itself into knots.

Imbalances in the seven centers can be corrected in two ways. One is to live, while in a physical life, in such a spiritual, holy manner that the centers become spiritualized. The second is to learn how to become silent and meditate. When a human quits all outside earthly activities and becomes quiet within and meditates, then God comes to that human on Earth and, in a slow process, with God's help, the seven centers are gradually spiritualized.

Remember that God put a veil of forgetfulness over each soul's memory, before it was born into human form, as the mark of the soul's original disobedience in entering Earth. This is the original sin which each human is born with: that it willfully and disobediently put itself in a situation where it forgot God. Because this act of forgetting was caused by the souls' free will choice, *forgetting God* now had to become an experience that was part of each Earth soul's consciousness. The Christian sacrament of Baptism symbolically washes away this veil of not knowing God. But what a soul does not get back with a symbolic act such as Baptism is its own conscious remembrance of God that it originally had as a spirit soul in heaven.

Because God placed this veil over the memory of each new born infant, God took the responsibility of guiding and training each soul to know the difference between right and wrong until it matured and could make adult free will choices. God made sure that there was never a time in a human's life when a teacher sent by God was not available to guide and instruct at an awareness level equal to that section of humanity's evolved consciousness at that time. These teachers have been known as medicine men and women, shamans, high priests and priestesses, prophets, saints, enlightened beings, sages, and so forth. To these specially selected teachers and to God itself fell the responsibility to guide and train the emerging consciousness of mankind.

Ideally there are also adult humans available to all souls, from infancy to adulthood, who are their teachers and the guardians of their developing consciousnesses. This is a God-designed pattern of personal guidance and intervention into the affairs of the young human that is usually necessary until the child becomes fully grown.

After children become adults, they must make their own decisions and choices with free will, and be responsible for their own actions. But just as an adult can come back to its parents and teachers for advice, so also can a human always go back to God for help. If the request is appropriate, God will intervene to help and guide any human who makes such a request (though frequently not in the way envisaged by the human). But each adult must make a free will choice to ask God for help; help is no longer automatically given as it was to the child.

From the beginning of its emerging consciousness, mankind has also been trained directly by its own higher self, which does *not* have a veil over its memory. This training is accomplished while a person is sleeping and in a dream state. At this time the events of each day, and/or unresolved earlier problems and situations, are reviewed in dreams and one's higher self attempts to instruct the human's daily evolving consciousness in the appropriate conduct for the situation.

The higher self always uses symbolism in these dreams as a way to teach that the life in physical matter in which human consciousness finds itself each day is *not really reality, but a physical symbol of reality.*

To get its original soul awareness and memory of God back, each Earth soul must make free will choices which will develop its new human consciousness back to a God-aware state of mind. In other words, in the exact same way that disobedient souls made free will choices that caused them to *forget* God, now as humans they had to make free will choices leading to the *remembrance* of God.

If souls on Earth chose not to know or accept God and proclaim themselves atheists, then that was a free will choice God had given them the right to make. However when a soul makes a free will choice to become an atheist, this becomes a "Catch 22" situation because of Earth's *law of duality,* where any given choice sooner or later attracts its opposite. On Earth it is as dangerous for a soul to push itself into becoming a saint as a sinner. The very act of trying, in a world of dual opposites always seeking balance by an interaction of opposites, always attracts to itself the very opposite of what the soul intended.

Souls on Earth find that desire is a pendulum which keeps them endlessly swinging from one extreme to another. If an Earth soul wants to be free, then it has to learn the Buddhist secret of remaining balanced at its center, successfully resisting the temptation to drift to either of its opposite extremes of consciousness.

To put it more simply, after one has had many lifetimes as both a sinner and a saint and realizes that these are opposite extremes of the same thing, then the soul gives up the struggle and stays centered. In this center the soul can contemplate and discover the wisdom which *both experiences together* can give. The soul then becomes balanced—neither sinner nor saint—and contemplates a third choice: how to stop incarnating on Earth.

Anything a soul started on Earth as a learning experience had to be finished on Earth, even if it took coming back once, or a thousand times, in the process called reincarnation. The disobedient souls had to continue incarnating in matter to perfect their evolution if they ever hoped to again become pure spirits that could continue their evolution within God's consciousness as spirit, not flesh.

After an Earth body died, the soul as spirit would leave that body and would be met by special angels and heavenly souls whose job it was to guide it, from the instant of death, back to the spiritual plane halfway between heaven and Earth. Here a soul would immediately be met by a group of angels and advanced souls who would show it, by a form of mental picture telepathy, what its mission had been in going onto the Earth. Its lives on Earth would be reviewed, and the newly arrived soul would decide if a lesson that gave wisdom had been learned or if the experience needed to be repeated.

Before souls could again incarnate on Earth for a physical life experience, two conditions had to be met. The first condition was that they had to agree, as a free will decision, to return to Earth and again strive for perfection. These souls could also choose not to incarnate into matter again because the experience could be so painful. Those souls who made a free will choice not to return to Earth could remain in purgatory, but without ever achieving a complete memory of their original knowledge of God.

The second condition that a candidate for a new Earth incarnation had to meet was to wait for an Earth body and a time in history which most closely matched the lessons that particular soul needed to master. For instance, if a soul had continually caused chaos and upheaval in the affairs of others during past incarnations, then it would accept a life to be lived on Earth during a time of great social upheaval and chaos.

The trouble is, and always will be, that a perfect match between an incoming soul's needs and the type of physical body just conceived by the Earth parents, or the perfectly matching period of history, almost never happens. So a soul would accept as close as match as was possible.

But even with all these advance choices made before an Earth incarnation, sometimes when death occurred a soul would realize it had accomplished nothing and the lifetime seemed to have been wasted. When the sad realization came over a soul that it had just wasted a lifetime on Earth, it would go in front of a Board of Elders. The Board would immediately correct the just-returned soul's thinking, pointing out that each free will choice made on Earth was a valuable learning experience even if the results were negative to the soul's progress toward reuniting with God.

This was because of the way God had set up the Seventeen Rules. No matter what a soul did, it was really only one-half of an experience. If a soul spent a lifetime stealing, robbing, and killing, this simply meant it would have to spend another lifetime, or many lifetimes, giving back to each something that had been taken, even if it was a life.

If the soul took on this mission as a free will choice for another lifetime, the soul would have the opportunity to balance each negative experience with a positive one. If the soul refused to accept the responsibility of doing the physical acts necessary to balance the experiences, the opposites would occur anyway. For each thing a soul had stolen, it would have something stolen from it in an Earth life; for as many times as it had hurt or killed, so would it experience the same things as a victim that its victims had experienced when it was the attacker. This would be written of in the Christian Bible as "an eye for an eye, a tooth for a tooth".

But this didn't have to happen. The soul could accept life missions where it could willingly correct bad experiences with good experiences. In this way, it would meet those it had stolen from and give them gifts of equal value. Thus the victim would experience the pain of having something taken from it and the pleasure of receiving, both from the same soul. This same experience could become a balance for both—each one would learn wisdom from the experience and they need not meet again.

When souls as humans hear the singing of birds, the bubbling flow of mountain streams, the roar of waterfalls, the thunder after lightning bolts, the sounds of winds and breezes, and the sounds of rainfall, they know and understand at least unconsciously that they are hearing the sounds of a physical God on the Earth plane.

All that could ever be known of God was expressed somewhere, in some form or part, on and in the Earth. It would take the wisdom gained from many lifetimes before souls on Earth could discover again what they had already known in the beginning: that the physical Earth is a manifestation of God's consciousness alive in physical form.

SIMILAR PATTERNS OF GOD, EARTH, AND HUMANS

Creation is a fractal design that continues to expand, a design created by God's mind by the use of its conscious imagination. The imaging of forms and the life given them by God means that all things exist and evolve within the consciousness of God. So in a sense, God is also expanding its own consciousness with the expansion of a fractal design.

When this combination of one large and many small internal patterns is allowed to evolve long enough, the whole design reforms: it re-normalizes back into its original design, except this time the whole design is larger. This renormalizing pattern can repeat itself forever, which allows God's conscious imagination, and all of its created free will micro patterns, or souls, to also expand forever.

The original design that began as *First Creation* can still be seen in matter as the concept of an expanding universe. This is the reason stars, galaxies, and nebulas are born, expand, collapse and die. They then become a part of a larger evolving mass in a re-creation process that typifies a fractal design.

The humans, other animals, plants, and even land masses on Earth evolve, live, and die in this same pattern. However, on Earth where the concept of *duality* was put into the evolving pattern, nothing can exist as a whole unit or as a complete design by itself—both halves of each micro pattern have to evolve as separate entities. For example, it is the task of a separated male or female soul to balance the two opposite natures of itself by having a desire to either mate with, or in some other way intimately interact with, a member of (usually) the opposite sex. Since born within each human is the lesser presence of the other sex, sometimes this can be done within the individual person by using the two halves of his or her own consciousness and merging with them. In either case, an interaction between the two halves occurs that duplicates how God's own inner and outer awarenesses interact upon each other.

God's *conscious energy* in spirit form can be thought of as an interaction between its own inner and outer awarenesses which produces thought and creative image making or imagination. Imagination flows from the negative pole of female awareness, and is the result of interaction with the male awareness part of mind. It was the brief merging of these two types of awareness for a millisecond of time that resulted in the formation of the new form of God consciousness that was active rather than passive in its nature, and therefore able to create energy.

The duality principle on earth is the Ying/Yang or polarity movement of energy. In electrical energy, this becomes the positive and negative poles between which a flow of energy is possible. The micro pattern in our physical world of how God created thought energy to create and control a universe can be found in simple bar magnets and in electrical generators. When two magnets can circle or spin around each other and their magnetic force fields intersect, a flow of electrical current is induced and made to flow. This is the principle of alternating current (A.C.). All animals produce their own electrical energy and some, like the electric eel, can produce amounts large enough to kill other animals.

The total makeup of God consists of four distinct parts. The first two are the aspects of space and emotion. The other two parts are those of inner and outer awareness, or mind and energy. Since God is made up of these four forces as part of its design, all things that are created in a fractal design pattern will personify one, two, three, or all four of these forces in the design. The four primary forces flow out into the universe as design concepts and they also return back to God. Because of the circular flow of these four forces, it is believed that God has a mystical center. It is from this center that all forces go out and it is to this center that all forces return.

Since everything that is a part of God's macro design must also have a corresponding micro design in physical matter, this mystical center of God is duplicated on Earth. This is the point in the center of a bar magnet where all the force fields of electromagnetic energy leave, and to this same center all electromagnet energy returns.

The four forces or characteristics of God, souls, humans, and Earth which are evolving as self similar patterns are space, emotion, mind, and energy. These are expressed on Earth in the four elements of water, fire, air, and earth.

SPACE

Space appears as the shape of God that is without a beginning or an end. In the beginning there was only God, not God *and* space. Therefore, space is an aspect of God that defines its shape.

As each thing is created by God, it is given its own space. For example, even atoms have their own space. Space defines the individuality of each thing. Space appears as the shape of souls, and helps to give souls an individual identity.

Space appears as the shape of the human body that is physical and also, because of duality, has a spiritual equivalent which incarnates and changes appearance so that it always corresponds to the physical body. This shape then forms the identify of a soul on earth.

Space appears on Earth as the shape of the Earth, which is round, a shape that has no beginning and no end. Because of duality, it has two physical components: solid/liquid or rock/soil, and water/vapor.

The element of Earth has two parts, which can almost be considered an outside and an inside. The outside part of the Earth is solid while the inside, rock, like the planet itself can be part solid and part liquid following the fractal concept of a pattern within a pattern.

The solid rock outer core can be considered the skeleton shape that all else will be hung on. Soil, minerals, insects, plant and animal life are the interacting parts of the whole that will have fire, water, and air acting and reacting on and in them.

EMOTION

Emotion appears as the total love of God.

To souls in heaven, emotion appears as the ability to give and receive love as a form of nourishment to a soul's own consciousness.

Emotion appears as the emotional potential a human body and mind can express. The emotion of God is pure love—but pure love can have many parts. It is these many parts of God's pure love, broken into their individual parts, that can be examined on Earth in animals, including the human animal. On Earth one can see the pure love of God personified by animals as either love or as its opposite, hate. Because of duality, the pure emotion of love can be separated into its opposites, love and hate. Because of the principle of free will, a human is free to indulge itself in any part of, or in all, the range of emotions that make up love so that it may better be understood.

Fire is the element on Earth that represents the *active emotions* that are within consciousness. As heat it can be creative and nourish life, when it is under control. Fire out of control is a destroyer. When our bodies are in control, we maintain an even body temperature of 98.6 degrees, but out of control, fire becomes a fever that can destroy the body.

As love, fire is a creative emotion and kindles the sweet passions of life—however it also can kindle destructive obsession; as hate, fire's dual opposite of love, it destroys life. Fire on the planet Earth represents the heat of emotion that is in consciousness. Fire is like a passion that heats and stimulates thought into action, then acts and interacts within the very thought it made move.

Emotion appears on Earth as the element of fire. As love can be creative and hate destructive, so also does fire have the same potential to be creative or destructive. As humans matured on Earth and better learned to control their emotions, so in a corresponding manner did man learn to control and use fire. Fire as fuel has progressed from wood to coal to gas/oil to atomic fusion. When the emotion of love is not materially manifested on Earth, ice ages and dark middle ages appear.

MIND

Mind appears as God's inner and outer awarenesses which interact to create. The element of air represents the individual thoughts of God that go around freely inside its own consciousness. They are *always circulating* in God's mind.

Water represents calm intellect which has reasoning ability that can wear down resistance to change. It can be creative, helping to bring growth and to support life. It can also represent emotions, but most often represents God's intellect, although with the idea that God's intellect can become emotional.

Water also symbolizes total conscious thought in one place, as with the oceans and seas of the world. The top half of an ocean represents God's outer awareness and the bottom half, God's hidden awareness, or the deep, deep part of God's mind. This is because an ocean can symbolize both the conscious and the unconscious mind at the same time.

Just as God could not be considered alive without intellect and emotion, so it is that no living thing on Earth can be alive without water.

Mind appears in souls as their ability to think and to produce imaged forms, or imagination, which is creative.

Mind appears in a human body as a new born consciousness known as human consciousness. But in the companion spirit body which also incarnates with a soul into a human body, a memory of all past Earth incarnations is carried. This mind is called the subconscious.

In a physical model of the mind of God, air, as the symbol of thoughts, permeates all things and acts like thoughts do in a conscious mind.

So, if air on the planet Earth represents thoughts that fly in and around God's consciousness, then we can assume that when thoughts no longer move within a consciousness, that consciousness can be considered *dead*.

Air is moved by heat. When the sun or another source warms air, it rises and flows toward the cold. Cold will draw heat out of the air. Heat is the emotion or fire symbol and this means symbolically that emotions can make a thought move, or block off a thought's movement by a lack of emotion. This is a self-similar pattern of matter and consciousness acting and reacting the same way because on Earth, heat is a source or force that makes air move as wind, and in our minds, our own emotions can make our thoughts fly or they can chill them out to a stop.

Mind appears on Earth as the element of water. In the duality of Earth, it can be solid as in ice, a vapor as in steam, or a liquid as in water. It can be either hot or cold. It can be either a constructive and destructive force as rain, rivers, and oceans. It can be seen as vaporous clouds that race across the sky as thoughts race across mind or it can be stationary as the great oceans and represent the unconscious potential of mind.

ENERGY

Energy is the thought of God that flows out of God's mind now that it is active rather than passive.

Energy appears in souls as the ability to project themselves by action of their thoughts into other planes of God's awareness, or into physical matter.

Energy appears in humans as a direct result of their thoughts. If human thought is kept positive and creative, then a corresponding rush of physical energy invigorates the body. If human thought becomes negative and non-creative, then depression and fatigue will enter the human body. Human thought creates human energy!

Energy appears on Earth as the element of air; as energy in motion it appears as the wind and as moving water. Energy is created by thought, then forms of thought's equivalent, which is water, appear with wind as clouds in the sky. In a dual world, energy can be destructive or it can be creative and constructive.

Because duality splits the four basic characteristics of God into so many fractured patterns, human consciousness is in a constant conflict with the duality of its character. A human's unconscious mind senses the exact similarity of itself to Earth and to God, so our human conscious mind mixes up the three as if each were descriptive of any one of the others—as a much criticized process of anthropomorphism and pathetic fallacy.

Because of this correspondence between the physical earth and human consciousness, all of the rules of physics which govern physical matter apply also to our minds and emotions. For instance, there is a law of physics which explains how matter that is at rest will tend to stay at rest until a force is applied to begin movement. The equivalent law of consciousness is found in mental procrastination, where a person puts off doing something until an outside force is applied.

Friction is a physical law that defines how motion of an object is slowed by resistance to this motion. Resistance to change is a mental concept that keeps people from going forward, or stops them after they have started movement.

Gravity is the law of physics that holds all things that are in orbit in a state of equilibrium. The individuality of a galaxy is caused by the force of gravity which holds all the many pieces together as a cohesive unit. As an individual galaxy can have its own identity in a universe of millions of galaxies, so also does a human have its own identity in a world full of billions of people. The human mind keeps all of its fears, beliefs, assumptions, emotions, and thoughts within that person's consciousness in a state of equilibrium so that the person may create its own personality or individuality.

So that we may see and understand the cycle of birth and death on a faster scale, it is duplicated for us in the micro pattern of the day/night cycle in each twenty-four hour time period on Earth. At midnight, on one side of the world, a day begins in darkness, a period of rest, of self-contemplation not unlike God at the beginning. Earth has the appearance of being asleep, most of life is asleep; it is a day which is still in a dream state, a state of self-contemplation.

About four a.m., a restlessness starts to stir the night into a state of half waking, half still sleeping.

The morning stars fade into a twinkle of goodbyes as the birds begin their morning songs, songs that seem to float in and out of the trees in harmonic chirps of greeting. The air stirs awake and moves as a gentle breeze rustling tree leaves in rhythm with the birds' songs. It is nature's Hallelujah Chorus, a fitting way for a day to begin.

The sun sends a little light over the eastern horizon, then in a splash of glory and pride crashes over the horizon itself, colors flowing from its center in pastel hues of soft reds, oranges and gentle yellows, spreading and tinting the sky. Flowers begin to open their blossoms to receive the sun's energy, and some turn to face it. Birds fill with pride, feathers puffed out, and sing their calls in clear bell-like notes that welcome a new beginning, a new day.

As the sun rises higher, it shines with the harsh light of reality which illuminates and reveals; that which it cannot shine through forms an image of itself in black, as a shadow. Everywhere at once the dualities, the black and the white of nature are evident.

At noon the sun reaches its fullest height, marking the end of a beginning and the beginning of an end. In a hot, unyielding light, it begins its slide from the fullness of day into the cool twilight of evening.

At four p.m., a feeling comes over the land that the day is almost over. The majority of the creatures put aside the activities of the day to begin to think about what they will consume to give them the energy they need until a new beginning starts anew the next day.

As evening phases in, those of the Earth's inhabitants who are not nocturnal begin to relax. They enter into a period of inactivity that synchronizes in some strange way with the fading of light and energy from the earth.

The western sun begins its descent and, in a sense, its death. Yet, even as the sun closes out a day, it cannot help but do it with the same splendor it showed when it arrived. And why not? Isn't a beginning an ending and an ending always a beginning?

It is as if the sun is trying to say, "Look! Look at what I'm doing... it is just as splendid a thing to die into a new beginning as it was to be born and flow towards an ending... the cycle is endless."

As the sun disappears, the night begins. There is no gap in sequence—one flows into the other seamlessly, effortlessly. In the strange flowing pattern of beginnings and endings, at the same instant that the sun fades and sets in our West it begins to rise in others' East: our sunset is their sunrise.

You can see how emotions and thoughts act and interact with each other by watching a storm form and then seeing a bolt of lightning from "out of the blue" strike a tree and the tree start to smolder. Then a breeze begins and the moving air stirs the smoldering tree ablaze. This is self-similar to the state that occurs when "out of the blue" an action hits our human consciousness which makes us hot and we start to do a "slow burn". Maybe this was caused by an unkind word from another, or an insult or intentional hurt. Or maybe it was not intentional, but it still hurts. If we can ignore it and move on, the heat from the hot desire for rebuttal or revenge will go out. But if we fan this hot desire with our thoughts, then the action of thoughts (like moving air) will make the smoldering resentment erupt into the bright flame of anger.

If we are able to use our intelligent reasoning ability, symbolized by water, then we can put out this bright flame of instant anger by the coolness of our reasoning. We say to ourselves, "Cool it... chill out!"

If one puts just a little bit of water on a flame, it turns the water to steam or to a vapor that gets blown away by air. Isn't this also what happens in an emotional situation? If we try to use just a tiny bit of reasoning and we are dealing with an emotion that has gotten so hot that a small bit of reasoning will no longer have any effect, it just boils off like steam and is carried away by the full force of thought that is fanning the emotion. A small bit of reasoning like "I really shouldn't be acting this way, but..." is not enough, and then another wave of thought feeds the emotion hotter and the small bit of reasoning gets boiled away like drops of water on a hot fire.

If we aren't able to use our intelligent reasoning ability to put out the inner fire or rage, then the inner anger will flame up with an intensity that is destructive to ourselves and all those who surround us.

Our human bodies are what our minds work on and interact with by the use of thought, emotions, and intelligent reasoning. It is why worry causes ulcers, fear causes chills, anger makes our faces red, and intelligent reasoning can control all of these if we can access it appropriately.

To clarify this concept of how the four elements, earth, air, fire, and water, are self-similar to the conscious forces of earth as space/shape, air as thoughts positive/negative, fire as emotion love/hate, and water as conscious reasoning, I'm going to describe two different storms and show how they have self-similar patterns.

AN EARTH STORM

Out above the middle of an ocean, the sun is heating up the air over hundreds of square miles. As the air rises, because of its heat, it takes moisture from the ocean water which has evaporated, because of the sun's heat, up into the sky.

High in the sky, this moisture starts to condense because of the coolness of the upper atmosphere. The moisture turns into clouds which form at first as individual wisps. These wisps join together to form single clouds, then the single clouds form together to become a huge lowering mass that may extend ten to fifteen thousand feet up into the sky.

This mass of evaporated moisture and heat continues to churn up from the ocean and cloud cover begins to form over hundreds of square miles. Finally the cloud mass becomes so huge that the rotation of the planet causes the entire enormous cloud mass to start spinning as one unit.

This spinning cloud mass has now become a tropical storm known as a hurricane. As it spins faster and faster around itself, an inner core forms that is called the eye of the storm. Often this eye is miles wide.

Now this spinning storm starts a forward movement and as it gathers speed it gains inner wind velocity because the spinning motion speeds up. As the hurricane crosses the ocean, it gathers more moisture and more strength, with winds reaching speeds of one to two hundred miles an hour.

As long as the hurricane is over ocean water, it does no damage except to churn up the ocean surface and drop moisture in the form of rain back onto the ocean from which it came.

When this happens, the total effect is a cleansing action of the ocean water and of the air. The ocean water went into the sky as a pure moisture evaporation process; when it fell as rain, it carried with it dust and particles that were in the skies, so the air was purified. And since rain water is purer than salt water, the process was also cleaning the ocean. If one didn't happen to be caught in a hurricane while on a boat, the storm had little personal meaning to humans.

When a storm is forming over either the ocean or land, the barometer, which records atmospheric pressure, starts to fall. When it is a clear sunshiny day, the barometer rises. A falling barometer is an indication that a storm is coming. It is interesting to note that one of the descriptions of a hurricane is a tropical depression. In humans, when an emotional storm starts to form in their minds, they often go into a mental condition called a depression.

When the storm or hurricane leaves its place of birth in the ocean, its forward movement often takes it across land mass. Approaching land, its outer edge is seen as white fluffy clouds and a slightly increased wind.

As the wind increases, the clouds become darker and more dense. Thunder can be heard from afar and lightning is seen in the sky. Soon great bolts of lightning strike across the clouds, and from the Earth up into the sky. Rain starts in little droplets that soon get larger and faster until they seem to be a curtain—sheet after sheet of water. The rain ebbs and flows, up and down in velocity, in concert with the wind.

The wind increases as a strong gust within a strong wind, following the same form as all else on Earth—a pattern within a pattern.

As a hurricane of great intensity sweeps across land, it begins to destroy all things not firmly anchored to the ground. They are either flattened down or blown away in a great swath of destruction that extends across the whole area of the storm.

At the center of this storm, the eye, there is no violence. Here, at the center, the violence that swirls around outside it is unnoticed. There is no turbulence and no destruction. The center of every human is also where they find their calm.

As the center passes over the land mass, the winds reverse. Those that seemed to come from the south now come from the north, and another period of destruction begins.

When the whole storm system has passed, a great calm replaces the violence. A fresh smell of clean air and newness is everywhere. Yet, also everywhere, is seen the great destruction that the storm caused. Trees and plants and buildings and cars have been uprooted and blown down or blown apart. Flooding is everywhere. All the clouds have gone away with the storm and the sun appears bright and shining. Birds begin to sing, animals come out from their hiding places, and the great peace after a storm comes over the land.

A HUMAN EMOTIONAL STORM

Now comes a self-similar human storm. Out in the middle of a person's total consciousness, its ocean of thought, the heat of a hot emotion is soaking its mind.

In this example, we will say that the person is a man who has just found out (or believes he has found out) that his spouse was unfaithful. At first, the information lies on his mind, sort of baking inside; it's like he is in shock. Then, from inside his unconscious mind, thoughts begin to float up into his consciousness, little mental images of the spouse in the arms of another. Then an image of the two of them kissing floats by. He begins to get flushed and feels hot in the face just thinking about the indignity that being betrayed makes one feel.

His body begins to move as he tries to sit in a chair while more visual images float across his inner eye. He feels tense, tightly wound, agitated. The more he thinks, the more emotion and anger come over him, and the more anger and emotion that gather up in his mind, the more hot and flushed his body gets. The thoughts already in his consciousness have floated up out of his unconscious mind and begun to spin around in his conscious mind, over and over, around and around, the same thoughts, the same mental images of infidelity, of holding, of kissing, of... the man gets up and starts to move.

His face is contorted in rage; it is red and flushed and as he moves across the room to where his spouse is, he kicks aside a coffee table. He wipes off the knick-knacks standing on the mantel with a swipe of his hand; he picks up a dish from the table and smashes it to the floor.

In a howling rage, he gulps great quantities of air and begins to scream obscenities at the unfaithful one. If a brain wave monitor were hooked up to this man, one would see huge spikes of energy as he emotionally goes up and down in the intensity of his screams of rage. It would look like lightning bolts recorded on a chart. His rage would become so great that moisture would well up in his eyes and tears would roll down his face.

Finally, he would stop, outwardly calm for a short period as he stands gasping for breath, fists clenched together. He would sit down, head in his hands, thinking. This is his center of the storm time.

Then just when it seemed to be over, the screaming would start again, the fury coming from another direction as wedding vows are remembered. More wreckage, more screaming, the fury would go on and on, with more tears of frustration and hurt rolling out of his eyes.

Then it would stop. Suddenly, for no apparent reason, it is all spent, all gone! The fury, the anger, the harsh words, and most of all, the tears, have stopped. Maybe, as the spouses looked at each other, they would come together to hug and ask forgiveness; maybe, after looking long at the other, the grieved one would simply turn and walk away, away from the hurt, the betrayal, the wreckage of the marriage.

In this case, nothing from the past was left; it had all been emotionally destroyed, torn apart and scattered and it would take a long time before new growth could begin. The emotional storm that had risen out of the man's personal consciousness had swept across them with the fury of a hurricane and destroyed all that wasn't firmly anchored.

Can you see how a mental and emotional storm is self-similar to a physical storm on Earth? Do you understand that if an angel was teaching a soul how dangerous emotions and mental storms could be to its own mental body, the angel would only have to take the soul for a view of a storm on Earth? They could also linger and watch how the physical Earth would heal and re-create itself with new plants and trees and, in some cases, end up in better condition than before the storm.

How does one put out an Earth fire? There are three ways. First, take away the fuel so there is nothing left to burn; second, remove the air or oxygen supply; and third, throw water on it to cool it off.

These are the exact same three things that will put out an emotional fire in a human. First, take away the fuel that is keeping the emotional fire going. This means to physically remove another person or the thing that keeps feeding the emotions. Second, stop thinking (the symbol air) about the problem, because thoughts feed emotion. Third, dump calm, cool mental reasoning (the symbol water) on the problem to put it out.

The four elements—air, water, fire, and earth—interact on the planet Earth in the same way their psychological equivalent of mental thought, calm reasoning, emotions, and our physical body interact on our own personal planet, our human body. This is because we, as human bodies, are micro patterns of the Earth; anything that can happen on Earth can happen to a human—we are self-similar patterns.

This is why humans have instincts, just as the other animals have, as fragmented psychological character traits. Sometimes we do things in excess, like pigs; sometimes we are cunning as a fox; sometimes we charge and kill with the savageness of a bear or a lion; sometimes we chatter on like a magpie or endlessly glide through life like a bird, just going along with the breeze, never wanting to land, never wanting to work at flying.

Sometimes we hunt our prey in packs, like wolves; sometimes we stink like a skunk; sometimes we live in the savage jungle river of a stream of consciousness like a crocodile, with only a snout and our eyes above water; sometimes we sit as a vulture in a tree, waiting for someone's death so we can pick apart the inheritance.

But there are other times when we can soar like an eagle, be gentle as a lamb, and flee nimbly from danger like a deer through a forest. Our smiles can be as graceful and lovely as a butterfly touching a flower, as we help each other in sorrow and pain, and as we dance and sing and share one another's joys and successes. These are the animal selfs that man must kill off and offer to God.

I have now explained as fully as I am able the results of my forty years of esoteric study which revealed new insights to me about the creation of God's own consciousness and the creation of the universe, including angels, souls, the Earth, and the human beings and other life forms upon it. The allegory section of this book is now complete, and I will continue in Section III with a discussion of human consciousness and what part it plays in the meaning of our lives.

PART III

RETURNING TO GOD SOULS' EARTH EXPERIENCES

SIMILAR PATTERNS OF HUMAN AND ANIMAL CONSCIOUSNESS

How has the Earth, as an alive consciousness, been identified by humans throughout the ages? The humans who did this identifying when we were in a more primitive stage of development were the shamans and medicine women and men. Our own Native Americans had, and some still do, a deep understanding of how God operates in nature. The Native American religions and the teachings of Christ fit hand and glove—because both are self-similar concepts of the consciousness of God. The Indians saw the pattern of God in nature, white men saw the pattern of God in Jesus Christ. Both are self-similar concepts.

If you want a quick understanding of how God's consciousness actually operates in nature, then have a Native American shaman, or a shaman from any other part of the world, if you have access to such a person, explain it to you. These people are the guardians of these secrets today.

If it wasn't for their all too human intertribal warfare, being as far from solving the problem of human aggression as the rest of us, the lifestyle of American Indians would be as close to my idea of perfection as it is possible for a human to live—because they lived in harmony with the Earth and with all of nature. They did so for many thousands of years. They made no attempt to create factories so they could spend all of their lives working in them just to buy more possessions that kept breaking or wearing out, requiring them to work even longer and harder to get new ones.

They didn't get carried away with farming in such a big way that the farms ran them instead of them running the farms. Can you imagine a lifestyle where all of a family's possessions could be loaded on a drag made of a few poles sewn to deerskin, strapped to and dragged along by a horse, or a woman?

One should remember that the Indians had a lifestyle totally different than the one shown in Hollywood movies, where they are depicted as savages who attack and massacre helpless white men, women, and children for no reason. In this lifestyle, where a human's daily existence was interwoven with nature like a vine wrapped around a tree, something happened. Without jobs to go to or the need to amass money, these people could study nature in a relaxed, reflective way.

They noted the characteristics of the four basic elements—air, fire, earth, and water— and considered them sacred. They saw that there were six directions (including above and below), and realized that they represented things that were happening in their own lives; the four seasons also symbolized seasons of their lives.

They learned the peace, the balance and harmony, of Earth, and because they were at peace with themselves and nature (though frequently not with other tribes), they spent great amounts of time just sitting in the beautiful virgin woods watching birds, animals, clouds, storms, fire, water, and earth. In some ways they arrived at a deeper understanding of life by observing nature than the white man was getting from his universities and theological theories of the day.

The Native Americans began to see the similarity between the way certain animals acted and the way different members of their tribe acted. They saw that some animals personify the love and joy that a family group of human parents, grandparents, and children have for each other in the way they play together, care for, and protect each other.

For example, a human who had the traits of an agile, quick, cunning mind was called a fox and everyone in the tribe knew what was meant.

They observed the work habits of beavers and saw that those animals over indulged in everything they did. Today, we call people who are busy as beavers, workaholics. The tendency to dam up one's emotions until they burst free, as a beaver dam breaking up, is also a beaver characteristic.

Rabbits were soft, fluffy, and gentle, capable of moving at great speed. The Indians noted their rapid movements and breeding habits and called people with those kinds of traits the rabbit people.

Geese could be relied on to arrive and leave at the same time each year, flying high to do so, and were considered steadfast in purpose.

Salmon had the trait of wanting to swim against the current to go back to their origins even if it killed them. People who want to go against the current of life, or public opinion, are like salmon.

Bears could be friendly and sleepy one minute and roaring, raging, angry beasts the next. People who have instant abrupt mood changes are like bears.

Elk walk with their antlers high, with great dignity and ceremony, through a forest. Their presence seems to be a calming influence to the animal life around them. Men with this kind of presence are thought to make good leaders.

Mountain lions are animals who like to go from rock to rock, ever higher and ever faster, sure footed and always in charge. This trait can be seen in political and religious leaders.

Snakes are the reptiles who can only move on the earth by making total contact with the ground. Therefore, they have great wisdom about the nature and form of matter. They also have the ability to strike out and injure or kill things that disturb them. Indians recognized that people who have great wisdom in material and spiritual matters can't be pushed too far. If they are, they will strike back with a force and venom that can kill. This trait of personality seems most common in politics.

Woodpeckers are the birds that beat at a tree, peck by peck, until they get the worm larvae they are seeking. This is the trait in humans who are seekers of knowledge and will dig hard, keeping at it, until they find it.

Porcupines represent a state of consciousness that is in eternal defense. Try to be nice to people who are overly defensive and you get nailed by a barrage of sharp barbs from an even sharper tongue.

The mental and emotional traits of humans are found in many other animal species. This is because a part of God's consciousness is personified and alive in animals, birds, and the whole planet. Indians recognized this Great Spirit of God and communicated with it verbally and mentally.

Birds in the sky represent the thoughts and ideas that flutter in and out of consciousness. Some are beautiful, while others are ugly and depressing. Birds represent ideals and ideas that swiftly move across consciousness, singing a brief song of greeting and then vanishing. Sometimes, like the birds in a forest, humans hear the song but can't identify or see the bird singing it. So it is with the half formed bits and pieces of ideas, sentences, and thoughts that fly in and out of their waking consciousness.

Eagles are birds of great nobility who live at breathtaking mountain heights. They glide and soar in the air with incredible majesty and dignity. They can see enormous distances and have few natural enemies.

So it is with human consciousness. Humans hold majestic high flying ideals and ideas which give them great insight and the ability to see far into the future. It is no wonder that the American Indians claimed the eagle had great medicine and that a feather of this bird was sacred and therefore worn in ceremonies. You see, long ago Indians figured out that watching an eagle fly was the same as watching an ideal of the Great Spirit in the sky.

As they watched the enormous variety and abundance of bird life, they realized that these small creatures indeed personify thought matrixes that fly. Sparrows travel in formations that are living evolving patterns moving in the air like air-blown oil on a water surface. Have you ever taken the time to watch a big flock of sparrows in flight? You look in awe, wondering how in the world they can move together like a chorus of musical notes into ever changing fluid movements and shapes. This is also how fish swim in schools in the ocean in a self-similar pattern to birds flying in the sky.

Flocks of birds and schools of fish moving in synchronized patterns, which can instantly change direction as if they are all one entity, symbolize to me how the collective consciousness of animals and humans can move as one entity, causing peace or war or beauty.

All of us have had a time in our lives when, beaten up by personal emotions, we almost literally collapse and negative thoughts, our personal vultures, come and seem to pick the flesh from our egos. Our own thoughts will pick and eat at us until we are exposed to the bare bone. Isn't this really what a vulture represents? A personal, negative thought that picks us apart?

It is no wonder that the American Indians so loved nature and the land that they were willing to die rather than be driven off by so-called civilized man.

Wolves always seem to me to personify my conscious mind under attack by negative emotions and thoughts which I must either fight off or be devoured by. The archetypal instinct of wolves is to hunt in packs which act in concert to conquer. To overwhelm, wolves will sometimes send out decoys and scouts to look for their prey. They bite and nip at it in such a way that it turns away from the fake attack, and then the whole pack charges in for the kill. Sometimes wolves will flush one animal out of a herd toward the pack, which jumps all over it, going for the kill.

It's the same way when one desires to eliminate a bad habit, say smoking, as a conscious and emotional desire. For weeks you don't smoke and feel good about it. Then in comes the decoy, or scout: the thought "I'll have just one" flies across your mind, like a bird darting in and out of a forest, "one cigarette won't hurt." If you follow this thought, get a cigarette, light it up, and inhale, it should be over—you smoke that one and the thought should be satisfied. But it is not. That's when a whole pack of emotions flood in to overwhelm and conquer.

If you can't successfully get away from the first decoy thought, the whole pack will rush in to devour your good intentions, and you're instantly back to two packs a day.

Plants represent the beauty of form that thoughts or consciousness can have, like the complete blueprint or drawing that an architect makes of a single, individual house. Many individual houses form a community. So, also, do clusters of plants become forests, or hillside vegetation, or a wildflower patch.

Not only are the sight and feel of plants broken into dual opposites, but so are their scents, so that beautifully formed plants can have a foul odor and ugly plants may have a beautiful scent. Some are a pungent, strong odor, others light and faint like a mint or pine smell.

Sometimes, meanness and hate are represented as thorns, thistles, or poison ivy, but mixed with great beauty as in a rose bush. This means a rose is like some parts of our own consciousness, beautiful to look at, sweet to smell, but painful to touch.

It is really surprising how we use so many animals, plants, and earth places as symbolic representations for conscious states of our own mind each day, yet we never make the connection that all of life and our whole planet is a symbolic representation of consciousness.

We say things like gentle as a lamb, sweet as sugar, a real sour pickle, he's burned out, a watered down personality, her habits are growing like weeds, she's solid as a rock, he's flighty as a breeze, stands tall as an oak tree, anger crossed his face like a dark cloud, frustration boiling inside like a volcano about to explode, tears flowing like rain, acts like a bear with a sore hind end, like a horse feeling her wild oats, busy as a beaver, acts like a rat, and on and on.

I haven't studied all the Indian beliefs, but I know they understood dying. They knew that when they died they went back to live in spirit form because they understood how death cycles back into life in all parts of nature. They knew that by dying, they would live as freed spirits.

When something on earth dies, what really happens? Why has the spark of life, which is an essence of God, gone? What is this essence of God? It is God's own consciousness that has entered into a plant, an insect, an animal, a human, and yes, even a rock.

Now you may think this is going too far! How in the world could a rock have a spark of life in it? We don't see it because it is patterned on a different time scale than animal or human life. If one takes a sample of rock and a sample of human flesh and looks at them through a powerful electronic microscope and keeps magnifying, eventually one sees that both are nothing more than molecules with atoms and electrons moving in space. Both are made of the same substance.

"Yes," you say, "but we move!" So does rock, as lava. "That's different," you say, "that's the energy or pressure inside the earth pushing it." Then, I ask, what is the force or pressure that moves *you*? Actually, it's a conscious thought. The conscious thought of God moves the lava because God is the pattern. "Well, but we are warm, and we live and die." So is the rock warm and alive, and it also dies.

"This is foolishness," you say. "We, as humans, can act and react. Rocks can't do that!" Yes, they can, they just have a different time scale.

"Well, those are just coincidences. After all, *we* can think. Don't tell me rocks can think!" I'd say, "I don't know. Maybe they weren't designed to think. Does a tree think? It is alive. The point I'm making is that rocks are part of the consciousness of God made physical as the earth. The whole planet is alive because it has the spirit, the essence of God in it, and that includes rocks. Rocks are only an isolated part of a whole pattern, the earth."

What happens when something on Earth dies? Actually, life on Earth never really dies. What dies is the form that life was inhabiting. When the spark of God we call life leaves, there is death. The only thing that is alive in the universe is God.

Let me repeat this. *The only thing alive in the universe is God.* All else is inanimate forms of matter that do not live until God inhabits them with its spark of life.

Remember, in the beginning there was only God! *There was not God and life,* there was only God. God is a life consciousness. *Life is God!* When there is death, then the life essence that is a spark of God goes back to be a part of God. This is the same thing that all earth matter does in a multi-fractal pattern imitation.

Take water, for an example. Water is collected in a solid mass called an ocean. By an evaporation process, it drifts away from the mass to collect in the skies as cloud mist, which is tiny, tiny bits of water which form into a bigger drop. This drop of water is exactly like the ocean water except it doesn't have the salt or mineral content, which really aren't a part of water anyway.

This drop of water falls near a plant which absorbs it and uses it as liquid nourishment, and so it becomes part of the plant's sap which circulates throughout the plant like blood circulates in a human body.

When the plant dies, it shrivels because the heat of the sun draws out the moisture and the original drop of water goes back into the sky to once more form into a tiny drop of water which falls on the earth. This time, it lands in a stream and starts a journey back to the ocean from which it came.

The element of air follows the same process. Individual molecules with atoms and electrons moving inside are breathed in as air by an animal. They enter its bloodstream and move deeper to become part of the semen used to create another life. This passes from the male body to the female body and is part of the making of cells that split, split again and again in a fractal pattern that becomes self-similar as a lion cub, or whatever the species is, and becomes matter as flesh.

At the death of the animal, or some time during its decay cycle, the molecules are released back into the air to join with other molecules and become something else, a tree perhaps. They never die; they just evolve into something else.

So it is with the spark of life. It never dies. It either goes back to the source or it enters into something else in matter form or matter matrix and causes it to become alive.

The question is: what is it that dies?

What dies is individuality! What is dead is the sense of conscious individuality that a particular plant, rock formation, mountain goat, insect, or human expresses. Individuality is the only thing that can die.

Everything on earth—plants, minerals, insects, and animals—is really a three dimensional matrix, a bit piece of individuality of God's consciousness. Only by looking at the whole creation can we see the whole God. A star, a planet, a fox, a gardenia, and a human are each an individual expression of God.

When a plant, rock formation, insect, or human dies, then what dies is what that particular form represented or symbolized as a physical expression—its individuality.

What is individuality? It is what makes a person, place, or thing unique. It is the sum of all the qualities that make that one thing different from all others.

Using this definition then, each rose, mango tree, rock formation, wart hog, and wasp has individuality.

And that is what dies—this individuality. Take a giant oak tree that is in your front yard. There are millions of other oak trees that look much the same, but as there can only be one living oak tree in that space in your front yard, so can there be only one Mt. St. Helens and... so can there be but one you! When that oak tree dies, what is gone is the individuality of that particular tree.

And when you die, your individuality is dead, but *you* are not dead. Because just as molecules are the living energy of God, so it is that you are a soul, a drop of God that cannot be destroyed. When you die, your consciousness flows back into your own oversoul. This is that part of you that is the sum of all your earthly incarnations and the sum of all of your mistakes, failures, and successes. You are an oversoul in training to become a co-creator and companion with God.

Since we can now see that any plant, animal, particular place or thing has a sense of individuality, we can know and understand how each thing on earth is a living expression of a part of God's individuality.

Matter is always, endlessly, trying to change back into pure energy by a death and decay process. Matter can only stay physical by the use of some kind of internal spirit that forces energy to continue its existence as matter by having a form of life consciousness.

Isn't this the same physical law which says that "an object with no external energy source tends to approach a state of equilibrium as time passes? These objects' energy source must be constantly replenished or they die.

Isn't this law really a definition of how death occurs in animals and plants? And it is also a definition of how matter was created and how matter stays locked into a physical form rather than instantly vaporizing back into pure energy. Matter continues to remain matter because an internal force or energy is keeping it from returning back to pure energy. What is the internal energy force?

It is *the consciousness of God*.

As humans became less primitive and more educated, they came up with three little words defining the extent of our contemporary understanding of God's consciousness in nature.

The first is *anthropomorphism*. The other two are *pathetic fallacy*. Webster's *New Universal Unabridged Dictionary* gives the following definitions of these words:

1. An-thro-po-mor' phism - The attributing of human shapes or characteristics to God, objects, animals, etc.

2. Pa-thet' ic fal' la-cy - The literary device of portraying inanimate nature as having human feelings and character. Examples: The angry sea, a stubborn door, etc.

In the past, I had often wondered why inanimate nature was portrayed with human feelings and also why the shape and characteristics of humans would be attributes ascribed to God. To my mind, it was never enough to have someone say, "Oh, that's a bit of pathetic fallacy or anthropomorphism!" because I would always ask myself, why? I knew the world wasn't a flip/flop accidental design, so when something kept making a good fit for so long a time, there had to be an explanation.

As self-similar fractal patterns are the design of creation that is endlessly evolving as a pattern within a pattern, then it is within this pattern that one can find the footprints leading back to God's First Creation, and to God itself.

This concept finally satisfied my endless questions of Why? Why was I born? Why are men shaped differently than women? Why is the world made with a strange dual pattern so that nothing can exist unless it has an opposite? Why have cause and effect? Why is the world created so that its ecology system is (or rather, was, before humans over-reproduced, thoughtlessly misused their technology, and began destroying the balance) in perfect balance because of the action and interaction of its billions of life forms? Why, if we are made in the image of God, is it even necessary to be human? And as humans, why do we need a Christ, or a Buddha, to serve as an example of how to live our lives so we can be saved? Why do we even need to be saved? Saved from whom, or what? Maybe from ourselves—but why?

Creation has a very orderly, precise design with a series of large and small built-in checks and balances so that it can't unwind and fly apart. This means that for every "Why" I have ever asked myself, there is a precise answer. There is a precise reason why animals (including humans, obviously) were created with a built-in desire to kill each other for food when they could just as well have been created to absorb energy from, for example, the air. Why do some humans also kill each other and other animals for emotional satisfaction, not hunger? No other animals do this.

Why are most humans drawn to nature? Why do we go to scenic places? Why do we like to walk in cool, tall forests and go down paths that weave through thick vegetation? Why is it that some of us don't like to go into caves because they fill us with fear or make us uncomfortable, yet we get a feeling of peace and inner contentment in a deep, cool forest?

Why is it that the bubbling and running of a small stream over stones is such a delightful sight and sound? Why is it such a pleasure to walk barefooted on moss and thick grass?

These things both thrill and content us because each of the earth scenes is a physical manifestation of a psychological bit of the mind of God. Since we are made in the image of God, each scene is also a physical manifestation of our own human mind. In the forest, we find the duplication of the deep serenity of God's consciousness, and of our own.

We sit in silence in a forest, back against a tree, watching soft shafts of light seek openings in the tree tops and filter to the ground in angles of light. We hear birds chirping and far away a singing answer comes floating back, serenading God's splendor, displayed as sight and sound.

We watch sunsets and sunrises time after time and we never tire of the experience. We swim in warm water and let a soft breeze and a hot sun dry us off, and we do this as often as possible, year after year, and we never ask ourselves why we get an emotional feeling of peace and contentment each time. People who ski enjoy the sharp, crisp beauty of winter scenes, so different from the warm green lushness of summer. Whatever the season, each has its own unique beauty.

So it is with our lives. Each decade brings a new wonder, a new enjoyment, a new way of looking at life, a new way of enjoying life. So it is with the seasons.

We lie on our backs, legs bent at the knees and crossed at the ankles, and unconsciously reach for a blade of grass to chew while staring into the sky. We watch human faces and animals form in white, fluffy clouds, and we relax and become peaceful and happy. Why? Why should this be? Sit in front of a man-made building and you will find no mind change. Yet in nature, there is. A part of us, somewhere deep inside, still remembers the meanings of the hidden mysteries of nature and we respond at a soul level.

A human, in periods of great mental anguish and torment, will often find relief by leaving his dwelling of brick or wood and going out into nature, drawn to a forest and to nature like a sick animal seeks mud and water for healing. Humans at soul level instinctively know that nature will often heal their psychological and emotional wounds.

Nature is a psychological balm that heals by touching all the senses. The sicker we are mentally, the more relief we get from being with nature. Yet we humans, in our ignorance, kill other animals, destroy our ecology system, and laugh at the efforts of the Sierra Club and other nature conservation groups, of the American Indians, to preserve and venerate nature because it is God's consciousness made physical in matter. So many humans today see value only in what humans have created—a pattern of calamity known to the ancient Greek tragedy writers as *hubris* which always and inevitably brought death and destruction.

CHAPTER

HOW HUMAN CONSCIOUSNESS FORMS

The physical human body and human consciousness work together in harmony, both being micros created from the same macro pattern: God's consciousness. In this same way, the human body is created in a self-similar pattern to the human mind. This means that *our concept of physical reality is created in our human world by... our minds!*

In the beginning, the newborn human baby is helpless in its ability to care for itself and must be completely cared for by adults. And just as food and water are needed by the child's physical body, so is input from its own five senses: the five senses are the food, and the emotional flow of love is the water, which the child's mind must have to survive and flourish. A baby will begin to explore itself by touch as it plays with its hands and fingers and toes, then by taste as it puts objects in its mouth. As the five senses explore the world the baby lives in, these sensory inputs are registered on its memory and the birth of an individual consciousness begins. The baby learns to recognize the voices and faces of its mother, father, or other primary care givers, and its own voice as it cries. Eventually, it learns to recognize its own body and its own self. As physical growth occurs, a corresponding growth occurs in the mind or consciousness.

This developing human's individual Collective Consciousness begins to guide and influence itself with hunches and desires, with intuitive thoughts and feelings telling it to continue or dispense with a particular course of action. For this reason, the urges and desires that come into one's mind should always be explored to see if there is a real physical and/or soul reason why one's own self is pushing for a particular action. However, the desire can also be a negative one that would best *not* be indulged in because of the damage it can do to the Self.

Like a robot being manipulated, the human body reacts to these thoughts, urges, and hunches of the unconscious and conscious mind to initiate a series of events. These events end as *changes or new creations* in the physical and spiritual life experiences of the soul-in-matter and create new consciousness.

"Consciousness" is described in *Webster's Universal Dictionary* as:
1. The knowledge of what is happening around one; the state of being conscious.
2. The totality of one's thoughts, feelings, and impressions; mind.

In other words, consciousness means knowing what is happening around and within oneself. Using this definition, the human beings on Earth, living in physical matter, were creating a new consciousness by their physical and mental actions.

To understand how both the human body and the human consciousness are similar in design, one should realize that a woman's body symbolizes the inner consciousness of mind. If this is so, then it follows that there must be significance to the way her body prepares itself for creation each month by becoming fertile so new life conception can take place, and to the way a human's inner awareness also creates new mental concepts that become physical.

An opportunity for new soul growth will come out of the unconscious mind as a seed or an egg of an idea, just as an egg comes from a woman's ovaries. This thought or idea from our own unconscious mind will bring new growth into our life, if accepted.

For a certain time period, this new idea will stay alive in our mind, fertile and active, ready to be impregnated by outer awareness so it can begin a new life of its own. Or, we can ignore the new idea and it will go away.

If accepted, we carry this idea in the womb of our mind until the idea starts to grow because we are feeding and nurturing it with our attention. It will grow from the seed of a small beginning to become rounded, filled out, and fully formed. At this point, our little idea has gotten a life of its own. When this happens and we allow the idea to grow further in our minds, sooner or later we have to give it a physical birth. We do this by writing the book, starting the business, painting the picture, composing the music score.

This is the same sequence the female human body will use to create. A human baby begins as an egg that comes from a woman's ovaries (symbol of the unconscious). It lies for about fourteen days in her womb (symbol of inner human consciousness). Then, if it is impregnated by a male sperm (symbol of outer male consciousness), conception occurs. Now the fertilized egg stays in the womb, growing, and is fed and nurtured internally. It will grow from the seed of a small beginning to become rounded, filled out, and fully formed. It then begins to have a life of its own and must be born as a human baby.

It is the instincts and emotions common to all animals that have caused the human consciousness a great deal trouble, because they can become so active and violent to the body forms we inhabit. Sometimes, more than anything else, a soul at the beginning of each incarnation desires to kill of or crucify as many of its animal instincts and emotions as it can. Yet, these are necessary not only for mere survival, but also for the complex development needed if a soul is finally to become a co-creator with God. Anger, for instance, can be very destructive, particularly if acted out thoughtlessly. Yet the failure to fully experience and acknowledge (this is different from acting them out) *all* of one's thoughts, feelings, impressions, etc. means that full consciousness is not achieved. The human who is not in touch with his intuitive faculty, with the inner urgings of her or his unconscious mind, is generally doomed to act these urges out without consciousness and without choice. This unexamined activity generally causes great damage to oneself and others.

In Genesis, 3:21, God gave Adam and Eve (symbols of the newly born human consciousness) animal skins as garments to clothe themselves. This is a symbolic way of showing that animal instincts, urges, and emotions have to be worn by this newly formed human consciousness as part of its protective shield and that they form an important part of its resources.

In other words, *Just As* we use clothes to protect our human bodies from temperature and physical harm, *so also* does the newly formed human consciousness have to use its animal instincts and emotions to protect itself from the emotional or animalistic attacks of others, or from itself.

For example, if the soul mind decides that being aggressive is a negative animal instinct used by lions and leopards to hunt and kill prey that doesn't belong in its human personality any longer, then it works long and hard to eliminate those traits from itself.

The problem is that one can't completely kill them off while living as a human mind. We *have to* clothe ourselves with some of these animal emotions because we need some, or most, of these instincts and emotions to survive life as a human on earth.

A person who becomes too much of a passive non-violent follower type finds that life begins to charge at it and kick it around. And, when it recognizes other undesirable traits in its mental makeup, it can't do anything about them because it now lacks within itself the righteous indignation and anger, the drive and determination that aggression gives one to conquer other personal faults.

Besides, if anger and aggression are wrong, why are they a part of God's consciousness here on Earth? Why is the killing and eating of other life a part of God's Consciousness?

To answer these questions, we have to go back and examine the reason that God created earth as a physical model of the workings of its own mind. The working model of God's mind was made to show how thoughts and emotions play off each other in God's mind to produce a third result—reaction of consciousness. There is a place or reason for every thought and emotion in God's consciousness. If they are kept in balance and used at the right time and in the right place, there is nothing wrong with showing aggressive or angry emotions or mixing them with any other possible thought to get a reaction.

Sometimes overly passive non-violent people find out that the very thing that would allow them to counteract an action directed toward them is now gone—because they subdued it in themselves. This is why Jesus is shown losing his temper in the temple and scattering the money changers in a rage of righteous indignation.

A new individual consciousness is born each time a soul is born into a human body as a baby, a new baby body and new baby mind, self-similar patterns. As the child grows up, it lives a lifetime on earth much as an actor accepts a part in a gigantic stage play.

Like an actor, a soul will play a part in that lifetime that was written for it by itself as the oversoul. It may be a starring role, for self confidence to be learned. It may be a minor role—a street walker or homeless person, a cripple or a beggar—so that humility may be learned.

We role play human parts of consciousness to learn wisdom. Often we have been like actors in a movie; we have learned our own role and performed it well, but we haven't yet seen the play in its entirety; we don't understand how our part fits into the whole of the play.

In the last twenty years or so, we have discovered a great deal about the complexities of the human mind and know that we role play different personalities all day long. We start out in the morning looking at ourselves in the mirror. If we are married or in a significant relationship, we greet the other and say and do those things necessary to promote harmony in the relationship. If we have children, when they come to the breakfast table we talk down to them as leaders and counselors, telling or advising them to do things in certain ways—things that often we don't do ourselves.

We meet strangers and nod and smile, or frown and avoid them, because this is the role strangers play with each other. At our place of work we accept the role of boss or worker.

For there to be harmony in life, each has to play the role he or she agreed to take. Just as in a stage play, the drama can only run smoothly and be a success if each actor plays only his or assigned part.

This is a harmony lesson to be learned from nature. A bear doesn't act like a wolf and a wolf doesn't act like a bear; they stick to the role or part they were given to play in life. So do we have to learn to role play our lives.

Of course, figuring out exactly what those roles are is a whole other problem. And a person's role may be to throw over his or her *apparent* roles for the true ones required by his or her higher self.

Humans not only create their own individual consciousness, but together as a whole create also a collective consciousness. And as a smaller pattern, groups of people who live together in the same area over time begin to form a mini-consciousness which becomes the regional group consciousness. This regional consciousness can be discovered, if one is observant, in the certain ways the common beliefs of the group are expressed by its individuals. These group beliefs, prejudices, fears, and political and spiritual preferences can be seen within tribes, communities, towns, cities, states, and nations. The form and content of the different group consciousnesses and cultures varies considerably as they develop. Cripple your mind with false beliefs and some day in the future your body will become crippled. Keep thinking that life and your family are heavier loads than you can bear, and you will end up with back trouble. If you have created a closed mind, you will constantly say to all who try to help you, "I can't see me doing that!" Then your eyes will get weaker. Your glasses will get thicker and stronger. Maybe you can go so far as to make yourself physiologically and/or psychologically blind.

So, you ask, where do you go from here? What exactly is this life you must live if you are to wash the conscious mind and be free? Do you have to fast for forty days in the desert and fight off the devil, then go out and teach the masses while doing miracles like healing the sick, the lame, the blind, and raising the dead—only to then be crucified on a cross and die?

Yes! You are going to have to do all of those things. But here's the surprise: it is *yourself* that you must do all those things to, to your own United States of Consciousness, to all the many characters you role play each day of your life. Some of this is done symbolically, some literally.

Certain parts of your personality are blind; you will have to help them see. You will have to cast your own evil spirits into a herd and drive them over a cliff; these are your negative beliefs that must be destroyed.

You are going to have to let die instincts and emotions that are not becoming to the *new you*. No more judgment of others. And you will have to forgive *yourself* as well as the others, seventy times seven or as many times as it takes.

My own forty day period in the desert—symbolic of taking a period of time away from others for self cleansing and contemplating yourself in your own mind—took forty years.

In this period of our lives we feel lonely even when we are with others. We interact with them, but deep inside we are alone in our own desert, in the loneliness of our inner selves, seeking answers to the two main questions that cycle over and over in our minds: "Who am I?" "What am I doing here?"

What is happening is that remembrance is starting to come back. It passes through our consciousness like wisps of clouds crossing the sky; we get a wisp of remembrance here, another there.

We begin to look at wild animals and nature in a different way. We may join the Sierra Club or other conservation groups; we protest the use of animal fur because deep down, it seems wrong. Just for a fleeting moment we may realize why, then quickly the thought passes over the horizon of our awareness.

We can see how consciousness an evolving fractal pattern of endings flowing into beginnings by the way we begin to forget things at the end of our lives. As humans go into the winter of their later lives, remembrances of their childhoods, their parents, their school years become more vivid and clear in their minds. Their consciousness is flowing from their ending (the present time) straight into their beginnings (the childhood time).

However, at the same time that the beginnings are becoming clearer, present lives become vague. Things that happened an hour, a week, or a month before are quickly forgotten. Their consciousness, like a fractal pattern, is evolving into new beginnings as their lives move toward an ending.

This is the same pattern that the consciousness of the human race as a whole is finally beginning to evolve into.   We look at the clouds in the sky and watch them drift out of our range of vision, over the horizon, and think that maybe this means something.

We watch sunrises and sunsets puzzled and bewildered as to why, all of a sudden, we are looking at the sky, at sunrises and sunsets. Why do we like to take long walks in the forest and in scenic places? Why does a gentle breeze with the freshness of salty sea water scent stir our insides?

Why do we stare at flowers or waterfalls, or in the evening listen to the crickets, whose chirping seems to have such a peaceful rhythm to it? Why do we get upset seeing animals shot or caught in traps? We know there is something wrong with killing whales, or any other animal.

Some of us protest nuclear testing because deep inside we sense this is wrong; it is wrong to blow up atomic bombs inside the earth. Some people sense that it is like putting a bomb in their own insides and exploding it, and they think what a strange thought that is.

What is happening all over the planet is that remembrance is coming back to the human race. Many of the souls now inhabiting earth as I write this book are some of the most aware, most advanced souls created by God.

Old souls and spiritual leaders from the distant past are now back on earth, and because of their efforts a new shift in consciousness is coming.

As we come to the end of the twentieth century, our individual and our Universal Consciousness have reached a place of maturity and sophistication so that a new awareness of life as a whole can be understood—by those souls who have done the necessary work.

We must become our own saviors of our personal worlds. This pattern within a pattern enables us to start to remember that we are souls, sons and daughters of God, rather than mere fragmented individual humans helplessly afloat in a hopeless puzzle of bits and pieces.

What is your personal world? Your personal world, my friend, is what is stored up in your mind and copied by your body so faithfully.

CHAPTER

AN EVOLVING HUMAN CONSCIOUSNESS CREATES RELIGIONS

Human beings learn their beliefs from family members, from their peers, and from other persons they respect, and from introspection and self awareness. As individual human beings explored the new human consciousness, including the input from their five physical senses as well as their thoughts and emotions, they began to reason out mental conclusions. These conclusions congealed into beliefs. And it is from human beliefs that the varieties of religious experience have flowed from humans as water flows out of the ground as a spring.

The meaning of the word *religion* is as diverse as the people it serves. These are the definitions in *Webster's Unabridged Dictionary*:

Religion:(-lij'un, n (oFr. *religion*, from L. *religio* (onis), religion, piety, conscientious, scrupulousness, from *religare*, to bind back; re-, and *ligare*, to bind, to bind together)

1. belief in a divine or superhuman power or powers to be obeyed and worshipped as the creator(s) and ruler(s) of the universe.
2. expression of this belief in conduct and ritual
3. (a) any specific system of belief, worship, conduct, etc. often involving a code of ethics and a philosophy; as, the Christian religion, the Buddhist religion, etc. (b) Loosely, any system of beliefs, practices, ethical values, etc. resembling, suggestive of, or liken to such a system; as, humanism is his religion

Religions seem to come from the unfathomable depths of consciousness of primitive humankind, then become focused and crystallized through local teachers and sages who appear when the human consciousness of the particular area or regional group is ready to hear them: "When the pupil is ready, the teacher will appear." Some of the teachers came from royalty, others from humble beginnings.

The first form of religion was a primordial type that explored the individual spirit consciousness found in insects, plants, animals, man, and the Earth itself.

Male and female shamans appeared as the teachers and healers within each tribe wandering the earth.

Surrounded by nature, they were the first humans to explore the spirit consciousness of God in matter that is living insects, plants, animals, humans, and the Earth.

Then another great awakening of human collective consciousness began far, far back in the mists of prehistory, around 10,000 B.C., in India. The Hindu religion was passed on orally for many thousands of years and developed instructions on everything from correct agricultural practices to the nature of reality. Its ancient wisdom, added to and extended over the millennia, was eventually preserved in writing in the *Vedas* and the *Upanishads*.

In Hinduism, God creates the world through self sacrifice, self dismemberment, or self forgetting, so that the One becomes Many, this One expressed mythologically in hundreds, even thousands, of different God and Goddess images: Brahman, Vishnu, Shakti. The life of every sentient being on Earth (not just the humans) is a part, or role, in which the mind of God is absorbed. There is therefore no problem of evil in Hinduism: the higher self of *every* individual—saint, murderer, thief—is the veiled Godhead experiencing the world of form which the Indians call *maya*.

Examining almost every aspect of how humans lived their daily lives, Hinduism laid out rules for proper conduct which included tolerance of other religions and people. Along with the ancient Chinese, they were the first to discover and develop the special state of consciousness called meditation.

Meditation had to be developed by humans so that they could understand their own human consciousness, so that they could understand that a God, angel, and soul consciousness were already created and in a state of growth called evolution.

Meditation was a way to quiet their own human consciousness and begin to access these other forms of consciousness to accelerate human conscious growth and begin to control the creative abilities of themselves.

As souls began to inhabit the earth in human form, they learned, to their horror, that it was just as easy to be creative in a negative way in a dual world as it was to be creative in a holy way; it was just as easy to be a great sinner as it was to be a great saint.

It was in India that psychological probes into the human mind began and mystics found and identified the seven chakra centers in the human body that correspond to the seven levels of conscious awareness found in heaven.

A soul, as a human, could train, learn, and work itself up through the seven spiritual centers in its own human body by the actual way it lived and thought during its lives on Earth.

The seven spiritual centers, or chakras, are the places where the memories of all past lives' successes and failures are carried within the body. When a soul enters into a human body to begin another incarnation, its spirit carries the memories of past life patterns, like the memory in a CD. These vibration patterns go into the newly formed seven spiritual centers and reside there. Each center has the ability to influence different parts of the human body.

Say, for example, the soul which just entered a new born human baby had strong emotional problems not yet resolved. These emotional patterns would be imprinted in the third spiritual center, the solar plexus. The result would be a human who, even as a baby, would have a very sensitive stomach and as an adult whenever it became emotional its stomach would seem to tie itself into knots.

Imbalances in the seven chakra centers can be corrected in two ways. One is to live, while in a physical life, in such a spiritual, holy manner that the centers become spiritualized.

The second is to learn how to become silent and meditate. When a human quits all outside earthly activities and becomes quiet within and meditates, then God comes to that human on Earth and in a slow process, man, with God's help, begins to spiritualize the seven centers.

When we pray, we, as humans, are talking to God. When we become silent and meditate, then God talks to us. We should realize that since the earth and our bodies are simply physical manifestations of God, God can find us, in meditation, in an instant.

Deep, silent meditation is one of the most cleansing experiences a human can have. Just as a warm bath or shower will cleanse and refresh the outer body, so will half an hour of meditation cleanse the inner body.

It is not difficult to learn to meditate. Sit in a comfortable chair in a quiet room with the hands folded across the abdomen. Next comes the slightly hard part—you must completely relax your body and your mind and become still. Many people silently say a mantra five or six times as they relax more deeply such as "Be still and know I am God" or "*om-mani-pani-hum*" or another mantra of their choosing.

Have your eyes looking down the line of your nose so they don't roll back, then gradually close your eyelids as you relax. Silently repeat the mantra as you still your mind.

It will take a while, but as you learn to still the mind and become relaxed, a gradual vibration will start in circular motions in part of your body; it could be in your hands or in your legs or around the center of your body. Often, when younger people first start the meditation procedure, they will begin to feel a vibration in their groin areas, then become aware of sexual desire arising in them. Thoughts of a sexual nature will flow into their minds, upsetting them and causing them to wonder what in the world is the matter with them.

Here they are, sitting quietly in a chair, hands across their middles, getting ready to have God itself visit, and they are having sexual desires and thoughts. This is because the first chakra to be spiritualized is the testes in men and the ovaries in women. These represent the creative centers in humans and as they become spiritualized, sexual thoughts and emotions are driven out into the mind from the body so that the mind can expel them as old stored energy.

These sexual sensations will go away after a period of time and are not to be considered as wrong or a source of embarrassment, but as a normal part of the beginning process of spiritualizing all seven centers.

As one is spiritualizing different centers, the normal darkness a person sees as the eyes close will change into colors; sometimes the red or orange of the lower chakras will appear; sometimes the green healing of the heart chakra will be seen instead of darkness.

When one has finally spiritualized all seven chakra centers, a white light will appear. This shows that all the colors of the seven chakras have been purified, and as happens when all colors are combined, they produce a white color. Therefore, the spiritualizing of all seven centers will produce the white light of illumination sought by all saints and mystics.

The seven physical chakras are as follows:

1. Gonad Chakra Center or Base Chakra:
   This center is located at the base of the spine and opens to receive the energy of the earth. It is why it is good to sit on the ground and walk barefooted. The emotion of fear is stored here, because fear is of the earth, not heaven. It controls and affects the adrenal glands, the kidneys, and tension in the spine. Its color is red and it vibrates to the musical note C.
2. Lyden Cells or Sexual Chakras:
   This chakra is located below the belly button in the ovaries of women and in the testes of men. It controls the pelvic sexual organs and is the lower seat of creativity for the physical and mental self. This is the center where a man feels his masculinity and the female, her femininity. Its color is orange and it vibrates to the musical note D.
3. Solar Plexus Chakra Center:
   This chakra is located above the belly button. As anyone who has ever had a stomach ulcer or upset stomach knows, this is the center where sadness, rage, anger, hostility, and threats to our personal power come to rest. It affects the health of the liver, gall bladder, spleen, pancreas, and stomach. A person who controls this chakra will be good in emergency situations because he or she stays calm and collected. This center's color is yellow and it vibrates to the musical note E.

These first three chakras are known as the three lower chakras.

4. Thymus Gland or Heart Chakra Center:
   This chakra is located near the heart in the thymus gland and, as the first of the three higher chakras, it deals with love and harmony. It controls the heart, blood, and circulatory system. When we balance or control this center, we feel in harmony with ourselves and nature, which is how people who are in love feel. Its color is green, the color of healing and of growth in nature, because when we love, we both heal and grow. Its musical note is F.
5. Thyroid or Throat Chakra Center:
   This center is located in the throat and deals with communication by both thought and the spoken word. It is here, when one gets control of this center, that clarity of thought and speech can be achieved. We can begin to get detached from our physical bodies and to realize that we are more than just bodies; we become aware of our minds and souls for

the first time. This is the center where judgment of others rests and where we contemplate the wisdom of making judgments. It is where free will is located. Its color is blue, a deep blue, deeper than the sky, and it vibrates to the musical note G.

6. Pineal or Third Eye Chakra:
   This center is located in the pineal gland between the eyes, about one inch high on the forehead. It is where women from India wear a dab of color or a jewel. This center is the seat of a higher type of creativity than is found in the sexual chakra. When this chakra becomes activated after a spiritual life or a training period of prayer and meditation, one begins to become clairvoyant, with intuitive feelings or visions and paranormal happenings. We begin to understand how a spiritual and physical life are related, how they are actually two versions of the same thing. This center is where imagination and idealism come from; it guides us toward those things in life that will uplift and free us. Its color is indigo and when activated, a pulsation feeling comes between the eyes. When the eyes are closed in meditation, a deep indigo color appears. It vibrates to the musical note A.

7. Pituitary or Crown Chakra:
   This chakra is located above the third eye chakra, right at the hairline on the forehead. When this chakra is stimulated, it is a miniature combination of the other six and holds them in balance. It brings the bottom three chakras (physical) and the top three (spiritual) chakras together in balance. It deals with our divine purpose on earth or our destiny in life.

We use this chakra for a complete understanding of God because once we have mastered the three lower and the three upper chakras, we reach this level of spiritual development and have earned the right to be given a complete God understanding. This center also deals with things that language cannot describe and that are beyond logical understanding. Its color is violet and it vibrates to the musical note B.

Hindu contemplation of the human condition found four basic needs or desires that all humans have in common. The first, pleasure, is considered good and normal as long as the rules and laws of society are not broken in this pursuit: the physical world can be a beautiful sensual experience, so why not enjoy it? Hinduism knows that, because of the law of duality, there will come a time when a person will no longer find any pleasure in pleasure. It's a sort of "get it out of your system now, then get on to finding out there is more to life than the pursuit of pleasure".

Each human inwardly senses that each lifetime they live has some great significance, but cannot quite grasp what that significance is. The second basic need thus surfaces: the desire to be a success, to make a success out of each life lived. However, the person soon finds out that success is laid out in plateaus. When the top of a particular ladder is reached, instead of achieving permanent success the person has come only to a landing which contains yet another ladder. There is no end to this striving for success as practiced and achieved on the physical, or human, level: monetary, intellectual, religious, political, or any other category you can think of. Therefore, success can never bring lasting satisfaction.

The third need is the performance of duty. Here one gives of self to others for the pleasure this gives back to oneself.

The fourth fundamental need is liberation from the first three desires, from anything that keeps souls from experiencing the infinite bliss of Self-knowledge and reintegration with Brahman, or God. The final purpose of Hinduism is the description of the state of consciousness, of the *experience*, of liberation, Self-knowledge, or Self-awakening: the soul's realization of its original identity with God, or Brahman. This awakening can only be accomplished by *having the experience*—never by comprehending the words describing it, which are only meant metaphorically anyway.

From the most ancient times there has been a strong tradition in India for the seeker of liberation to abandon ordinary life and divest himself of his caste—his social and economic position and obligations. This is the external sign that his true Self *belongs to no classification whatsoever*. The path of liberation is then to discover, usually through working with a teacher, as well as through meditation and asceticism, who one *is* when no longer identified with any of the conventional world's roles or definitions. "If I still exist when divested of *all roles whatsoever*, who am I?"

Or, to say this in a modern way: "If I still exist when I am divested of my role as a mother/father, friend, lover, brother/sister, saint/sinner, doctor, lawyer, Indian chief, then who am I? Who or what is my core?" This thought begins one on the road to becoming a Seeker, the journey that ends when the Seeker says: "I am that I am!"

Siddhartha Gautama, born around 563 B.C. as a prince in a small Indian kingdom, was in complete accord with this tradition when he abandoned his conventional worldly life as a prince, husband, father, son, abandoned his caste, to become a forest sage in search of liberation. He had already received training from two renowned masters in Hinduism, and after working with a group of ascetics for a while then left the group and, in solitude, struggled for seven years of meditation and asceticism to find the cause of the enslavement of human beings to *maya*: to find his eternal, real self. But he struggled in vain. All he could find was his own effort to concentrate.

At the end of the seven long years of complete failure, Siddhartha simply gave up, relaxing his diet and eating some nourishing food. At that point, a feeling of some extraordinary change coming over him, he sat down under a nearby tree and vowed never to rise until he reached enlightenment. He sat there all through the night until, with a first glimpse of the morning star, he suddenly and instantaneously experienced perfect clarity and understanding: "unexcelled, complete awakening".

Siddhartha Gautama at that point became the Buddha, a word which means the enlightened or awakened one. There had been buddhas for thousands of years in India, but it was Siddhartha who became the personification of *the* Buddha and whose own experience of complete awakening formed the new path of liberation named Buddhism. Perhaps Buddha became the first human to realize that he was a soul aware of being in a human body. He personifies the awakening of soul consciousness within a developing human consciousness. Perhaps Buddha, too, knew the meaning of the phrase "I am that I am", or I am Siddhartha, that has a God patterned consciousness within me.

Buddhism has no gods, goddesses, or other supreme beings: there is simply clear awareness of the world as it really is, achieved through attention to direct experience rather than being confused with labels and names. When asked basic questions about the universe, the Buddha is said to have kept a "noble silence", then commenting that these kinds of questions were not relevant because they did not take an aspirant into the *experience* of awakening. "Do not accept what you hear by report," Buddha preached, "be lamps unto yourselves." When asked if he were God, or a saint, Buddha would always answer: "No, *I am awake*".

Similarly, the doctrine that there is no Self is *not* saying that there is no real or higher Self underlying consciousness, but rather that there is no such Self, or basic reality, which can be *grasped*.

Buddhism teaches that there is a state of consciousness called nirvana. It cannot be "attained", which implies grasping; it can only *arise spontaneously* after it is finally and completely understood that all of one's intentional acts to attain it are futile. The mind then achieves a state of indescribable peace, because the mind has returned at last to its natural state. This is not a state of inactivity, but rather one of true spontaneity in a world perceived directly as it really is, unconfused with abstractions and ideas such as good, bad, past, future, permanent, impermanent. One can now live in complete spontaneity without even trying. "Spring comes, and the grass grows by itself."

The Far East, as we Westerners call it, is far away in miles and even farther away in the nature of its consciousness. In considering the great Chinese religion/philosophy of Taoism, it's important to realize that East and West are not merely *different* in their regional developments of consciousness; comparing the two is like comparing chalk and cheese. They don't begin with the same assumptions, they don't make the same basic categorizations of experience, and they frequently don't honor and pursue the same methods of thinking.

For example, in Western thought the word "fist" is a noun—an object—and the opening of one's hand is an action. But what about the question: "What happens to my fist when I open my hand?" Within the framework of Chinese language and thinking, the question doesn't even come up. Many words in Chinese serve as both nouns/objects *and* verbs/actions. So if you think in Chinese, it's easy to see that objects and events can be interchangeable, and therefore see the world as a system of processes rather than entities.

The Eastern mind can be described as vertical, each moment preceded and then followed by another; it is the progression of the moments that is of interest. This is a sharp, spotlight kind of vision with little to no interest in the periphery. Western science is based on causality. Yet modern physics has shown that every process in the universe is subject to some degree of chance, or chaos, and that the observer is always a part of what is observed. The Chinese mind seems chiefly interested in this chance aspect of things. The Eastern mind works more on a horizontal and the interest is directed toward every single detail contained in that one horizontal moment. This involves at least some degree of letting go the spotlight vision for a less focused, but more inclusive, view of the whole contained in that one moment.

The foundations of Chinese consciousness date back to mythical antiquity, and the work which presents them is the *I Ching*, or *Book of Changes*, which has been in continuous use for thousands of years. Ancient tradition assigns a connection between the book's sixty-four mysterious signs and the underlying order and reality of the world. I Ching is also used by the Chinese to help explain how duality creates change in ones life.

Dualism is defined in *Websters New Universal Unabridged Dictionary*.
Du'al-ism (L. dualis, of two, from duo, two); 1. The state of being divided into or made up of two distinct but related parts; duality; 2. In philosophy, the doctrine that recognized two radically independent elements, as mind and matter, underlying all known phenomena; opposed to monism; 3. In theology, (A) the recognition of two radically different principles in operation, one good, the other bad; (B) The doctrine that man has two natures, physical and spiritual (Author's Note: Strongly implied by many religions is the idea that the physical is bad and the spiritual is good. What if both are good and are actually self-similar patterns, one in matter, one in spirit?); 4. In chemistry, the theory of Lavoisier that every definite compound consists of two parts having opposite electrical activity.

Therefore, the basic premise of the *I Ching* is the idea of change, which itself is founded on the eternal interaction of the two fundamental principles of the universe: *yin* (receptive, feminine, yielding or flexible, Earth) and *yang* (creative, masculine, firm, Heaven). A late 18th century Taoist sage, Lui-I-ming, commented that the ancient work "...is the study of principles, fulfillment of nature, and arrival at the meaning of life".

The Chinese have never considered the *I Ching* the specific property of any one religion or philosophy and the two great and enduring developments in human consciousness which occurred in China and which are so different from each other, Taoism and Confucianism, both have their roots in this ancient work.

Lao-tzu, born around 604 B.C., taught mainly by the spoken word, but at the end of his life produced a short manuscript titled the *Tao Te Ching* or *The Way*. This *Tao* (pronounced Dow) is that it is fundamental reality and order of the universe which spontaneously produces the world. It is also the "way", or path, of liberation. As with the Buddhism developing in roughly the same era in India, Taoism is concerned with the *direct experience of life*, which requires liberation of the mind from conventional thought and representational thinking.

Lao-tzu perceived the human mind as unstable and all too vulnerable to the conditioning of abstract conventional knowledge, to influence by thoughts and emotions related to mere objects, rather than to true reality, the *Tao*. The two levels of consciousness are not seen as separate, but as different parts of the totality of human consciousness. For the Taoist, the rational part of the mind, though useful in its own way, is of far less importance than that part of the mind capable of experiencing the world directly and truly.

The Taoist learns how to let the mind alone, and comes to understand that the mind works best by itself. As in the *I Ching* and in Buddhism, this process is not a matter of striving or effort. The legs know how to walk by themselves; walking is only interfered with if we try to pick up our legs with our hands to expedite walking. In the same way, the mind must be trusted to do its work spontaneously.

The incredible spontaneous creative power of the natural mind is blocked when the conventional mind is in control. The idea is to access one's innate intelligence, which can only function truly when it is not being forced, but is allowed to appear by itself spontaneously.

It is anathema to the Taoist that nature be exploited or abused. Taoist Temples, unlike later Greek, Roman, and Christian sacred buildings, were not placed on the highest point of land so they would be imposing and stand out. Instead, they were carefully designed to blend in with the landscape. In matters of social values, too, Taoists tend to be low keyed and informal. To indulge in pomp and ceremony is considered foolish. (If blue jeans had been available at its inception, Taoists would have been the first to wear them to work and to ceremonies.)

Kung Fu-tzu, who became known as Confucius, was a younger contemporary of Lao-tzu. He put trust in the natural man, as does Taoism, but Confucius primarily concerned himself with the functioning of man in society. His doctrines address the forms of conventional knowledge which make society work smoothly: the law, ethics, and rituals which give society its buffers and its guidelines. Humanness, or human-heartedness, is always preferable to righteousness because reasonable (human) men are able to compromise, while those who worship an idea or ideal have lost their humanness and become fanatics; fanatics are the enemies of the natural man and of life itself.

Confucianism is one of the most stable and workable patterns of social convention the world has ever known, and quickly became an inextricable part of the Chinese mentality. Until this century, young Chinese school children began their school day by memorizing and then repeating one of Confucius' sayings. Because of his teachings, scholars and teachers were held in greater esteem and considered more important than soldiers for thousands of years.

More than a thousand years later Buddhism found its way to China. With its continuous unbroken culture of at least two thousand years, under the influence of the *I Ching*, Taoism and Confucianism, Buddhism became in China a more practical sort of endeavor for ordinary human beings with families, jobs, and the normal assortment of appetites and passions. Zen Buddhism eventually emerged from roots both Taoist and Chinese Buddhist, and has had its greatest flowering in Japan. Zen emphasizes instantaneous awakening: *nirvana* cannot be found by grasping for it, therefore it can't be attained by the slow accumulation of insights—it must happen in a single instant. The Zen *koan* was developed in Japan to help provoke just such an event. Questions such as "What is the sound of one hand clapping?" are designed to wear down the conventional mind of the seeker to such a point that his mind simply collapses, gives up, as Buddha's did. And then, presto!—he or she is instantaneously pushed over the line into complete and unexcelled awakening.

In the Near East in the small country of Ur (present day Syria), another unique religion emerged around 2000 B.C. The large desert area was inhabited by nomadic tribes of Semitic peoples, among them the Hebrews. Yahweh, or God, a spiritual personal being like the other gods in the area, sent an angel to the Hebrew Abraham declaring himself to be the one true God. God told Abraham to get himself out of Ur and go to a country that God would show him. God further told Abraham that he would make of him and his descendants a great nation. If they would follow the path of the eternal father (God) with virtue and justice, God said, "all the nations of the earth shall rejoice in you".

Judaism was the first religion on earth to conceive and acclaim a single, one and only, true God of the entire universe, and the first to boldly proclaim itself as a religion which was *created by the divine intervention of* [this] *God*. The main and most important thrusts of Judaism are therefore the revelations that there is only one true God (monotheism), that God continually listens to the prayers of his followers and intervenes in the affairs of humans, and that God, if listened to and his teachings obeyed, will lead his people back to life, after death, of eternal glory in heaven.

In addition, Judaism was the first religion to use its own history as part of its religious ritual and as a teaching tool. The books of the *Torah*, as this account is named by the Hebrews, contain power struggles, sex, betrayal, relationships with Yahweh, relationships with other humans, alcohol use and abuse, slavery, bravery, cowardice, wisdom, foolishness, persecution, failures, and triumphs of the Hebrew people as actual case histories. In this way, his Chosen People could learn the forms of action pleasing to Yahweh in virtually every human situation conceivable.

At first, this religious history of a tiny nation and its people (a micro-nation only one hundred and fifty miles long and fifty miles wide) would seem like nothing more than the purely literal history of a people emerging from slavery. But in fact, the books of the *Torah* were primarily to be understood as an allegorical or symbolic account of the path of consciousness that individual humans must travel if they seek to be reunited with God. They can also be understood as a way humans can escape the bondage of their own limited personal beliefs and how they, too, must do battle, as did the ancient Hebrews, to conquer those negative forces that would keep the true self enslaved.

The daily events of their history were presented to the Chosen People so that they could begin to understand cause and effect in their own lives, as the Chinese did with *I Ching*. They could learn that it wasn't right to do certain things, not because of the penalty, but because of the effect the action would have on the development of their own souls and their human consciousness. As described in the Old Testament of the Bible, the female, Eve, is created by God from the rib of the male, Adam. This symbolizes human consciousness split into male and female parts, or into an outer and an inner awareness. Eve is eventually led astray by the serpent (the spirit of rebellion which each soul has, along with free will) and seduces Adam to take a bite out of the apple from the tree of wisdom (which is duality). In this way, soul consciousness is no longer pure spirit, but falls into physical matter and the cycles of birth and death begin as described earlier in the allegory section. This spirit of rebellion against God's wishes, symbolized by the serpent, results in the expulsion of Adam and Eve from Paradise (the full awareness of God), and the two become the first humans to die because of this act of choice. In this way, awareness of suffering and death became part of human experience and consciousness.

In Judaism, sex was a gift from God and was to be enjoyed within the rites of marriage. The uses and abuses of alcohol were also explored.

It was by this use of written history that the daily actions and reactions to events was put into historical perspective so the Jewish tribes could begin to understand cause and effect in their own lives.

If one wanted to understand why they should not get drunk, then they need only read about the effect this action had on Biblical figures. Each sin and each virtue that a human may encounter is personified in the Bible as an actual event so one can understand the pleasure and pain these things can create in a human.

To be sure that this written history was done in a correct manner, God sent prophets who taught both orally and also wrote out the significant parts of Jewish history that best personified mental, physical, and emotional traits of humans. This Jewish history would later be collected together in one book and become known as the Holy Bible, the inspired word of God.

One man, Abraham, was chosen, as was one woman, Sara, Abraham's wife, to start this new nation of Hebrews who would then and forever after refer to themselves as *God's Chosen People*.

And they were. To these people was given the duty and responsibility of living their lives in such a way that when their lives were recorded in the Bible it would be seen as an allegorical representation of how all humans should live their lives.

In order to faithfully represent the path that each human must walk through life, both the successes and the failures of individuals and the Jewish people as a nation would be depicted.

Now for the first time in one book could be found all the information about how God continually guides humans with dreams, visions, visits from angels, the sending of great teachers and prophets, and finally with acts of divine intervention by God itself. In this way, by free will choice, the Jewish people, as individuals and as a nation, would be seen as the new pattern of how God would lead humans to salvation by the predicted coming of a Messiah.

The books from Genesis to Noah give a symbolic account of the forming of the consciousness of God; the books from Noah to Abraham tell the symbolic story of the forming of human consciousness from embryo to birth; the stories from Abraham up until Jesus, who the Hebrews repudiated, are symbolic descriptions of the forming of human consciousness from birth to mature adulthood. The New Testament is a symbolic description of the Savior or Christ consciousness that allows consciousness to overcome matter or the human experience.

As Judaism developed, teachers, or rabbis, were chosen to study and then interpret the writings of the *Torah* by consensus agreement. A certain amount of editing was done on these books, which are considered to have reached their final form by about 500 B.C. Judaism also has a non-written body of wisdom which is passed on orally. Over the centuries, Judaism has become a religion concerned more and more with ethical behavior with an extremely strong emphasis on scholarship and teaching.

To lead mankind successfully and also as a way to establish a path of perfection that could be copied, God chose to do something quite remarkable. God promised the Jewish people that a Messiah or Savior would be born of their race. God chose to enter into matter and live a human life exactly as souls were expected to do. Why? Why would God want to live in the limited awareness world of matter, where only by the use of the five physical senses could one understand matter, when in the spirit world one already had unlimited awareness? Because God as a leader wanted to live a series of lifetimes in such a manner that both a human consciousness and a human body would evolve into a state of God perfection. In this way, souls' projection into matter could finally be overcome. Therefore, the redeemer of mankind would be God itself, living a life as half man and half God.

It was this perfected human body and perfected human consciousness that God wanted to evolve forever as God's own consciousness that was now designed as a fractal pattern. God did this feat by allowing his first soul, Jesus, who was the first soul to complete all the steps needed to re-unite with God, who then became the same as God, to enter the earth as a prophet, teacher, and sometimes as an ordinary man with a wife and children within the Jewish race.

Of all the decisions that God had to make to save the fallen souls, the decision to allow the first soul who had evolved into a full companion to God, as God, to enter into matter grieved God the most. This is because of a very real danger that this soul could also fail on his mission to establish a path of salvation for all humans living on earth *and* become trapped in matter.

One of the reasons God had deep, deep reservations about giving Jesus permission to enter into matter was because both God and his first soul, Jesus, knew that after the first two incarnations as a teacher, a veil would then be placed over Jesus' God aware consciousness each time it was reborn as an infant. To really establish a true path of salvation for humans, both God and Jesus knew that the path or pattern that was to be created could not be faked. It had to be a mission, a path of lifetimes actually lived.

In secret esoteric writings, these many incarnations of Jesus came to thirty-two.

The American psychic Edgar Cayce said that Jesus began his mission first by just projecting his consciousness into matter and then by causing energy to form as a matrix into a physical body that was human in appearance. As a projection of thought energy, his name was Enoch and he became known as a great teacher. After his message was delivered and was received in a time frame of many generations, Enoch left earth and waited in heaven for human consciousness to evolve further. His second thought projection lifetime was as the great prophet and mystic, Melchizedek.

As part of the process of re-weaving a pattern that duplicated the actual path that fallen souls had taken, it was necessary for the first two incarnations of Jesus to duplicate how the disobedient souls actually traveled and created their path that led to them becoming humans in matter rather than evolving continuously as pure spirits.

The third projection of Jesus' consciousness came when he projected himself into Adam after the great ape form of animal had been divinely guided so it could evolve into a human form. This intervention by God to evolve a physical form for souls to inhabit was to duplicate the pattern of intervention that would also be done as human consciousness also evolved, because the physical and conscious patterns of humans have to be a perfect match.

Jesus' consciousness is split apart to conform to earth's laws of duality and Eve, as Adam's inner aware consciousness, is drawn out and so now Jesus will evolve as two separate male and female patterns of consciousness, the same as each soul would do.

As Adam, being seduced by Eve to take a bite out of the apple of wisdom (which is duality), Jesus is duplicating the pattern of the fallen souls when they allowed the inner aware part of their own consciousness to tempt them into entering earth.

The snake or *the Devil* is a symbolic representation of the *spirit of rebellion* that each soul has along with free will as part of their personal conscious pattern.

During the millennia in which these and more transient religious doctrines were taking form in the Far and Near East, the religious consciousness of the West remained for a long time in a primitive state. Early Western civilization is famous for its wars and for its great conquerors and explorers: Alexander, Hannibal, Caesar. Often, or even usually, what Western consciousness has not understood, it has destroyed—as for example the sacking of the great libraries of Alexandria by "barbarians" from a more primitive culture.

Eastern consciousness, while it also was engaged in plenty of wars, was an inward looking kind of thought concerned with inner awareness. Western consciousness, in contrast, when it began to emerge was an outer-aware, masculine type of awareness characterized by aggressive, linear, forward searching thought and action with much time and energy spent on the conquest and destruction of other groups of people in order to grab their material possessions.

It is said of those engaged in Eastern thought that when they find a problem, they love to endlessly examine it without really caring whether or not they ever find a solution. Their attention is always to the past and the present. It is said of those who engage in Western thought that when they find a problem, they either solve it or discard it to find another problem. Their attention is always to the present and to the future and when they bury their dead, *they stay buried*. There is no ancestor worship evidenced in Western thought.

It is not surprising that it would then be within Western consciousness, that loved to solve problems, that never looked back, that had its attention grounded in the present and its eye focused on the future, that the birth of modern science and technology would evolve.

And so it was that only after a long sleep during which Eastern consciousness was already awake and exploring itself, did Western consciousness begin to wake up. In the Near Eastern desert countries of Persia, Egypt, Assyria, Babylonia, and others, a form of human conscious outer awareness began to develop. Since human outer aware consciousness personifies the male trait of linear aggressive forward searching thought which is meant to compliment the female trait of deep inner circling self examining thought, a balancing of the thinking process of the human race was beginning.

When Western thought first awakened, it expressed itself as a desire to expand by force and material expression. It is out of Western thought that armies, conquest, and wars began as physical counterparts of mental urges.

Humans were not the first animals to express outer aware consciousness in this manner. The use of spies, decoys, fake thrusts or feints to the center of an opponent while making a flank attack to the sides is a familiar tactic humans use as strategy when armies attack each other. In fact, it is also the strategy used by ants and viruses as they attack an opponent. Hawks and larger birds that are harassed and attacked constantly by smaller birds while flying remind WWII buffs of a B-19 or B-29 bomber being attacked by fighter planes—or of guerila warfare in Vietnam or other places.

More complex religious and philosophical doctrines emerged around 1200 B.C. on the Greek island of Mycenae and developed from there to great heights on mainland Greece. Although the specific *religion* of the Greeks is long cast aside and made no contribution to

Western consciousness, their poetry, philosophy, art, and politics stand at the very foundations of Western thought much as the *I Ching* does to the Chinese. To the Greeks we owe our emphasis on rationality, on observation of the natural world with a cause/effect focus and the attempt to deduce causes from this observation—in fact it is the West's great faith in the cause-and-effect workings of the Universe which forms the starting point for its amazing developments in science and technology. Buddhism and other Eastern systems of consciousness concern themselves with a reality beyond the world we ordinarily see, while the Greeks dealt with the world as it appears.

We owe to the Greeks the unique concept of democratic government which reached its height in the fifth century B.C. city state of Athens. Democracy was considered a paragon of equality for all of its citizens (males only as in all other parts of the world at this time), freedom of speech, law, politics, good economic conditions for its citizens—a paragon which above all was governed by a *constitution* that guaranteed these rights. Individual citizens were involved directly in the government of the Greek city-state, both in forming policy and in all areas of administration.

It was the Greeks who first began the shift toward a center of interest dominated by the *individual* human being and away from a tribal consciousness, which would have incalculable consequences as Western consciousness developed.

Greek civilization essentially self destructed over a period of several centuries through its endless internal warfare, and its final remnants were easily gobbled up by an emerging young and energetic nation called Rome.

Along with the territory and the art, the Romans took over the entire pantheon of Greek gods and goddesses, gave them Roman names, and devised tales of their intervention in human affairs which tended to be amorous and rather lightweight. They also took over Greek ideas, including the Greek political form of government called democracy, which now became representative instead of directly participatory. Augustus was the first Roman head of state to allow himself to be declared Emperor and the existing Roman Empire—no longer a Republic—was officially acknowledged.

The Greeks had been great thinkers in philosophy, and their art and literature reached heights of beauty and distinction that have never been surpassed. The Romans were a more down to earth people, and their talents were practical rather than philosophical or artistic. Romans had great skills in organization and administration; they were the first bureaucrats. They were better than anyone before them at organizing armies, at how to get large numbers of troops from here to there with their supply lines intact, which is logistics. Their temples were no match for the famous Parthenon or the temples at Delphi, but they built superb roads, aqueducts, and gigantic structures for large numbers of people, such as the still standing Coliseum. They showed the world how to govern a huge empire of people who were all different, democracy in action—no piece of cake even back then—and they did it pretty well, achieving after their extensive conquests the famous *Pax Romana* which lasted for hundreds of years. If the Greeks were the theorists of early Western civilization, the Romans were the technologists. A great deal of what makes Western civilization work today comes from the Romans.

CHAPTER 27

THE CREATION OF A NEW CONSCIOUSNESS

A living, evolving, fractal designed pattern is never the same this moment as it was the moment before. So the design of God is never the same from one moment to the next. God is now a living, creative, evolving God rather than the single, passive God of old.

The idea that "God always was and God always will be" is correct. But what wasn't correct, after God's own self creation began, was the idea that "God will forever be the same". God is now, and forever will be, in a state of constant change. It is this same mini pattern of creative change that we humans see happening daily in our lives.

In God's fractal creation of consciousness, everything that happens to an angel, a soul, a human, a nebula, a planet, a solar system, an animal, a tree, or even a butterfly, happens to God. This is because each of these things is a micro fractal pattern that is evolving within the greater macro pattern of God's evolution.

As these micro patterns expand their individual awareness, so also does this cause God to expand its macro awareness, or God's Collective Consciousness.

The history of the human race is the story of its own evolution, of its human Collective Consciousness. This evolution is seen in physical matter as ebb and high tide cycles of successive civilizations, each having a birth, a growth, a period of maturity, and then a death.

As the Twentieth Century comes to a close, humans can now look back thousands of years into their collective past and see in vivid detail the rise and fall of past civilizations.

Even something as small and individual as plant life has this same pattern. When a plant dies, it decays and turns into fertile soil, and from out of this soil a new plant is born and grows. In this way, plant life feeds off the death and decay of its parent and surrounding plants, its nourishment actually coming from its own past.

In this same pattern, each civilization dies and decays into the fertile soil out of which a new civilization will be born and grow. And its nourishment will come from the civilization that is dying, so that it, too, is living off and evolving from its own past. This is why, for example, the Roman Empire had Greek influences interwoven into it.

So, too, will an individual human consciousness, which is veiled with forgetfulness at birth, feed off its past, its own forgotten earth incarnations—its Collective Consciousness. And each individual also feeds off the mind energy of the past human collective consciousness of its race and of all humans who lived before.

We can see this happening in smaller patterns as individuals absorb from their parents, their town or city, their country, their religion, the customs that form their culture, work ethics, art, and even architecture. Each of these forms of consciousness will be a type of either inner or outer awareness.

All forms of consciousness—of God, angels, souls, and humans—are real living creations that have the power to manifest themselves in physical matter. But it is human consciousness, which can evolve in physical matter in the same way God's consciousness does in the evolving fractal pattern of creation, that becomes the problem for God. Human consciousness is now able, in a very limited way, to recreate matter in the same way that God has the

174

power to recreate matter. One example of this is DNA splicing and manipulating of living physical forms by chromosome changes, artificial insemination, and cloning.

The physical equivalent of spiritual Collective Consciousness is human history. And everyone knows that history is always repeating itself. Why? This is God's way of giving humans on Earth an opportunity to clean up their acts, to get it right this time, by the use of their own free will. Wars, for example, will continue to rage over the earth until humans make free will choices not to commit violent acts, either mentally or physically, against themselves or others—until they make free will choices to negotiate their differences rather than fight over them.

The reality which a human has to learn is the *reality of consciousness* rather than *physical reality*. And it is by the use of symbols and of such processes as anthropomorphism and pathetic fallacy that the more mature conscious mind begins to slowly realize that physical matter is a duplication in matter of the spiritual consciousness which shapes and energizes living matter, or all life on Earth. When Western Consciousness is evolving as a male outer awareness, it is symbolized in nature by straight lines; a female awareness is symbolized by curves and swirls.

Even the architecture and art of Eastern Civilization reflects this inner circling examination, so that graceful half circles as arches, spirals, circles, and vivid colors are present in the design of their buildings, clothes, and art.

The architecture and art of Western Civilization reflect its own outer aware, straight ahead way of looking at and examining things. They tend to follow the classical Greek designs of straight lines and black and white as color contrasts.

It can also be seen that as art evolves throughout the centuries, it, too, has cycles whereby it is female Baroque in style, with emphasis on swirls, circles, and curves, with just a hint of straight lines, and then a male Ionic style which is all straight lines and squares, with just a touch of swirls and scrolls. This is an indication that the Collective Consciousness of humans keeps cycling from female inner awareness to male outer awareness within both Eastern and Western civilizations.

Even individual souls must follow this cycle of being a female of curves and then a male of straight lines so that humans can learn to balance and perfect both sides of their inner selves. What better way is there to learn how to perfect oneself than to live lifetimes as a male and then lifetimes as a female.

All my life I have been aware of my nightly dreams. It was in my late twenties that I started to record them in a spiral notebook that I kept by my bed. As I wrote this book I had guidance dreams at night that would clear up concepts which had seemed vague as I attempted to put them into written form during the day.

The following dream is one that I had at about this stage in the writing of this book. I think it is quite significant and I feel that it will serve as a good introduction to the final parts of this book.

The Dream:
I'm in the Navy. I seem to have the job of moving a submarine in and out of a water lock of some kind. I am in the ocean outside of the submarine and I am pushing it into place in the lock. (This water lock is the same kind that is used beside a dam to raise or lower a boat that is inside the lock to the correct water level.)

This is not a river lock, but a gigantic lock that is between the Atlantic and Pacific Oceans. There seems to be about a forty foot difference between the two ocean levels.

Suddenly, the lock gate that separates the two oceans is lowered and the higher water from the Atlantic Ocean rushes toward me as a wall of water forty feet high.

I'm still in the water beside the submarine I had been moving. As the high wall of water comes toward me, I am lifted up with the wave and then start to move rapidly with it.

I can feel the awesome force of the water wave and realize I am right at the edge of it as it continues to flow out. I can look down over the edge of the wave and I know if I fall off or get in front of it, I will drown.

My only hope is to stay right on the crest of the wave and ride it out, which I do successfully. Then, as the two oceans, the Atlantic and the Pacific, merge and their levels become one again, I find my submarine and submerge it. I then guide it down to the bottom of the ocean floor, where I find there is an underwater dock. I park the submarine inside the docking berth.

End of Dream.

This was an easy dream for me to interpret because I immediately understood both the symbols and what they were referring to. There are only six symbols in the dream:

Symbol 1:   The two oceans, Atlantic and Pacific, are symbolic of two huge stationary bodies of water that represent two huge states of consciousness.

Symbol 2:   The ocean lock represents a divide or barrier that now separates these two forms of consciousness. Naturally, since the Pacific Ocean is in the *east*, this is symbolic of the consciousness of the *East*, or the Orient, China and India. The consciousness of the *East* represents *inner awareness* or the feminine potential that is intuitive, self reflective—an inner, looking at self, type of consciousness.

I got mixed up interpreting the East/West symbols because the Pacific is to the *West* of the United States. The United States represents to me my own united states of consciousness. The consciousness of the *West* is pure *male* or outer awareness and is the *male* potential, in that it is aggressive, has a boldness of action and an assertiveness, and the ability to take charge and lead, which are things that Western Civilization has been doing, while the Eastern Civilizations of India and China continued to keep their attention turned inward.

Symbol 3:   The ocean wave is an interesting symbol in that it is the Pacific Ocean that is higher than the Atlantic Ocean. This means that since the Pacific Ocean is in the *east*, then it is the *eastern* consciousness, or *inner* awareness that is flowing over and overpowering the Atlantic Ocean or western consciousness, which is the male or outer awareness and aggressiveness of mankind.

Symbol 4:   The submarine is a vessel that can move over the ocean, but it is really designed to go deep inside the ocean. Therefore, *Just As* there is a vessel that can do these things, *so also* do I have a vessel or a type of consciousness that can safely move on top of consciousness or deep down in its depths, and I do it safely because this is what I was designed to do.

Symbol 5:   Myself as a sailor and the one who guides and controls the submarine. This represents the fact that I am the one who moves inside this submarine, or I can also be on the outside controlling it. This could represent my own imagination and dreams that are the vessel I travel with, either on the surface of my consciousness with imagination, or else deep down into my subconsciousness with dreams.

It also shows that even though I am on the outside of this vessel of consciousness (submarine), I still direct and control where it will park and moor after a voyage is over. Does this also mean that this is the part of my own consciousness that can travel inside of the Universal Consciousness?

Symbol 6:   The underwater dock. A boat dock is a place where a vessel that travels under or in the ocean can be parked while it is not being used. So, *Just As* a submarine can do this, *so also* do I have a place deep down at the bottom of my own unconsciousness where I dock. It is that part of my consciousness (the submarine) that has the ability to travel on top of or inside my total consciousness.

It is symbol number 3, the *ocean wave*, that is the most significant part of this dream. This represents the new wave of inner awareness, the *female principle* that is coming as a new wave of consciousness when the gate is let down, and it will overpower and roll over the old outer awareness, *the male principle*. When the two merge, then the aggressive form of Western world consciousness that has caused so many large world wars and small internal wars (always a pattern within a pattern) will be influenced by the female consciousness of the East. When this happens, then the lion and the lamb will by lying down together.

Now, as inner consciousness rolls over outer consciousness, they become balanced or level, which represents God's own Consciousness that is always level or in balance. More importantly, the two huge bodies of water, or consciousnesses, are *merging*.

What is interesting is that my dream shows me riding right at the edge of this new flowing wave. I can see it is a dangerous place to be, but I also see that I make it through this merging of the two forms of consciousness all right, along with the vessel I had been using.

Is this the new consciousness that has been predicted for mankind? Is this the beginning of the Millennium, the thousand years of peace when the devil is bound, which means human conscious rebellion is bound?

Did this dream mean that the two halves of my own consciousness were joining? Because of the size of the consciousnesses (symbolized as oceans), I feel that this means humanity's Universal Consciousness is about ready to come together.

This idea that the two separately evolving types of collective consciousness will merge caused me to do some serious thinking about collective consciousness as a whole.

I had never before considered the possibility that Eastern thought as an inner consciousness principle was evolving as a separate form of collective consciousness. Nor had I considered the idea that Western aggressive thought was also evolving as a separate entity. I had always thought of them as one entity: *human* consciousness.

Now, as I contemplated the dream of the two oceans merging, I could understand these things differently. The symbolism showed me for the first time that male awareness would penetrate female awareness, which is the "normal" way it should happen, normal because Western thought, or male awareness, had always initiated expansion as an outward form of movement. Even in the micro pattern of physical sex, it is usually the male who initiates the act if the female signals consent.

I could see the physical application of the merging of two conscious forms by the way the teachers of Hinduism, Buddhism, Zen Buddhism, and other forms of Eastern religions are coming to the West, to Europe, the United States, etc. in an effort to seduce Western Consciousness to join them.

History is the physical record of man's collective consciousness. And it seems to flow in an ebb, then high tide, sort of a motion. So that as one examines past history, it can be seen as a rising of great Eastern civilizations, such as the Chinese, Japanese, Koreans, etc. and that of India. Then a high tide is reached and a receding tide carries the sands, the bits and pieces of the civilization, back into itself.

The same thing can be found in the Great Western civilizations, such as those of Rome, Greece, Egypt, Persia, and the Inca and Mayan civilizations. They reach high tide, then recede back into the oblivion from which they sprang.

But now something different is going to happen to human consciousness. At the present time Western civilization, with its use of technology and wars of expansion, has reached its high tide, while Eastern civilizations that have long been dormant are awakening to tempt the West with their forms of inner wisdom. From out of this merging of two separate types of consciousness, a totally new human Collective Consciousness will finally form which is balanced: both a male and a female pattern.

One hopes that the new inner aware consciousness of the East, with its inner wisdom of itself, will merge with the outer awareness ability of the West to initiate action. Then human Collective Consciousness will become balanced as a fractal pattern that can endlessly evolve. The physical balance of the two types of civilizations comes when women are given equal rights.

An example of a balanced pattern in human Collective Consciousness that keeps renormalizing into larger patterns is the form of government—democracy—whereby people govern themselves. Democracy had its birth in Greece and keeps evolving and renormalizing in country after country as the centuries fly by. When equal women's rights are added, the pattern of democracy becomes balanced and will not self destruct as male dominated democracies do.

Perhaps all of the countries on Earth will become a collective civilization which in essence is one huge democracy when equality between the sexes and races is achieved. If not, the pattern will self destruct because it is out of balance.

As human consciousness evolves on a larger scale, so also, as a micro pattern, will individual consciousness continue to evolve. As individual humans evolve, they carry within their own individual collective consciousness the archetypal patterns of all the major and minor deities found in the Eastern and Western religions of the past.

For example, it was in the Far East, about 567 B.C., where a man was born who would become one of the great archetypal symbols in the evolution of human Collective Consciousness. He would come to symbolize the first great awakening of the soul, slumbering inside the human body and mind like a giant genie. This man was named Siddhartha Gautama. It was while he was in deep meditation that his human mind finally broke through into his own soul consciousness. It was like a ray of bright sunshine breaking through heavy clouds.

With this first breakthrough came the realization that he was actually a spirit soul inside a human consciousness. He stirred, became alert, and proclaimed, "I am awake".

He became the first soul, after the fall of the souls into matter on Earth, to awaken to his own divinity. For this accomplishment he was given the name Buddha, which means *to be awake*. His willingness to sacrifice earthly pleasures and to teach other humans how to achieve their own spiritual breakthroughs into a consciousness called *nirvana*, allowed Siddhartha to become an archetypal symbol.

My realization that I, as an American Christian living thousands of years later and thousands of miles away from India, now had a *Buddha Awake Consciousness*, came when I had the following dream.

THE DREAM

I am taking part in some kind of a Buddhist ceremony or rite. The Buddhist priests are looking for a new volunteer successor for the Buddha, whom they need to pick from those present.

I'm one of the few Americans at the ceremony. We are all gathered by a large lake. It will be from the results of a series of three coming events that the successor for Buddha will be chosen.

Somehow, as these tests progress, the circle of candidates gets smaller, but I am still there. As the final selection is about to be made, I volunteer to become the candidate because the others seem apprehensive about being selected.

As part of the test, I dive into the clear water lake and sink to the bottom. The water is so crystal clear that I can see all around me as if it were daylight and I were on dry ground.

Then I see that Tibetan monks are waiting at the bottom of the lake. They take me immediately to a glassed-in room on the lake bottom where I can breathe as if I were on land.

I realize that I didn't die because I allowed myself to be the sacrifice. But I now have this ability to live and breathe underwater in this clear, calm lake room.

Then I see a body image of the sacrifice that was me sinking down onto the bottom of the lake. But I realize that I am not inside that body anymore. I seem to be forever changed. Other Tibetan monks swim over to greet me and I am the center of attention.

End of Dream

It took me a long time to understand this dream. I thought about it for days and weeks at a time, but it was hard for me to interpret because I had no real understanding of Buddhism or any other Eastern religion.

The few books I had read on Buddhism seemed to me to be nothing more than walks through endless mind images. Often, halfway through an Eastern religion book, I would just stop and put it down; I couldn't grasp what looked to me like someone playing word games using abstract thoughts and sentences. So without Buddhist training, it was a long time before I could understand and interpret this dream. It was only when I decided that the whole ceremony was a passage from one state of consciousness to another that the dream became clear to me. I then interpreted it as follows:

MEANING OF DREAM

A large body of water has always been a symbol for the unconscious mind. The clarity of the water symbolizes clarity of thought. Obviously if I had been doing deep, clear thinking in my subconscious mind level, I would dream of being comfortable in deep, clear water.

Jumping into the lake is symbolic of my being willing to take the plunge into the depths of my own unconscious as a type of personal sacrifice.

But then I discover as I sink to the bottom of my own unconsciousness that it isn't as scary or frightening as I thought it would be and that I can see things as clearly when I am in the unconscious mind state as when I'm in an earthly, human mind state of consciousness.

The human body that I see floating down is my own human ego, or human consciousness, which I have sacrificed and left behind to jump into the unknown. This symbolizes that as I plunge into the depths of my soul consciousness, a part of my human consciousness will die.

The Tibetan monks who are waiting for me are the Eastern religion parts of my total personality.

The glassed-in room where I now live and breathe, as if I were in a room on the earth's surface, symbolizes to me that I now have a safe place inside of my own unconscious mind where I can reside as easily as in my conscious mind. I have been guided to this safe place because I was willing to take the plunge by sacrificing my own human ego.

When I finished analyzing the dream, I realized that I, too, had had a Buddha type awakening because of meditation and self sacrifice.

Further study of Eastern religions also led me to realize that they had discovered the concept of a mystical God. A mystical God is simply the idea that all things that exist in creation are God. This is the same idea that I have been trying to explain in this book since I discovered the fractal pattern design of creation. However, it is this idea that "All is God" that becomes a real problem for Christianity because it leaves no way to explain the presence of the devil.

In the beginning there was not God *and* the devil, but only God. Therefore, God had to create the devil. And if God created the devil, and God is a mystical God that is all of its own creation, then one has to conclude that the devil is a part of God.

The devil a part of God? God part of the devil? I can hear these concepts bouncing off minds like an echo bounces off mountain walls in an acoustically perfect valley.

The Hindu religion handled this problem nicely when they created Shiva, the destroyer god, as a minor deity. They did this after observing that in nature all four elements, earth, water, fire, and air, could be both constructive and destructive. Therefore, they rightly concluded that God can be both a creator *and* a destroyer... And God is!

This is a pattern copied from First Creation which began when God decided to destroy its single passive self so it could give birth to a new creation of many. This self sacrifice and dismemberment of God is part of the philosophy of the Hindu religion: God created angels, souls, and matter from itself, giving souls free will.

Free will cannot be given as a psychological concept unless a test of free will is also created. If there was not a test, then the free will concept would be just a theory that souls would know about, but couldn't practice. The test of free will is the creation, by God, of the psychological concept of rebellion. If souls had an awareness of and the actual power to rebel against God, then souls had, indeed, been given the gift of free will.

Souls have the power to create and the power to destroy because they were made in the image of God.

It is to learn how to discipline and control the two-edged sword that is creativity and destruction that free will is needed and was given as a gift by God. Evolving souls now had the ability to rebel against God and the parts of their own consciousnesses that they didn't like. This whole concept of the power to destroy and enslave free will by doing battle against the power to be creative and have free will is described allegorically in the Bible as the creation of Satan and his Legions of Fallen Angels. The Battle of Armageddon is the allegorical battle which had its physical expression as the Second World War.

Humans are always swinging from their creative selves to their destructive selves, and will continue to do so until they become quiet and centered. For it is in this mystical center that these two powers can be controlled. Man is both a devil and an angel.

Some examples of the devils we meet in life are alcoholism and other addictions. Addictions are destructive powers that destroy our creative powers. Sometimes, as members of Alcoholics Anonymous have learned, the only way the destructive power of an addiction can be stopped is by the divine intervention of God as a type of higher power. There has to be a time in addicts' lives when as an act of free will, they request God's help in the affairs of their lives.

Anything that tries to enslave a human is the devil within that individual, the power of that human's own mind to rebel and to be destructive in a creative way.

Before Jesus could begin his mission on Earth, he had to go into the desert of his mind to meet and conquer his devils in a series of three tests. In this same pattern, before humans can master themselves, they have to meet, conquer, and finally make friends with their own internal devils.

We have to learn how to make friends with our ability to rebel and our power to destroy. We do this by first identifying that ability and that power and then forgiving ourselves for them. We have to be able to forgive ourselves seventy times seven for the destruction and pain we have caused in our own self evolution. Then we have to learn how to forgive those people whose devils have caused great destruction and pain in our lives.

We develop a Christ consciousness, or a Savior consciousness, when we develop the ability to conquer and control our devils. Then this power to destroy becomes a power that creates. This happens because that which is destroyed creates a birth. Kill an addiction and out of its death a new self will be born.

In our Western religions, we need to replace our outdated concept of a devil who can enslave us and understand that hell is where we get trapped in our own fiery, negative passions by the creative power of our thoughts and imagination. We need to adopt an Eastern type Shiva god to replace our Satan. We have to understand that it is our own conscious power to rebel and destroy that has to be disciplined and controlled, not some mystical devil. We have to fight the mini Battle of Armageddon raging in our own minds almost daily.

After a lifetime of meeting and conquering many parts of my own devil, I'm familiar with the many minor deities, both destructive and creative, that exist as part of my consciousness. I believe that I have in my own collective consciousness a devil, a primitive shaman, a soldier/warrior who does his duty, a general as a conqueror, a Buddha for soul awakening, a policeman for order, a psychic prophet, a Confucius for social order, a Lao Tze for a Tao/Zen concept of how to live in harmony with nature, and a Jesus as a perfected man and a Christ as a perfected Savior consciousness.

I don't mean I have a multiple personality disorder, but only that these are archetypal symbols for states of my own consciousness. It is in my dreams that I meet these archetypal symbols as teachers of my own daily developing personal consciousness. These obviously don't exist as real people, but as conscious imprints that have already been made in mankind's Collective Consciousness by the way these people actually lived symbolic lives in the past.

Once I made this connection, it made my dream interpreting much easier. As I began to understand my own collective consciousness, I began to understand the Collective Consciousness of all mankind. As I understood these two patterns of consciousness, I began to understand the individual and collective consciousness of God. As I understood one, I understood the other, because the Kingdom of God is within each of us—as our own mind.

Each night as a human sleeps, in a self-similar pattern to God's beginning as a passive consciousness, our original soul that was created by God, and is now an oversoul, divinely intervenes in our evolving, human earth mind by the use of dream symbols. This oversoul, whom I have met as being symbolized as an American president (or the head of my United States of Consciousness) talks to me directly by the use of allegorical symbols, put into story form as a one, two, or three act play.

It is up to me to make a free will choice to train my virgin consciousness, which is my present human consciousness. My other human consciousnesses that I have developed in other earth incarnations have become my collective human consciousness. When I die, my present complete earth consciousness experience of a human, living in the twentieth and twenty-first centuries, will flow into this personal collective consciousness. This, in effect, keeps my collective consciousness evolving.

At no time does a soul have to reincarnate as anything but a human. It's bad enough that as a human we have to fight off the animal instincts and urges that are interwoven into our human consciousness without actually being an animal.

The need to sacrifice these animal urges from our human consciousness is told as the allegorical offering of Cain in the Bible. The practice of animal sacrifice that still exists in some religions today is supposed to symbolize this effort by humans of offering up their animal instincts to God.

Each of the dreams on the following pages are examples of the teaching dreams that have given me great insight into the workings of my own conscious and subconscious mind. People who can't remember dreams are imitating, as a mini pattern, that great black night of soul experience that is still part of the human psyche, the black night when souls could no longer remember God.

This next dream is an example of a shaman type dream, perhaps a medicine wheel type, in which I see myself being centered after being dismembered or split apart as is seen also in Eastern religions.

THE DREAM

I'm at a place which seems like an Indian medicine wheel location. As I enter the circle, the four parts of myself separate, or are split, into four different directions.

Then somehow I am also in the center of my four selfs as I dance round and round. As I continue to spin around, I see American Indians driving a white buffalo in front of them and coming toward me.

End of Dream

I also dreamed all that week of attending North American Indian ceremonial dances and being able to dance all night long. I interpreted this dream of being in a medicine wheel as becoming centered inside of self.

Then one night I had this unusual dream:

THE DREAM

I am at a place where I can examine things that have happened to me at different times in my life as if they were an exploded picture scene. I can then look at the exploded picture scene in a way that shows me how each individual sequence of events make up a complete scene or some one thing that had happened in my life.

By doing this, I can then go into the exploded scene and correct things that have happened in the past so that my future will be different.

End of Dream

I have had many of these types of dreams that show me changing my past, present, and future. I began to realize that if consciousness always was and always will be, then the concept of a past, a present, and a future are not real, but only conscious aware reference points.

I realized also that *time is the mental equivalent of space*. So if consciousness doesn't take up space, then a mind can instantly go anywhere in time or space just by becoming aware of where it wants to go. For example, if my consciousness is focused on my face and then I focus my mind on my feet, I don't have to do any kind of mind traveling; I only have to instantly change my awareness from one to the other, and I do this without a time concept.

Going into my past, while in the present, to correct my future, happens when I change a false belief for the truth.

Suppose I had a phobia like the fear of darkness and I succeed in completely conquering that fear today. When I do, I have, in effect, in the present eliminated a phobia from my past. And this will alter my future, since in the future I won't have to deal with a fear of darkness phobia.

When a false belief or phobia or anything else is eliminated in the present, then it doesn't exist in the future or in the past. This is why the concept of forgiveness is needed and should be used by humans. If we forgive our past, in the present, we change our future.

The next dream is an example of a teaching dream that helped to explain my own fears and duality to me.

THE DREAM

I am shown that there are seven forms of fear and they are laid out in three columns, with normal being the middle or balance point of each extreme. I am somehow shown that the first and most deadly fear is the kind that doesn't look like fear, but instead looks normal and therefore doesn't scare the person looking at it or experiencing it.
These fears are:

1. Strange	Normal	Familiar
2. Plain	Normal	Extravagant
3. Timid	Normal	Brave
4. Decent or Good	Normal	Bad or Evil
5. Happy	Normal	Sad
6. Rich	Normal	Poor
7. Weak	Normal	Strong

I had the realization that mockery or flattery are their names and they have the power to free or trap a human.
End of Dream

I thought that this was a different way of looking at the seven sins and the seven virtues which have to be met and conquered in a progressive order as each of the seven chakras are mastered.

Then I had another dream that was unusual.

THE DREAM

I am somehow weaving a pattern or patterns of lifetimes in a looping stitch so that all things that have ever happened to me in all my lifetimes on Earth are woven together in such a way that the pattern could just as easily be unlooped. I see that each lifetime lived on Earth has a finer loop design than lifetimes not lived on Earth. As I watch myself weave my own pattern of consciousness, it all becomes clear.
End of Dream

This has to be a dream whereby my pure soul consciousness (my superconsciousness or oversoul) is watching my human self weaving together a collection of human lifetimes into a form of collective consciousness. I can now see how mistakes or conscious free will decisions can unravel my tapestry of life just as fast and as easily as I have woven it.

The next dream happened in 1995 as I was reviewing what I had written so far in this book. As I did this review, I realized that I had never in my lifetime had a dream of Jesus or about meeting Jesus, even though I was a Christian. I also realized that I had spent my whole life praying and asking God the Father for help. So one night as I was ready to fall asleep, I asked myself why I had never met Jesus in a dream. That night I had this surprising dream.

THE DREAM

I am standing outside a great white temple. I go through the front door and go into a white room. I am met by a group of people who are dignified and quiet.

They point to a spiral staircase and one of the group, who wears the habit of a monk, leads me up the steps. At the top of the steps I turn right and find myself in a small white bedroom which has a single bed in one corner. I see a human figure lying on its back in the bed. I am surprised when I recognize the figure as Jesus, but yet it seems to be me. But this is not a live Jesus, but the dead body of Jesus which has been taken down from the crucifixion cross. His body is so stiff with rigor mortis that the bent position of the legs, from his slumped down position while hanging on the cross, keeps the body on its back.

Very carefully the guide who is with me lets me see the nail marks of the crucifixion in his hands and feet. Then I am allowed to place my hand in the spear wound in his side. After I do this, I am led back down the stairs and I go outside.

End of Dream

I woke up and wrote down this dream. I became very puzzled and concerned because I had just met a dead, crucified Jesus and not a live Jesus as I had been expecting. Also, my examination of the crucifixion wounds, plus the placing of my hand inside a spear wound, was strangely reminiscent of a Doubting Thomas, the apostle, symbol.

I wondered if this meant that I held, deep inside of me, some reservations about Jesus' resurrection, or did I doubt that Jesus ever existed? But I knew that wasn't right because I have had a strong belief in the divinity of Jesus since grade school.

Also, it was a dead Jesus I had seen as an answer to a request to meet a live Jesus. I believed that Jesus rose from the dead, so would a dead Jesus still be around waiting for resurrection? Especially a Jesus that seemed to be me?

After days of thinking about this dream, I realized that it was a purely symbolic dream about me. I had seen, as a dead crucified Jesus, that part of my human mind, my ego, that had died as a self sacrifice so that other parts of my personality might live. In a flash of inspiration, I realized that it wasn't a Jesus I saw that looked strangely like me, but Jesus as an archetypal symbol that his crucifixion and resurrection symbolized.

I knew then that the portion of my own consciousness, my Holy Savior consciousness, was still dead and hadn't yet had its resurrection because I doubted my divinity.

It is because of these kinds of dreams, and the days and weeks I spent trying to understand them, that I received the insight that great spiritual leaders from the past are also archetypal symbols for parts of any person's human consciousness. It also made my human mind understand Jesus' crucifixion symbols better.

The next dream occurred in July of 1996 during a period when the writing of this book was going badly. The person who was helping me by editing my original draft had pointed out so many mistakes and pencilled in so many corrections that even she got lost and had to retype pages and even sections of the book. When I saw the massive changes, I began to doubt that I had enough writing skill to ever complete the book. And as has happened so many other times in my life, many negative family problems which kept occurring at that time were a major distraction.

THE DREAM

I'm at a place where people get to write the script for the life they are going to live on Earth. I am given the job of writing my own life script.

The problem is that it had never been done before by anyone else so I have no guidelines to follow. This was lifetime number thirty-three and there was no model to copy from.

I didn't know how to write the life script because I hadn't yet lived the life. So I would have to write the script as I went along in life, which is why my life had seemed so hard, sad, and difficult.

End of Dream

After recording this dream, I realized it was a self-explanatory answer to the thoughts and worries I was having at the time.

I also had the following dream in July of 1996.

THE DREAM

I see myself as two separated parts. The edges of each part seem to be serrated or formed like the teeth of a wood cutting saw. Then, as I watch, the two parts of me come together into a perfect match like pieces of a puzzle being fitted together. I somehow know that this is my own inner and outer awarenesses coming together to make me balanced and whole.

End of Dream

After this coming together dream, which I'd been hoping to have some time in my life, something different started to happen to my consciousness.

It is my practice, every evening when it is nice and warm and a break in the Pennsylvania cloud cover allows for a beautiful sunset, to sit outside in a lawn chair and watch the sun go down.

As I sit facing the west in a comfortable lawn chair in a private place behind the garage, close to the woods, a calmness and peacefulness always comes over me as I watch the day end.

I enjoy sunrises and sunsets. Their splashes of color give a beauty to the clouds and the sky while birds and crickets sing background songs. And usually a soft, warm evening breeze will stir the grasses and rustle the tree leaves. I sink deeper into my chair and a sense of peace and relaxation comes over me as I watch and think.

Before my coming together dream, I had always hated poetry. I thought that if a person had something to say, he or she should just spit it out or write it in plain English. Besides, I always felt that poetry was for girls or sissies; it wasn't something that I, a steelworker, could be interested in. Period.

But in the summer of 1996, thoughts began to come into my mind that rhymed. I was thinking poetry! A complete change in my thinking process was occurring. As I moved my eyes, without stirring in the chair, and looked at the various scenes of nature that surrounded me, poetry describing what I was looking at flowed spontaneously through my mind. It was as if those lines of poetry were explanations of what I was seeing.

As a long time explorer of my own thoughts and consciousness, I decided to see how long the poetry process would last, and I found that it would go on for twenty minutes or more. Some of the sentences seemed like thoughts being directed toward me, so I began to take a spiral notebook and pencil with me each evening so I could write down what was happening in my thought process. I must have filled up thirty pages with poetry describing fireflies, grass, birds, sounds, clouds, sunsets, and all the other things I was seeing and hearing.

I was especially surprised by poems that seemed to be speaking to me personally. The lines of poetry would flow spontaneously as fast as I could write them down.

The following three poems are examples of the new flow of spontaneous thoughts that I experienced. I feel they are a good way to end this book.

Fireflies

How can fireflies' light be gold
When it's dark...and growing cold
Does their light warm the night
Or is it their job to make a light
That you might see...as you watch
A form of beauty that can't be touched.
Maybe their job is to show
That all life has a silent glow
That you could see if you would look
Into life's...tiniest nook
For it is there you see
That you can find me
And when you find me...you will see
That you are me and I am thee.

Walking in the Woods

When you walk through the woods
Life seems to flow the way it should
As you see the birds, bees, and butterflies
You sigh, you whisper, "Oh, my"
Sometimes your heart has such remorse
That it has become so very coarse
So speak with me as I hear
The songs of birds, the sound of deer
Don't leave me be, don't leave me out
For surely you know without a doubt
That the sun doesn't shine and the rain doesn't fall
Without giving a harvest to one and all
So listen as I say...
I'm glad you had a peaceful day.

Love

It is love, don't you see
That I have created for thee
Don't you know that when I recall
Each thought you had before your fall
That I know that it wasn't hate
That made you reject...even your mate
I know that it was haste
That caused you to waste
A life I give to you and all
In the stars...before the fall
So listen, as I recall
The glory, the light, that is in all
For never again will it be
That man will have no vision to see
Because my son became a man
You live, love, and don't give a damn
But be assured that the time is near
When you and all I hold dear
Will come back, you see
Just because...You love me